Sara Caldwell
11/02/08
LEHR 2007

THE OCCULT MIND

The Occult Mind

MAGIC
IN THEORY
AND PRACTICE

CHRISTOPHER I. LEHRICH

CORNELL UNIVERSITY PRESS
ITHACA AND LONDON

First published 2007 by Cornell University Press

Printed in the United States of America

Library of Congress Cataloging-in-Publication Data

Lehrich, Christopher I.
 The occult mind : magic in theory and practice / Christopher I. Lehrich.
  p.   cm.
 Includes bibliographical references and index.
 ISBN 978-0-8014-4538-5 (cloth : alk. paper)
 1. Magic. 2. Occultism. I. Title.

 BF1611.L435 2007
 133.4'3—dc22

                                            2006036025

Cornell University Press strives to use environmentally responsible suppliers and materials to the fullest extent possible in the publishing of its books. Such materials include vegetable-based, low-VOC inks and acid-free papers that are recycled, totally chlorine-free, or partly composed of nonwood fibers. For further information, visit our website at www.cornellpress.cornell.edu.

Cloth printing   10 9 8 7 6 5 4 3 2 1

For Sarah, who puts magic in my life

CONTENTS

ILLUSTRATIONS

PREFACE

⁙

Modern academe does not recognize a discipline devoted to the analytical study of occult, magical, or esoteric traditions. Work in these areas, though on the increase, remains hampered by various methodological and political blinders. The primary difficulty is simply explained: work on magic is tightly constrained by the conventions of the disciplines in which it is locally formulated. Early modern magic, a preoccupation of the present work, receives treatment within the narrow limits of intellectual history and the history of science. Most books advert to normative modes of evidence, analysis, and interpretation in those historical fields. Sociological and anthropological studies similarly present themselves in traditional disciplinary styles. And some important potential contributors, notably philosophers, have not as yet seen a reason to join the conversation.

Academic scholars working on magic have often been strikingly anxious to situate themselves indisputably within a conventional disciplinary framework, as though thereby to ward off the lingering taint of an object of study still thought disreputable if not outright mad. Many have encountered hostility, or amused disdain, from colleagues in more accepted fields. Thus it is no surprise that scholars of magic bend over backward to demonstrate just how "straight" they are.

But it should no longer be necessary to defend studies of magic, given the long line of distinguished predecessors in several disciplines. In the history of ideas, Eugenio Garin, Carlo Ginzburg, Paolo Rossi, D. P. Walker, and Frances Yates laid an eminently reputable foundation on which others have built. In the history of science, Brian Copenhaver, Allen Debus, Walter Pagel, David Pingree, and many others have legitimated previously disdained materials as essential to understanding the foundations of science. In anthropology, surely the name of Claude Lévi-Strauss by itself grants sufficient legitimacy, whatever one thinks of his conclusions, to say nothing of Lucien Lévy-Bruhl, Stanley Tambiah, and Robin Horton. In the history of religions, Jonathan Z. Smith has continually grappled with magic, as have in different ways and areas Hans Dieter Betz, Christopher Faraone, Fritz Graf,

Moshe Idel, and Joseph Needleman. One could continue such lists endlessly. Why then the desire—or need—to apologize?

The peculiar insecurity of scholars of magic has further prompted a failure to read across disciplines, or at least to do so overtly. Classicists do not cite anthropology, historians of science do not cite comparative religious studies, and vice versa. The exceptions are few and far enough between to prove the rule, and rarely developed on a broad basis; Tambiah's interesting look at Yates's work in *Magic, Science, Religion and the Scope of Rationality* serves more as a prolegomenon to a wider-framed anthropology than as an independent interrogation of magic.

One explanation lies in the difficulty of writing on an interdisciplinary basis. However fashionable the notion of interdisciplinarity, scholarship normally rests on narrow foundations and reaches outward for occasional inspiration. A work by and for historians must satisfy their criteria of evidence and argumentation, and if it draws on anthropology it need not by this token take entirely on board the disciplinary context of the ideas borrowed. Thus in the last few decades we have seen the rise of self-consciously theoretical history, which as a rule borrows notions from theorists of one sort or another and deploys them as tools to extend fairly traditional historical scholarship.

I do not dismiss the value of such works, in the study of magic or elsewhere, but one often finds problematic assumptions embedded therein, assumptions at odds with many of the theories employed. In particular, such work presumes a clear and distinct division between data and theory, primary and secondary source. One takes for granted that a Foucaultian study of sixteenth-century German witch trials uses Foucault as a lens through which to look at German data. But Foucault, like most poststructural theorists, insisted on the intrinsic invalidity of such a procedure: the methods and theories must be part and parcel of the analytical object, because the object is *constituted by the scholar*, not simply "there" to be studied.

To take seriously the theoretical developments of the last fifty years requires that such easy divisions be challenged, and furthermore that the challenge occur in the *doing* and not only in the abstract. Theoretically informed history must do theory as much as it does history, and it must at least consider the possibility that one might not always be able to tell the difference.

The truly interdisciplinary theoretical scholarship required for magic would, if formulated in the ordinary way, tend to make itself an artifact of *no* discipline—and furthermore unreadable. A genuine merger between history and anthropology, for example, would need to legitimate itself in the evidentiary and discursive modes of each discipline and would have to advance critically within both sets of questions and concerns. One book must do the work of two and also strive toward some further synthesis not normally requisite. If the number of disciplines at stake is large, as with the study of magic, even a single article soon expands to epic proportions.

The present book works somewhat differently. I have striven to include sufficient detail, from whatever discipline or area, to make the arguments comprehensible and allow purchase for critical engagement. To accomplish this, the chapters build on one another, both argumentatively and thematically: this is not a series of independent essays. In thus moving from start to finish, I try to provide enough data to elucidate my various forms of evidence. But the purely defensive gesture of disciplinary self-positioning is pared to the bone.

In a previous work, I attempted a first gesture toward the comparative theoretical methods employed here, focused on a close reading of a single major work in the history of magic; I also worked to constitute a dialogue between magical thought and modern theories. The present book, though it makes a similar gesture, has higher stakes and needs a larger array of materials, and as such the explicit documentation must be slimmer to prevent utter tedium. I have therefore provided extensive notes as a partial solution.

In composing this book as something of a preliminary to an interdisciplinary field as yet improperly constituted (or not at all), I have wished not to exclude those new to the field, or to early modern studies, or to various modes of theory. For this reason, I deliberately focus on works available in modern English editions. Where I draw on other languages, I downplay this in the text. I have tried, where possible, to suppress jargon and technical language—magical or theoretical—by simple avoidance or by defining terms where necessary and using them consistently.

Nevertheless, it must be said that this book makes some peculiar demands. Because I can have no knowledge of readers' prior familiarity with any of the various areas examined, I must on the one hand summarize everything and on the other not do so at length. I hope the readership is composed significantly of those not specializing in the history of magic, and I have endeavored not to mystify them, but it must be allowed that the nature of evidence and argumentation here cannot fully satisfy the disciplinary expectations of every reader. Thus I ask the reader to imagine this book as a product of a discipline that *could* exist but does not. For that reason it is only to be expected that its analytical conventions will be somewhat unfamiliar.

On the other hand, I hope that this book will act as a preliminary to an *in-*

terdisciplinary field of magic. A disciplinary formation is, I believe, impractical, but more to the point would foreclose a great deal of positive dialogical engagement among disciplines. Unfortunately, this is the direction currently taken by major voices in the study of magic (esotericism, occultism, etc.): though such is by no means their intent, these scholars move by constructing a narrowly delimited discipline to shut off collaboration and criticism from the "outside."

I hope that scholars whose primary interest is not magic will be led to investigate some of its claims—and mine. I hope other scholars who do work on magic will be encouraged to look seriously at the thin ice upon which we skate. And I hope that those who have felt constrained by a need to validate themselves and their work before the eyes of hostile or simply incredulous colleagues will find here some rudiments of a position from which to laugh back.

I should like to acknowledge Aleister Crowley's book *Magick in Theory and Practice*, which provided the subtitle for the present book. Although I have ultimately devoted minimal space to his thought, I have borrowed an epigraph for chapter 6 in token appreciation.

Although every work of scholarship incurs debts, of friendship, assistance, and intellectual stimulus, the wide-ranging inquiry of this book has made me lean on a particularly large community. I can hardly hope to detail every contribution; even if I could recall every one, this page would soon swell out of all bounds. I can only apologize to those whom I have neglected—assuming always that they would wish to acknowledge the association.

Michael Bathgate, Richard Blum, Bill Brickman, Steven Vanden Broecke, Stephen Clucas, Nick Clulee, Allison Coudert, Allen Debus, Alex Dent-Young, Sean Gilsdorf, Heather Hindman, Jason Ingram, Tom LaMarre, Armando Maggi, Chris Mills, Stephen Mulholland, Hajime Nakatani, Chris Nelson, Martyn Oliver, Richard Parmentier, James Pasto, Michael Prince, Frank Reynolds, Peter Schwartz, Amanda Seaman, Jonathan Z. Smith, Matt Smith, Chris Walsh, Melissa Wender, Jim Wilson, David Wolfsdorf, Elliot Wolfson, Rob Yelle, Anthony Yu, Elena Yuan, and Maria Zlateva, as well as the whole faculty and staff of the Boston University College of Arts and Sciences Writing Program, helped immensely in more ways than I can hope to explain.

My editor, Roger Haydon, had faith in this project even at its most awkward stages; my reviewers gave support to that faith. Hundreds of students contributed ideas, consciously or otherwise; I thank particularly Boston University's "Comparing Religions" students who started so many hares in my mind. Jere Genest, Ken Hite, Hajime Nakatani, James Pasto, and Allan Tulchin read the manuscript at a particularly difficult period. Tony Wallace went over the final draft with a fine-toothed comb and a stylist's eye. John Crowley very kindly blessed my borrowing of Ægypt, at the same time expressing extraordinary modesty about his own accomplishments in imagining magic; without his brilliant novels *Ægypt* and *Love and Sleep*, this book would never have begun.

The illustrations were more difficult to acquire than I had expected. I thank the curators and librarians at Houghton Library, Harvard University, and the Burndy Library at the Dibner Institute for the History of Science. Thanks also to Jean Morrow, director at the Spalding Library, New England Conservatory of Music; Alison Bundy and the staff of the John Hay Library, Brown University; and Timothy Young and the staff of the Beinecke Library, Yale University. Emi Shimokawa spared me a day's trip to Providence by cheerfully serving as my amanuensis at Brown.

A grant from the Boston University Humanities Foundation made these illustrations possible.

The lengthy quotations from Brian Copenhaver's translation of the *Hermetica* in chapter 1 are reprinted with the kind permission of Cambridge University Press.

Most of all, I wish to thank my wife, Sarah Frederick. In addition to constant guidance, support, and criticism, she provided invaluable assistance with Japanese materials and various modes of literary theory, without which several essays could not have come to fruition. Above all, she has cheerfully endured my obsessed ravings about magic and theory since the inception of this project long ago, and furthermore uncomplainingly read through draft after draft of material very distant from her own interests.

THE OCCULT MIND

I ⁛ ÆGYPT

Once, the world was not as it has since become.

Once it worked in a way different from the way it works now; its very flesh and bones, the physical laws that governed it, were ever so slightly different from the ones we know. It had a different history, too, from the history we know the world to have had, a history that implied a different future from the one that has actually come to be, our present.

In that age (not really long ago in time, but long ago in other bridges crossed, which we shall not return by again) certain things were possible that are not now; and contrariwise, things we know not to have happened indubitably had then; and there were other differences large and small, none able now to be studied, because this is now, and that was then.

John Crowley, *Love and Sleep*

The ancients were right. Long ago, the secrets of the cosmos were known to priests and poets and magicians, who manipulated spiritual powers to achieve mighty ends. With this magical technology they built pyramids, magic mountains that connected heaven and earth. They constructed statues that spoke prophecy when the masters inscribed the proper words upon them, cast yarrow wands and palm nuts and other mundane objects and read the state of the world in their fall. And they wrote epics in which we can still find guidance and answers despite their almost fantastic distance from the modern world.

The time was *illud tempus*; the place Ægypt. Not the Egypt of modern geography, nor of the dynasties recognized by archeology, but a special place and time, distant but perhaps not so alien as one might think. And through study, through close analysis, through the acquisition of vast knowledge and erudition about every subject imaginable, we can return to that time, restore our lost world to that distant Golden Age.

It is a pretty myth, and one that still resonates with a great many people in this (post)modern age. In a way, it is the scholar's great fantasy: the highest scholarship will of itself bring unimaginable material and spiritual rewards, not dependent on the vagaries of such tedious academic realities as peer review, departmental and disciplinary politics, or funding. And this myth is not entirely fantasy, either, for two scholars in particular have simultaneously analyzed and perpetuated this nostalgic story, and their visions inspire my examination.

In her numerous books and essays, Dame Frances Yates (1899–1981) revitalized the Egyptian mythos of the Renaissance by presenting in rousing prose its heyday. The heresiarch memory master Giordano Bruno (1548–1600) and the angel-summoning John Dee (1527–1608) are the heroes of this narrative, stolid Catholic and English lay authorities their ever-lurking nemeses.

Mircea Eliade (1907–86), Yates's almost exact contemporary, cast the nets of visionary analysis far wider and invented (or rediscovered) illud tempus, "that [distant] time," as the temporal location of mythological reality. In that time, Thoth created writing despite the warnings of Amun-Ra, Enki invented the arts of civilization, Prometheus brought fire to mankind, and Moses spoke to God on Mount Sinai.

Neither scholar invented from whole cloth but rather rewove the threads of history and myth to reinvent a powerful, even magical, narrative. Simply, Yates and Eliade analyzed the Ægyptian nostalgias of former ages, and in the process projected their own modernist nostalgia onto the texts they analyzed.

This book is not a project in "bashing"; I have no interest in denouncing the admittedly (now) clear failings of Yates and Eliade in their efforts to resuscitate a beautiful lie. To be sure, Yates's analyses of Bruno are now questionable, and Eliade's vast oeuvre often rests on tendentious misreadings of dubious secondary sources. But this is hardly news: many critiques, gently corrective or viciously destructive, have in the last twenty years challenged the bases of these scholars' works. Although she denied such claims, Yates was often accused of harboring occult or Hermetic sympathies. More seriously, it seems plausible that Eliade's scholarship, like that of Georges Dumézil and Paul DeMan, was colored by fascist sympathies.[1]

While such demonstrations may convince, they nevertheless have little utility. Contributions to the perennial sport of intellectual iconoclasm, they show that former paragons had feet of clay. But so long as we take care to apply rigorous, relentless critical methods to our predecessors' works and our own, we need not fall into their errors. Rather than dismiss them out of hand, I prefer to begin by assuming that these great revolutionaries, who were also visionaries, saw or imagined something precious, something irreplaceable, something worth saving at all costs in the texts they read—in

The Occult Mind

Code:	LEHR2007
Author:	Lehrich, Christopher I.
Title:	The Occult Mind: Magic in Theory and Practice
City/Pub./CR:	Ithaca and London: Cornell Univ. Press, 2007
Location	MINF

gypt *in illo tempore*, that place and time
esent book.

⁝⁝

he elite knew secrets of the universe, is
of its manifestations. In the Renais-
sca magia, a variant of the *prisca theolo-*
plified by the writings of Hermes Tris-
among others) noted, the notion of an
shaped many aspects of early modern
d similar conceptions appear through-
m, as well as in early Chinese thought

cult revival inaugurated primarily by
gical thought has rediscovered its nos-
isca magia. Lévi himself, by correlating
posedly Egyptian tarot deck with the
lphabet, brought together Ægypt with
s connection had some precedent in
eenth-century formulators linked Egypt
e builders of the pyramids and the Tem-
ever more magical utopias became ab-
atsky situated ancient knowledge in the
lost continents of Atlantis, Lemuria, and Mu; Alfred Watkins's theory of ley
lines presumed geomantic knowledge among the ancient Britons and
Druids; Margaret Murray (herself an Egyptologist) saw in witchcraft a pre-
Christian nature religion surviving underground into the present within European peasant society. More recently, New Age and neo-pagan thought
continue to expand the range of utopian pasts without altering the fundamental conception: that the ancients knew secrets now lost but recoverable
through personal occult study and practice.[4]

The remainder of this chapter concentrates on the first and most influential of the Western magical nostalgias, the documents that make up the Hermetic corpus or *Hermetica*. Written in the first few centuries of the Common
Era in Alexandria, these Neoplatonic dialogues came to define the nature of
the highest, holiest, noblest aspirations of European magicians.

But if we are to read these documents as *magical*, we must depart radically from the ordinary scholarly modes of interpretation. We must be cautious about questioning the validity and accuracy of Hermes' discourse—in-

deed, we must grant that Hermes knows what he is talking about, describes, and reflects upon a world different from our own. In short, we need to consider the *Hermetica* as texts from an alien world.

The obvious metaphor is archaeological: the world of Egyptian archaeology conjures up images of the pyramids, King Tut's tomb, Luxor, and the Great Sphinx—images of a grand and alien landscape. Yet if an archaeologist were to stumble on an unsuspected text or document, she would immediately look around the find for additional contextual materials. She would never presume that the text had no relevant connection to its historical, material, and geological situation. And, of course, the archaeological approach to the *Hermetica* is the normal one: scholars generally want to fit these texts into a larger historical and intellectual picture of Egypt in the early centuries of the Common Era.[5]

For us, though, mere historical and temporal distance will not suffice. In the history of magic, the *Hermetica* do not come from Egypt—if by Egypt we mean the historical time and place known to Egyptologists—but from Ægypt. In Ægypt, man and gods had constant communication, divinity and truth were always present, and magic worked. It was a land of wonders, and nearly every magician since entry to that land was barred has looked back on it with reverence, awe, and nostalgia. And it is Ægypt, not Egypt, that we fallen moderns must learn to explore and map.

⁙

The *Hermetica* are a loose collection of Neoplatonic dialogues composed in Alexandria during the first few centuries of the Common Era. They purport to be a series of conversations between Hermes Trismegistus (Thrice-Great Hermes), an Egyptian priest roughly contemporary with Moses, and various interlocutors, particularly Poimandres (the Divine Pimander, the demiurge itself) and Hermes' son Tat (equivalent to Theuth).[6]

As Yates demonstrated in the 1960s, Renaissance thinkers accepted the antiquity of the texts and discerned in Hermes the *fons et origo* of pagan learning. Marsilio Ficino (1433–99), for example, seems to have believed that all great learning came ultimately from either the tradition begun by Moses or that begun by Hermes. Such claims are essential here: as we read in the *Hermetica*, we must suppress that part of our critical faculties that immediately refers the texts to late Alexandria. The texts describe Ægypt, the magical place and time *in which they were written*. In short, we must for present purposes grant the internal assumptions and authorial claims of Hermes.

The Occult Mind

In the Latin *Asclepius*, the longest of the texts of the Hermetic corpus, Hermes prophesies the fall of Ægypt in ringing words:

Do you not know, Asclepius, that Egypt is an image of heaven or, to be more precise, that everything governed and moved in heaven came down to Egypt and was transferred there? If truth were told, our land is the temple of the whole world.

And yet . . . a time will come when it will appear that the Egyptians paid respect to divinity with faithful mind and painstaking reverence—to no purpose. All their holy worship will be disappointed and perish without effect, for divinity will return from earth to heaven, and Egypt will be abandoned. The land that was the seat of reverence will be widowed by the powers and left destitute of their presence. When foreigners occupy the land and territory, not only will reverence fall into neglect but, even harder, a prohibition under penalty prescribed by law (so-called) will be enacted against reverence, fidelity and divine worship. Then this most holy land, seat of shrines and temples, will be filled completely with tombs and corpses.

O Egypt, Egypt, of your reverent deeds only stories will survive, and they will be incredible to your children! Only words cut in stone will survive to tell your faithful works, and . . . barbarian[s] will dwell in Egypt. For divinity goes back to heaven, and all the people will die, deserted, as Egypt will be widowed and deserted by god and human. I call to you, most holy river, and I tell your future: a torrent of blood will fill you to the banks, and you will burst over them; not only will blood pollute your divine waters, it will also make them break out everywhere, and the number of the entombed will be much larger than the living. Whoever survives will be recognized as Egyptian only by his language; in his actions he will seem a foreigner.

Asclepius, why do you weep? Egypt herself will be persuaded to deeds much wickeder than these, and she will be steeped in evils far worse. A land once holy, most loving of divinity, by reason of her reverence the only land on earth where the gods settled, she who taught holiness and fidelity will be an example of utter <un> belief. In their weariness the people of that time will find the world nothing to wonder at or to worship. This all—a good thing that never had nor has nor will have its better—will be endangered. People will find it oppressive and scorn it. They will not cherish this entire world, a work of god beyond compare, a glorious construction, a bounty composed of images in multiform variety, a mechanism for god's will ungrudgingly supporting his work, making a unity of everything that can be honored, praised and finally loved by those who see it, a multiform accumulation taken as a single thing. . . .

The reverent will be thought mad, the irreverent wise; the lunatic will be thought brave, and the scoundrel will be taken for a decent person. . . . Whoever dedicates himself to reverence of mind will find himself facing a capital penalty. They will establish new laws, new justice. Nothing holy, nothing reverent nor worthy of heaven or heavenly beings will be heard of or believed in the mind.

How mournful when the gods withdraw from mankind! . . . Then neither will the earth stand firm nor the sea be sailable; stars will not cross heaven nor will the course of the stars stand firm in heaven. Every divine voice will grow mute in enforced silence. The fruits of the earth will rot; the soil will no more be fertile; and the very air will droop in gloomy lethargy.

Such will be the old age of the world: irreverence, disorder, disregard for everything good.[7]

For Hermes, the defining characteristic of Ægypt is reverence for the living gods. Worship here is not abstract faith but has an effect: "It will appear that the Egyptians paid respect to divinity . . . to no purpose. All their holy worship will be disappointed and perish without effect, for divinity will return from earth to heaven." It seems that Ægypt's reverence and worship keeps the gods present. After the fall, when the land is "widowed" by the gods, a series of important transformations occur; working backward, we can measure Ægypt's pyramids by the length of their shadows.

The primary metaphor for the transformation is a shift from life to death—"Then this most holy land, seat of shrines and temples, will be filled completely with tombs and corpses"—implying that those sites which later contain only the dead husks of divinities and people were, in Ægypt, populated by living gods. Thus the pyramids, for example, now appear as elaborate stone tombs or shells constructed around mummified remains; in Ægypt, however, divine presences dwelt within. The Egyptian tombs were once Ægyptian shrines and temples.

This transformation has far-reaching implications for our understanding of Ægypt as "an image of heaven. . . . the temple of the whole world." After the prophesied fall, this temple becomes a tomb, containing only dead shells of divinity. Even the outward appearance of the temple falls into ruin: "Then neither will the earth stand firm nor the sea be sailable; stars will not cross

The Occult Mind

heaven nor will the course of the stars stand firm in heaven. . . . The fruits of the earth will rot; the soil will no more be fertile; and the very air will droop in gloomy lethargy." By contrast, Ægypt is a fertile, vibrant land, in which the orderly regularity of earth and sea matches the stately, consistent motions of the stars in heaven.

Once this ideal condition has collapsed, what survives as evidence of the glories of Ægypt? We have seen that the temples and shrines do survive, but as dried husks of their former selves; the same effect occurs with Ægypt's language, the only survival described as such by Hermes, in an important passage: "O Egypt, Egypt, of your reverent deeds only stories will survive, and they will be incredible to your children! Only words cut in stone will survive to tell your faithful works. . . . Whoever survives will be recognized as Egyptian only by his language; in his actions he will seem a foreigner."[8]

Thus in widowed Egypt, the written and spoken languages will be divorced. The spoken language will survive, but without its attendant reverent actions; written language, now "only words cut in stone," will no longer be believed by the Egyptians, who will find the stories "incredible." Implicit in this division is a correlation of truth and action. In Ægypt, speech and writing were part of reverent action; in the ultimate Egyptian collapse, speech becomes action without reverence—"in his actions he will seem a foreigner"—while writing becomes reverence without action. In other words, the departure from reverence breaks the connection of speech and writing, so that ancient writings are not believed and speech does not serve proper action. Language in Ægypt was a divine temple but is only a tomb in Egypt.

This linguistic prophecy is extraordinarily important for our reading of Ægypt. We may briefly compare it to the Egyptian myth of the god Theuth's invention of writing as recounted in Plato's *Phaedrus*. There, Theuth (Thoth) invents writing as a remedy for memory, but King Thamus (Amun-Ra) realizes that the invention will poison both memory and speech. When Theuth claims that "this discipline . . . will make the Egyptians wiser and will improve their memories," the king replies, "The fact is that this invention will produce forgetfulness in the souls of those who have learned it."[9] Hermes does not subscribe to this view. For him, both arts are holy in Ægypt but fall into error when divine presence empties out of them. Thus in Ægypt, Theuth's vision was correct, but the fall into Egypt validates the king's prophecy.

Recall for a moment that in the occult history of the world, Plato was writing *after Hermes*—indeed, he was *inspired by* the great Ægyptian master. Reading from this peculiar perspective, it appears that Plato has tried to "correct" a story that does not make sense—or one that *no longer* makes sense. Ægypt had no need for a strong disparity of value with respect to linguistic forms, because the presence inhabiting them was divine and immanent. After the fall, when Plato writes, language no longer has a strong link to presence of any sort, and if there is presence, it is *human* presence. To put it differently, in Egypt (and not Ægypt) neither writing nor speech has any direct link to divine presence; speech apparently contains human presence through memory and the speaker's physical proximity, but writing constantly undermines this attenuated presence. Plato has conflated two different events: first, the failure of reverence caused divine presence to depart Ægypt; second, the departure divided speech from writing and forced them to make opposing claims on her memory.

Hermes' prophecy connects a number of issues of continuing importance throughout the present book. For him, reverent action—ritual of some sort—has theurgical effects, maintaining the link between humanity and the divine. We see this connection made explicit in the famous "god-making" passage of *Asclepius*:

> Our ancestors once erred gravely on the theory of divinity; they were unbelieving and inattentive to worship and reverence for god. But then they discovered the art of making gods. To their discovery they added a conformable power arising from the nature of matter. Because they could not make souls, they mixed this power in and called up the souls of demons or angels and implanted them in likenesses through holy and divine mysteries, whence the idols could have the power to do good and evil.[10]

An earlier passage clarifies the nature of these idols:

> "Are you talking about statues, Trismegistus?"
>
> "Statues, Asclepius, yes. See how little trust you have! I mean statues ensouled and conscious, filled with spirit and doing great deeds; statues that foreknow the future and predict it by lots, by prophecy, by dreams and by many other means; statues that make people ill and cure them, bringing them pain and pleasure as each deserves."[11]

The indwelling of the gods in statues and the divine immanence in the land and the language of Ægypt are strictly *homologous*, not merely analogous: they are linked causally, temporally, and substantively. When the gods depart, their temples become tombs, the land shatters into disorder, language dissolves into warring factions of speech and writing, and Ægypt herself becomes only a memory. Thus for Hermes, the presence or absence of

The Occult Mind

the gods connects space, language, and memory; much of this book explores various meanings of this distinctively Ægyptian complex in magical nostalgia.

Unfortunately, we cannot analyze this complex directly, because all our data is necessarily colored by the fall of Ægypt. Hermes' student Asclepius explains the problem to King Ammon rather neatly:

> My teacher, Hermes—often speaking to me in private, sometimes in the presence of Tat—used to say that those reading my books would find their organization very simple and clear when, on the contrary, it is unclear and keeps the meaning of its words concealed; furthermore, it will be entirely unclear (he said) when the Greeks eventually desire to translate our language to their own and thus produce in writing the greatest distortion and unclarity. But this discourse, expressed in our paternal language, keeps clear the meaning of its words. The very quality of the speech and the <sound> of Egyptian words have in themselves the energy of the objects they speak of.[12]

Hermes prophesies the fall not only of language but also of truth: what was true in Ægypt is no longer true and in fact could *never* have been true. And as we saw with Plato, this impossibility prompts corrections of Ægyptian texts, which are "no longer believed."

⁙

How can we interpret documents from a land and in a language so alien to ours? We can have no context, no further information, none of the ordinary materials with which every historian, archaeologist, or sociologist works. We must work comparatively, for only a comparative methodology will permit us simultaneously to interpret texts and ideas from multiple, unrelated cultures. We need to choose our comparative texts carefully, rigorously establish the foundations of and justification for the comparison, and then differentiate analytically to shed light on these mysterious and alien artifacts.

Great magical texts are commonly systematic and as such readily comparable to other systematic analytical structures, such as modern scholarly theoretical systems. As a preliminary demonstration of this hermeneutic possibility, I propose a comparative conversation between Hermes and the two modern scholar-visionaries who first provoked us to read the *Hermetica* in this fashion, who first attempted to map Ægypt in our time and in our scholarly language: Mircea Eliade and Frances Yates.

In *Patterns in Comparative Religion*, Eliade set out to reveal what he called the "morphology of the sacred."[13] This phrase should be taken seriously: Eliade does not construct a *history* of religious conceptions in the ordinary sense, and his use of Goethe's (and Rudolf Steiner's) morphological theories entails that such apparently value-laden terms as "degraded" or "expanded" take on technical, structural meaning.[14]

Eliade's morphology sought to elaborate the nature of religious forms, of patterns or archetypes in religion, in such a way that his analyses would not be subject to historical or psychological criticism:

> The *history* of a religious phenomenon cannot reveal *all* that this phenomenon, by the mere fact of its manifestation, seeks to show us. . . . All these dreams, myths, and nostalgias . . . cannot be exhausted by a psychological explanation; there is always a kernel that remains refractory to explanation, and this indefinable, irreducible element perhaps reveals the real situation of man in the cosmos, a situation that, we shall never tire of repeating, is not solely "historical."[15]

For Eliade, the sacred was strictly analogous to Goethe's "leaf," that primary archetypal form to which all other botanical forms relate by a strict economy of logical progression and degradation. Just so, every particular manifestation of the sacred (in Eliade's terms hierophany, kratophany, etc.) had a discrete and analyzable relationship to the sacred itself. By understanding the processes of such morphological change, it would be possible to formulate religious ideas, movements, and structures *without reference to history at all*. Like Goethe's *Urpflanze*, the perfectly ideal sacred would enable us to describe religious objects of which history "shall be jealous."[16]

Goethe's morphology provided him a mode in which to speak of multiple plants as having relationships that resemble historical ones but are not temporally ordered. That is, Goethe examined a given botanical phenomenon as a development from some other phenomenon without that development's implying temporal causality; instead, he could interpret all botanical forms as interrelated by endless *dynamic*—literally *vital*—processes. Thus he classified multiple plants with respect to one another on the basis of their internal structures—from their own points of view, as it were—without reference to historical models. This morphology was significantly a reaction against Linnaeus, whose means of categorizing had nothing whatever to do with the plants' internal dynamics and only related to the external qualities that botanists *perceived* in them. The historical perspective on biology did

The Occult Mind

not, at that time, have a strong scientific basis—that would not come until Darwin—and we may read Goethe's project as an attempt to formulate *a history-like structure in the absence of any actual history*. Goethe's intent was not antihistorical as such; rather, he knew that (at the time) one *could not know* the history of plants, and he sought an alternative mode of classification that would nevertheless respect the internal economies and dynamics of biological structure. Late in his life Goethe seems to have shifted to the proto-Darwinian camp, although he recognized that his morphology could not be overlaid directly on an evolutionary model.[17]

Eliade's rationale is importantly different. It has always been clear that one *can* write histories of religions (for example, a history of the Lutheran Church), but they are necessarily limited in scope. Eliade sought instead a way to talk about the history of *religion* rather than *religions*; that is, he wanted to study an object with no historical existence, an object outside history. To put it differently, Eliade presumed from the outset that there *must* be a "leaf" in all religious manifestations, and that one could thus formulate the entirety of religion backward: if in comparing two religious phenomena previous scholars had commonly assumed historical connections or causation (evolution, diffusion, and so forth), Eliade wanted to refer phenomena to an *exterior standard*, one he could not observe directly but had to postulate. In a sense, he reverses the historical context of the Goethean project: botany moves from exterior classification to internal logical classification and then to history in the form of evolution, whereas the study of religion moves from history to internal logical classification.

Did Eliade imagine a Linnaean classificatory endpoint to this progression? For our own part, we might legitimately wonder whether such a move would not solve a good many problems. Goethe's objection to the Linnaean system was that it privileged the botanist rather than the plant, classified on the basis of an artificial rather than a natural order. To do the same with religious objects would have the advantage of self-conscious abstraction: to say that two religious objects relate in some particular way would imply nothing whatever about history, causation, or valuation, because it would be accepted from the outset that the classificatory system had no ground but scholarly convenience.[18]

But Eliade could never have accepted such a system—nor would most contemporary scholars of religion, for that matter. It presumes that the best way to compare religious phenomena would be to disregard history entirely, to insist always that particular similarities are analogous and not homologous except with respect to a scholarly construct, to assume that there are no generalizable *reasons* for the particular manifestations of the sacred that we analyze: religious manifestations are the way they are, and are similar and different in the ways they are, for no reason at all. By this logic, no framework can properly be applied—not the motions of historical causation, not the articulation of some dialectic of the sacred—to *explain* anything. Goethe stated that morphology's "intention is to portray rather than explain. . . . Without exception it considers itself the handmaiden of biology."[19] It is hardly surprising that Eliade disregarded this essential point, for neither he nor almost anyone else who studies religion wants to discard a priori the possibility of explanation in favor of representation or portrayal, and certainly Eliade would not wish to make his morphology of religion "the handmaiden" of a historical analysis to which all explanatory possibility is referred.

Ultimately, Eliade had to ground his morphology in a fixed principle in order to retain the possibility of explanation. Furthermore, as we have seen, Goethe's method requires that any explanatory principle be *historical*. Eliade's solution to this seemingly intractable difficulty is elegant, if perhaps fallacious. According to Eliade, *homo religiosus* orients himself with respect to history in two ways that exactly parallel the dichotomous relation we have found in Eliade himself. First, *homo religiosus* experiences a "terror of history," a fear that the relentless onslaught of temporality will annul meaning; this is precisely homologous to Eliade's concern that historical analysis must overlook the ahistorical meanings bound up in sacrality. Second, *homo religiosus* refers his most meaning-laden behaviors to a *time outside historical time*, that is, to illud tempus, thus holding fast to ahistorical meaning through nostalgia; this is again parallel to the ahistoricity of Eliade's morphological method, which is founded (as it was not in Goethe) on an *antagonistic* relation to the historical.[20]

Thus Eliade's understanding of the nostalgia of *homo religiosus* has a twofold origin. On the one hand, it arises from his analyses of religious thought and behavior, as well as his own modernist nostalgia for a time before the disenchantment of the world. But more interestingly, this conception arises from his quest to develop morphology as a method for analyzing historical-cultural data.

At this point we can bring Frances Yates into the same conversation. I will examine Yates's methodology in more detail in subsequent chapters; for the moment, it suffices to recognize this dialectic of nostalgia at work in her analyses of Giordano Bruno.

In *Giordano Bruno and the Hermetic Tradition*, Yates explained in ringing tones that the Renaissance revival of Hermetism depended on a colossal historical error: they utterly failed to see that Hermes was not in fact a prophet pointing forward to Platonism and even Christianity but rather an invention of Alexandrian thinkers well *after* the rise of Neoplatonism and Christianity.

> The great forward movements of the Renaissance all derive their vigour, their emotional impulse, from looking backwards. The cyclic view of time as a perpetual movement from pristine golden ages of purity and truth . . . was thus of necessity a search for the early, the ancient, the original gold. . . .
>
> These are truisms. . . . But the returning movement of the Renaissance [which sought] . . . return to a pure golden age of magic, was based on a radical error in dating. . . . [Hermes] was not returning to an Egyptian wisdom, not much later than the wisdom of the Hebrew patriarchs and prophets, and much earlier than Plato and the other philosophers of Greek antiquity. . . . He is returning to the pagan background of early Christianity, to that religion of the world, strongly tinged with magic and oriental influences, which was the gnostic version of Greek philosophy, and the refuge of weary pagans seeking an answer to life's problems other than that offered by their contemporaries, the early Christians.[21]

Thus for Yates, much of the interest of Renaissance magic such as Bruno's is its poignancy: it could only exist under conditions of misrecognition, of believing in a miraculous proof of all their nostalgic desires, and within fairly short order this necessary error would be destroyed by new philological accuracy in dating. Of this end, this "bomb-shell," Yates writes:

> The dating by Isaac Casaubon in 1614 of the Hermetic writings . . . is a watershed separating the Renaissance world from the modern world. It shattered at one blow the build-up of Renaissance Neoplatonism with its basis in the *prisci theologi* of whom Hermes Trismegistus was the chief. It shattered the whole position of the Renaissance Magus and Renaissance magic. . . . It shattered even the non-magical Christian Hermetic movement of the sixteenth century. It shattered the position of an extremist

Hermetist, such as Giordano Bruno had been. . . . It shattered, too, the basis of all attempts to build a natural theology on Hermetism.[22]

In essence, Yates interprets the magical Renaissance as a moment when the world was once again enchanted because of a terrible historical error. Renaissance magic begins dramatically, with the discovery of miraculous texts, but ends with a melancholy reassertion of reality by a careful historian-philologist. This interpretation of the sixteenth-century magical moment is certainly a nostalgic one; we cannot help but feel Yates's poignant attraction to the magical:

> "Hermes Trismegistus" and his [early modern] history is important. . . . [The seventeenth-century moderns] may have discarded notions on mind and matter which, however strangely formulated, may be in essence less remote than their own conceptions from some of the thought of to-day. In any case we ought to know the history of what they discarded. . . . And that history uncovers the roots of the change which came over man when his mind was no longer integrated into the divine life of the universe. In the company of "Hermes Trismegistus" one treads the borderlands between magic and religion, magic and science, magic and art or poetry or music. It was in those elusive realms that the man of the Renaissance dwelt, and the seventeenth century lost some clue to the personality of that *magnum miraculum*.[23]

Here we see a kind of antagonism to history, like that we encounter in Eliade and Hermes himself. Yates does not understand herself to be antihistorical but rather projects a nostalgic vision of an enchanted time—a time whose enchantment contradicts the facts of chronological history, "based on a radical error in dating." Where Hermes denounced Ægypt's fall into irreverence and mundanity, so too Yates evokes a sense of loss in her portrayal of a moment when European intellectuals stood briefly outside mundane reality, outside history, *in illo tempore*—when they lived a moment in Ægypt.

Eliade seems to have taken Yates's reading for granted.[24] Admittedly, he was no expert on the Renaissance, but he must surely have found Yates's reading congenial. In her interpretation he could find traces of a sophisticated, elegant, scholarly articulation of the same old dialectic of the sacred and its attendant nostalgia. Thus for him Hermes could only be read as a product of Alexandria, not as an Ægyptian prophet. In effect, the desire to project and interpret nostalgia, to see a momentary reenchantment of the world, so overwhelms Eliade that he blindly sets aside his most fundamental

The Occult Mind

ahistorical principles. Hermes must be read as Yates reads him, because otherwise the whole poignancy of the Renaissance vision collapses.

In Yates's reading, Bruno conceived of religion and magic as closely connected, both receding backward in time to the *prisca theologia* and *prisca magia*; for him these were essentially identical, with their origins in Hermes. Thus if Eliade would read Hermes as himself articulating nostalgia, Yates reads Bruno as nostalgic with respect to Hermes.

To be sure, both readings may be accurate. But in the process of so neatly aligning all these perspectives, we have elided difference to an excessive degree. Most particularly, we must recognize that what we have called Hermes' nostalgia is only *analogous* to nostalgia as Eliade or Yates understood it. If nostalgia implies looking backward to a pristine origin, Hermes claims to stand *within that origin*; his apparent nostalgia is nothing of the sort, but rather a prophetic revelation of the future fall. To put it differently, Hermes gazes forward on Egypt from Ægypt, prophesying all that will transform the latter into the former; Yates and Eliade look backward on Egypt, trying thence to project back into Ægypt. What is ordinary, unstated, obvious in Hermes, is precisely what Yates and Eliade—and we ourselves—most wish to know: the nature of that reality variously called illud tempus and Ægypt. Thus the nostalgias of Yates and Eliade have their strongest parallel in the *prophetic voice* of Hermes. If the visions of Yates and Eliade are mediated by history and memory, it is rather the blinding wind of divine prophecy which enables that of Hermes. Memory replaces prophecy.

Comparative analysis always depends on a double gesture. On the one hand, there is the analytical construction or abstraction of the particular object of study, outside of broader context; on the other, there is the contextualizing process, in which the object takes its place in a larger framework that explains it. The former method is traditionally the morphological or structural, the latter the historical.[25]

But as Jonathan Z. Smith has famously noted, these two activities have parallels in Sir James Frazer's formulation of magical logic, divided between the homeopathic, based on similarity, and the contagious, based on contiguity.[26] Having first encountered and noted the object of study because it seems familiar, *similar* to something we already know, we then move to contextualize it, make it *contiguous* to known data.

In the abstract, this procedure is not so much problematic as inevitable: we become interested because something catches in Coleridge's "hooks-and-eyes of the memory," to borrow Smith's deft allusion, and then we try to make sense of it by finding its place in a pattern. The danger lies less in the handling of the object itself than in the contextualizing. The morphological procedure, seeking similarity, invites us to wonder what *other* object the first reminds us of. Then, using all the various contextualizing techniques, we try to establish an objective validity to that similarity: we want to find that the interesting mental connection has a causal, external basis.

Smith's criticism, while devastating, subtly distorts Frazer's magical logic. For Frazer, the objection was different: the magician thinks that because his doll looks like (is similar to) his enemy, or contains pieces of (is contiguous with) his enemy's hair or fingernails, there is therefore a causal connection between the doll and the enemy, such that a pin stabbed in the doll's head will produce headaches. From a scholarly perspective, this is indeed a misapplication of logic, but only because of the general arbitrariness of the sign. The problem to which Smith directs our attention is rather that the comparative scholar *elides homeopathy and contagion*, arguing that because there is *similarity* there must also be *contiguity*. It is as though the magician believed that because the doll *looks like* his enemy, it is therefore *made of* his enemy.

At the same time, this analogy between scholarly method and magical thought is suggestive for our present analysis. If some analogy obtains among Eliade, Yates, and Hermes, how exactly does it function and what importance or meaning can be ascribed to it? The three scholars in this preliminary study of Ægypt can to a significant degree be aligned with the Frazerian magical logic. Eliade's morphology, which in its most rigorous phases sought to define archetypes without regard for historical connection, is clearly an application of the Law of Homeopathy: similar things are connected, though not in a preexisting ontological sense; they have no *causal* connection, but in the future they can be treated together. Yates's impressionistic history of ideas, in which all connections and parallels arise from historical influence and contact, depends on the Law of Contagion: objects once in contact are always in contact, thus the advent of the Hermetic corpus in the early modern intellectual world must have crowning importance for an understanding of all later Hermetic-like intellectual ideas. And finally, we have the position of Hermes himself, which elides homeopathy and contagion: similar things must also touch, and contiguous objects must also be (or become) similar, as in his theory of speech and writing bound by the immanent presence of the gods. Thus in a sense it is Hermes' method that is most directly critiqued by Smith; or rather, Hermes becomes a peculiarly essential forefather of comparative scholarship.

As a preliminary excursion into Ægypt, in this chapter I have raised more questions than I have answered. We have seen that Hermes Trismegistus can be read as a precursor of modern scholarship, and that doing so elucidates a number of important problems in magical thought. Further, we have discerned in Hermes' modern interlocutors several points of congruence. In particular, the problem of Ægypt manifests a complex relationship of nostalgia or antagonism to history, an interest in linguistic and symbolic issues, and a strange half logic not unlike that which Frazer described.

Although it would be interesting to extend this comparison, we cannot go on indefinitely. None of these three thinkers is sufficiently systematic to permit rigorous comparison at the analytical level, and simply continuing the conversation would likely lead to sterile repetition. For the present discussion, it was sufficient to demonstrate a somewhat peculiar comparative method and to show its utility for the analysis of magical and theoretical texts. But to follow the labyrinthine threads we have found, we will need additional guides. If we widen our vision to include more precise theoretical and magical texts, we will be able to seek answers in stranger, more obscure corners of Ægypt.

2 ⋮⋮⋮ THE LEY OF THE LAND

I sat upon the shore
Fishing, with the arid plain behind me
Shall I at least set my lands in order?

T. S. Eliot, *The Waste Land*

Across the Great Schism, through our whole landscape
Ignoring God's vicar and God's ape

Under their noses, unsuspected
The Old Man's road runs where it did.

W. H. Auden, *The Old Man's Road*

In 1921, Alfred Watkins had a vision. A traveling salesman for his family milling and brewing business, as well as a respected amateur photographer who invented the Watkins exposure meter, he stood on a high ridge top, gazing down at his beloved Herefordshire countryside. As he looked, comparing to a map, he saw "that various prehistoric places, such as standing stones, earthen burial mounds, prehistoric earthworked hills, and other such features fell into straight lines for miles across country."[1] In this "flood of ancestral memory," as he called it, Watkins saw the ancient landscape beneath modern Britain.[2]

Briefly, the idea . . . holds that the early inhabitants of Britain deliberately placed mounds, camps and standing stones across the landscape in straight lines. As time went by later structures were added to these sites. Some Roman roads followed the leys, Christian churches were built on what had been ley markers in order to take advantage of the age and sanctity already attached to them, and the keeps of mediaeval castles were sited on mounds that had marked leys millennia before. As a result it is still possible to trace these alignments on maps.[3]

This theory, while it engendered the Straight Track Club and innumerable picnicking searchers, was flatly rejected by the professional archaeological community. This rejection was in some sense vindicated by the occult transformation of leys into invisible "lines of force," proposed first by Dion Fortune in her 1936 novel, *The Goat-Foot God*, and made central to the theory when in 1938 "Arthur Lawton, a member of the Straight Track Club, wrote a paper in which he claimed that leys were lines of cosmic force which could be dowsed."[4] By 1948, however, the Straight Track Club had closed, due to a near-total lack of interest, and leys themselves disappeared once more from the cultural landscape.

The revitalization of ley hunting in the late 1950s and '60s is well told by Paul Devereux, a leading modern ley hunter who has little time for the more extravagant occult theories:[5]

> From 1960 the ley theory took on a new lease of life, one that has led to the modern New Age notion of "ley lines." An ex–R.A.F. pilot, Tony Wedd, was very interested in flying saucers, or UFOs. He had read Watkins' *The Old Straight Track* and also a French book, *Flying Saucers and the Straight Line Mystery* (1958) by Aimé Michel, in which it was (falsely) suggested that the locations where flying saucers landed or hovered very low during the 1954 French flying saucer outbreak or "wave" fell into straight lines or "orthotenies". Wedd made the excited conclusion that Watkins' "leys" and Michel's "orthotenies" were one and the same phenomenon. He had also read an American book by Buck Nelson called *My Trip to Mars, the Moon and Venus* (1956) in which [Nelson] claimed to have flown in UFOs, and to have witnessed them picking up energy from "magnetic currents" flowing through the Earth. In 1961, Wedd published a pamphlet called *Skyways and Landmarks* in which he theorised that UFO occupants flew along magnetic lines of force which linked ancient sites, and that the ancient sites acted as landmarks for UFO pilots. It all relied very much on the notions and experiences of an old-fashioned terrestrial airplane pilot, rather than intergalactic extra-terrestrial creatures!
>
> Wedd formed the Star Fellowship, which aimed to contact the Space Brothers. The members of the club enlisted the aid of a psychic called Mary Long in their ley hunting, and she started referring to "lines of force" and magnetic nodes in the landscape. She also channelled communications from a Space Being called "Attalita." In 1962 a Ley Hunter's Club was set up with Wedd's encouragement, and by 1965 it produced the first few copies of *The Ley Hunter* journal.[6]

With the publication of John Michell's *The View over Atlantis* in 1967,[7] ley hunting divided into two camps, those who seek "lines of force" of a possibly Atlantean or extraterrestrial (or both) origin, and those who prefer ar-chaeological reconstruction. In order to clarify the epistemology of occult history, let us examine the intersection of the various forms of ley hunting with disparate institutional-scientific views.

Consider the claims against Watkins. First, the leys seem peculiarly hap-hazard given the claims for their organized use. In many cases, a ley consists of only four points—two or three close together, and one at a considerable remove. Given that two points indicate a line, and that the English country-side is littered with old objects, presumably one would need rather more than three or four points to see them as evidence of deliberate construction.

Interestingly, this issue was taken up in a presentation before the Royal Statistical Society by Simon Broadbent, a distinguished statistician who seems to have been introduced to it by David Kendall, whose analyses of the "megalithic yard" hypothesis of Alexander Thom may be familiar to some. Broadbent's discussion, although at times beyond my technical competence, demonstrates conclusively that the statistical likelihood of finding a passable line of three or even four points within a random distribution of fifty or so points is exceedingly high, indeed a great deal higher than even a statistician might guess:

> Unaided intuition can in fact easily be surprised in this area. If 50 points are uniformly and independently distributed in a square, how many tri-ads will we find at an acceptance angle of ½°? The reader might like to pause here and guess the answer. It is shown below [in Broadbent's paper] that in this case the mean is 57.01 and standard deviation 8.34, so to observe 60 or even 70 triads is not really significant.[8]

In other words, if we cluster every three points to make a great many tri-angles, and then we only examine triangles whose largest (flattest) angle is within ½° of a straight line (180°), we expect to find nearly sixty such trian-gles within a square containing fifty randomly distributed points. Ulti-mately, Broadbent shows that, contra Watkins and most ley hunters, it is not a question of finding so many points more or less in a line: this proves noth-ing. Simplistically, it is necessary to show that a given number of points fall in a line in a fashion significantly outside the statistical norm for all such points in that geographical region.[9]

Second, and more interesting, the existence of leys would require that an-cient peoples be exceptionally well organized, capable of long-term earth-working projects on a large scale. But of course, Stone Age societies were quite primitive, incapable of any such projects—at least, this was the usual

The Occult Mind

perspective in the early part of the twentieth century. Modern archaeologists accept the dense and sophisticated organization of these ancient cultures, and recognize that on numerous occasions (notably Stonehenge, Avebury, and the like) they organized enormous earthworks across spans of centuries. At the same time, scholars remain deeply skeptical about claims coming from well outside their own purview, analytically or otherwise. To quote from the megalithic yard and ancient astronomy discussions previously mentioned:

> Obviously it would be wrong to reject these theories on the facile ground that they do not accord with the previously generally accepted picture of prehistoric Britain. Our failure to find evidence of sophisticated intellectual activity among the barrows, cairns, standing stones, stone circles and henge monuments of 4,000 years ago cannot mean that such evidence does not exist. It need only mean that most of the archaeological profession was not equipped either by training or temperament to discover it.
>
> Equally, however, the theories should not be accepted uncritically and it would be just as scientifically naïve to assume that they are correct simply because the data collected has been subjected to impeccably accurate and skilled mathematical analysis.[10]

Statistically, then, there are many *possible* leys, but the great majority of them are certainly accidental or entirely modern. From Watkins and his enthusiastic admirers we thus have a large quantity of data from which to discern a much smaller number of actual lines, if any at all. That other societies, notably the Nazca people of ancient Peru, found it worthwhile to lay down vast networks of straight lines makes it not inherently implausible that such lines might exist. What is required is not empirical proof as such, since no evidence within the data set itself could ever constitute proof, albeit it is hypothetically possible (if unlikely) that one might find such fantastically improbable evidence that it would be difficult to challenge—a run of twenty equidistant points, for example. Instead, leys need confirmation from without: additional data of another sort, or, in the abstract, a *reason*. That is, supposing one could verify the likelihood of even a few actual leys, of long, straight tracks across wide expanses of countryside, executed with great care over long periods of time, the question would not be *whether* they exist, but rather *why* ancient people had constructed them. And Watkins's theories might or might not be accurate—but then he recognized the provisional nature of his work.

In the explosion of occult perspectives in the second half of the twentieth century, however, the question of leys returned in a new manner simply unacceptable to archaeology, leading in part to the unwillingness of even modern archaeologists seriously to consider the data for leys.[11] Specifically, the claim has arisen that these lines and earthworks, along with the Nazca lines, the Great Pyramid of Giza, and Chinese geomantic (*feng shui*) "dragon lines," all represent evidence of a previous great civilization, one that recognized the earth powers and telluric forces and tapped into them to perform mighty works—the Atlantean civilization.

This new theory of leys began in earnest with John Michell, an old Etonian with a penchant for UFO research, archaeoastronomy, and numerology, who became convinced that UFO sightings indicated something rather different than was generally assumed (by believers). Not that UFOs are not alien spacecraft—though Michell seems increasingly wary of this theory—but, as Wedd had suggested, they may have used and continue to use leys as sighting points and navigational beacons in their long trans-terrene flights.

In Michell's formulation this idea responds directly—and negatively—to the earlier theory of Erik von Däniken, presented first in *Chariots of the Gods?*[12] Von Däniken considered it impossible that primitive peoples could have constructed such massive and complex structures as the Egyptian pyramids, the Nazca lines, Mayan temples, the Easter Island statues, and so forth, so he proposed that these structures had been constructed with help from advanced alien beings.[13] He then analyzed a series of images, such as what others have interpreted as Aztec soldiers in ceremonial headgear, and noted certain similarities to photographs of modern astronauts. Adding to this collection a number of idiosyncratic measurements, a great many attractive photographs, and a chatty, slightly incoherent prose style, the Swiss former hotelier and his theory became a popular sensation.

Michell's theory of leys uses much the same monumental evidence, but projects backward in time rather than forward. That is, he is perfectly willing to accept that ancient civilizations could build practically anything they wished. At the same time, he thinks that these societies must all have collapsed, in a relatively short span, as adduced by the lack of later monuments on the scale of Tiahuanaco, Stonehenge, or the Great Pyramid. Combining this general perspective—a more traditionally nostalgic one, let us note—with a highly modified version of Immanuel Velikovsky's catastrophe theory of geological history, Michell proposes that the original leys and the best of the ancient monuments were the work of Atlanteans.[14] After the collapse of their civilization in the disaster described elliptically by Plato, later peoples tried to emulate the great works that still lasted among them, with mixed results.

The Occult Mind

This mixture of truly ancient and merely old provides an explanation for the confusing ley data. Those leys that do seem to pass smoothly for many miles of otherwise trackless countryside, as well as the great monolithic structures of England (Stonehenge, Avebury, and so on), come from the Atlanteans. The later structures and lines that produce such indifferent and confusing data must represent the work of post-Atlanteans. The same theory covers the works of Egypt: the Great Pyramid is Atlantean work, and the other, less perfect ones are later, post-fall imitations.[15]

Setting aside the more apparent problems with this theory, it is essential that we understand *why* Michell, as well as much of the Earth Mysteries industry that has sprung up more or less in his wake, believes leys were constructed in the first place. After all, if one is going to propose a radical theory—and a theory involving Atlantis and UFOs is hardly conservative!—there needs to be some result, some product that justifies the radicalism.

For Michell, leys are actually representations of underground currents or lines naturally existing in the earth's magnetic field. These lines form a vast grid or network and were tapped at important or convenient points by master scientist-magicians. He suggests that standing stones, for example, essentially act as acupuncture needles into the currents of the earth, allowing one to divert, draw from, or strengthen the telluric forces present. By these means, the ancient Atlanteans had unlimited free power, which they used to hold up their flying vehicles, just as today UFOs are held aloft on these same currents. They could communicate great distances without any need for phone lines. And all this extraordinary technology required no destruction of the earth—indeed, it required *understanding* and *nurturing* the earth, as opposed to drilling and gashing holes in it.

Thus at least one purpose here is ecological and political. In the old days of Atlantis, one could have power without ecological disaster, and these wonders were provided freely by a learned elite. Neither is true now, but they *could* be, if only scientists and ordinary people would come together to investigate the ancient magic of Atlantis, whose keys are still to be found in their cryptic ancient monuments.

Michell describes here a kind of illud tempus, and a very specific one. Not unlike Ægypt, to which it is closely related through the many discussions of the Great Pyramid and its occult geometry, Michell's Atlantis was a time of wonders and understanding, of peace and decency, when ecological harmony led to comfortable and spiritual living. Like Mircea Eliade, Michell dreams of a reactualization of this magical time, and he imagines this encounter occurring by means of a better understanding of space and place.

In many of his works, Eliade proposed a theory of sacred space as qualitatively different from other spaces, just as sacred time differs from other times. In particular, he argued that sacred space and time were constant, continuous, and wholly other.[16] Where ordinary space and time are organized sequentially, such that one can never step into the same river twice, sacred space and time exist in heterogeneous atemporal blocks or units, and one can enter the same sacred space and time repeatedly, through ritual. Thus every Mass *is* the Last Supper, for through the ritual acts, participants actually encounter the living space and time of Christ: "The passion of Christ, his death and his resurrection, are not simply commemorated in the course of the offices of Holy Week; they really occur *thus* before the eyes of the faithful. And a true Christian must feel himself *contemporary* with these *trans-historical* events for, in repeating it, the theophanic time becomes present to him."[17] This process of entering a sacred space and time outside ordinary reality, and in that space and time encountering an always-present sacred event, Eliade dubbed "reactualization." And this idea, this conception of the nature of ritual as well as space, requires rethinking in a magical context.

We have already encountered Eliade's nostalgia for contact with the sacred, for an Ægypt in which gods walked among men; here he projects that nostalgia as central to human religiosity. That is, Eliade conceives of religious man—*homo religiosus*—as perpetually nostalgic for mythic time, for *illud tempus*. At the same time, however, this apparent nostalgia has a peculiar nature: archaic peoples do not experience true nostalgia for illud tempus because, through ritual, they can enter that time. This is reactualization.

To recognize in ley hunting a similar perspective, it is only necessary to perceive the self-validating structure of reactualization when it comes into the historical. In a number of studies, but particularly in *Cosmos and History*,[18] Eliade argued that Judaism, by proposing an absolute and irreversible Fall, as well as by setting itself in temporal relation to an illud tempus from Creation to Sinai that could never be reiterated, began a process of discovering in time a new hierophany, a new modality of the sacred:

> Historical facts thus become "situations" of man in respect to God, and as such they acquire a religious value that nothing had previously been able to confer upon them. It may, then, be said with truth that the Hebrews were the first to discover the meaning of history as the epiphany of God, and this conception, as we should expect, was taken up and amplified in Christianity.[19]

The Occult Mind

Ley hunters too perceive time as distance from illud tempus (prehistory, Atlantis, Ægypt), and thus the historical mapping procedure of rediscovery becomes reactualization with a messianic tinge. As we have seen in Michell, reading the ley of the land entails the possibility of renewal.

·····

If for Eliade reactualization provided a means of describing and understanding a central principle of the archaic ontology, especially in ritual, it also amounts to a kind of magical hermeneutics, a way to read the landscape. The worth of this method, or of reactualization itself, in the analysis of ritual is an issue for another study; here, let us continue to trace the line of thought. Given that reactualization can be a goal and focus of magical reading, can it serve this function when reading magic?

The rewards and dangers of such a methodology are admirably demonstrated by the work of Frances Yates, whose many works on early modern magic occasioned an initial tremendous excitement, followed by perhaps inevitable disillusionment—a trajectory that might also describe the fortunes of Eliade's work.

The daughter of a naval architect, Yates nevertheless inherited sufficient funds to work as an independent scholar after receiving her master's degree in French theater at University College, London, in 1926; that she had done this almost entirely through correspondence study already points to the oddly para–academic course of her career. She began primarily as a Shakespeare scholar, but over the late 1930s and '40s, during which time she first visited and then joined the staff and then the faculty of the Warburg Institute, she became increasingly interested in the early modern history of ideas, in 1947 publishing *The French Academies of the Sixteenth Century*, in 1959 *The Valois Tapestries*, and in 1964 *Giordano Bruno and the Hermetic Tradition*, which, together with the 1966 *The Art of Memory*, catapulted her to academic stardom.

A skimming of her prolific article publications during this crucial period is revealing: in 1942, "Shakespeare and the Platonic Tradition"; in 1945, "The Emblematic Conceit in Giordano Bruno's 'De gli eroici furori' and in the Elizabethan Sonnet Sequences"; 1951, "Giordano Bruno: Some New Documents"; 1954, "The Art of Ramon Lull"; 1960, "Ramon Lull and John Scotus Erigena" and "La teoría Luliana de los elementos"; and in 1963, "Giovanni Pico della Mirandola and Magic."[20] Here we have an unusually clear progression, and one that tells us much about how Yates worked: she dug into a problem, then read backward and around the material in any way she could, following threads however tenuous and simply never letting go. Few historians have been so traditional—yet her conclusions were rarely so.

Immediately after *Giordano Bruno*, Yates at last received her LittD from London University, then retired as an honorary fellow from the Warburg in 1967 but continued to work and publish; she also received an Officer of the British Empire in 1972 and was made Dame of the British Empire in 1977. In 1969 she published *Theatre of the World*, a study of the Vitruvian architectural tradition in Elizabethan public theaters; in 1971, *The Rosicrucian Enlightenment*, a controversial reconstruction of a secret intellectual tradition in the seventeenth century; and then from 1979 onward, a series of volumes of articles, some revised from their first publications. At the time of her death in 1981, Yates was controversial but admired, as much for her charm and scholarly generosity as for her groundbreaking work.[21]

The historiographer of science H. Floris Cohen muses:

> Frances Yates has more than once been identified, with greater or lesser caution, with the Hermetic views she wrote about. To this she used innocently to reply that, rather than being an "occultist" or a "sorceress," she was just "a humble historian whose favourite pursuit is reading." Yet the questions raised about her personal views were not altogether unjustified. There remains something mysterious in her writing about these subjects. In reading her work one feels that she tries to define some ineffable core by circling around it and approaching it from all kinds of different viewpoints—her ultimate message is left to be guessed by the reader. This approach is quite appropriate to her subject, which is itself about things that lend themselves better to intuitive grasp than to logical analysis. . . . There remains the lingering suspicion that Frances Yates may have glimpsed truths about the origin of early modern science whose full import still eludes us.[22]

The idea that Yates might have had occult sympathies has little to recommend it. Yates denied the claim, and nothing in her work suggests that she practiced magic. In addition, little of the modern occultism available to her could have commended itself to an expert on Renaissance magic, as even the most intellectual and sophisticated of the modern approaches bear little simple relation to their early modern forebears, and furthermore derive much of the their impetus by the admixture of South Asian and East Asian concepts alien to her. I suspect that Yates may have experimented with the art of memory, as do many intrigued by her book, but that is a far cry from attempting to recapitulate the magic of Giordano Bruno.

The Occult Mind

THE SCHOLAR'S CHOICE
25 Franklin St. #1260
ROCHESTER, NEW YORK 14604
800-782-0077
information@scholarschoice.com

CUSTOMER'S ORDER NO.		PHONE			DATE	
R S A					4/5/08	
NAME		Sara Caldwell				
ADDRESS						

SOLD BY	CASH	C.O.D.	CHARGE	ON ACCT.	MDSE. RETD.	PAID OUT	

QTY.	DESCRIPTION	PRICE	AMOUNT
	Deciphering the European Emblem		15 —
	Occult World		20 —
			35 —
	#339		
		TAX	
RECEIVED BY		TOTAL	35 —

All claims and returned goods MUST be accompanied by this bill.

100039

Thank You

At the same time, the notion of Yates as occultist is revealing. Like most historians, Yates tried to make the past live again, to overcome the strangeness of Bruno and his magical worldview. Her success was remarkable, judging by the excitement provoked by her publications among not only Renaissance scholars but also the educated public.[23] To produce the desired effect, Yates makes three important methodological moves: first, she strives for ringing, powerful prose, rendering her books vibrant textually as well as conceptually; second, she suppresses much of the historian's technical voice, going in the opposite direction from her contemporary French-influenced theoretical historians by reducing methodological discussion to nil; and third, she blurs the line between her discussions and those of her subjects, such that it is often unclear whether we are reading Yates the historian or Yates the paraphraser. To return to Eliade, Yates strives in her books to *reactualize* Bruno's magic, to make it actual and present in text. It is no surprise that some interpret Yates as an occult practitioner, since she attempts to make magic a living worldview once more.

In a devastatingly accurate review article, Brian Vickers followed Yates's tracks through *The Rosicrucian Enlightenment* and discerned a fascinating paralogic.[24] To explain Rosicrucianism as a powerful, secret movement in seventeenth century Europe, Yates set herself the task of reconstruction from essentially no evidence, leading her into ever wilder speculation:

> In many places argument disappears altogether. Some of the recurrent words are "if," "may," "perhaps," "would have," "surely," "must have," a sequence which often culminates in the positive form "was." . . . [This] process is cumulative, as speculations at first tentative gradually harden and then become the base for further speculations: . . . Newton was interested in God—evidently mathematics "had not entirely satisfied him. Perhaps he entertained, or half-entertained [a telling qualification], a hope that the 'Rosicrucian' alchemical way through nature might lead him even higher." "At any rate," Newton drew on Ashmole, who drew on Maier, who drew on Dee, so that it would "*not* be historically *fantastic* to *entertain* as a *hypothesis basis* for future study, the *possibility* that a 'Rosicrucian' element, in *some revised or changed form no doubt, might* enter into Newton's interest in alchemy."[25]

Like a ley hunter, Yates sighted hypothetical points from known ones, then further hypothesized from the first, until she had produced a revelatory track through the byways of Renaissance ideas. As with Watkins and his "flood of ancestral memory," it seems at times that she had a vision from which she worked backward, tracing possible tumuli, mounds, and barrows filled with rich historical treasure.

Vickers notes, and deplores, the occult quality of Yates's methods:

> It does seem, indeed, that Yates has suppressed her critical faculties. Admittedly she is dealing with the occult, and not every aspect of that activity is susceptible to rational explanation. But even after making such allowances there are passages in which the entire absence of any skepticism about the occult's methods and aims must raise the reader's concern that on this level, too, normal processes of evaluating evidence have been temporarily suspended. . . . What are we to make of the later discussion of [John Dee's] *Monas* as a "mysterious epitome" of alchemy combined with mathematical formulae, where all qualifications have disappeared? "The adept who had mastered the formulae *could* move up and down the ladder of creation, from terrestrial matter, through the heavens, to the angels and God." What now? Has Yates identified with Dee's beliefs? Does she simply accept them, and has she deliberately converted them from the possible—but as yet untried—to the actual? It seems as if she has, for a few pages later she writes . . . that in Rosicrucianism "magic was a dominating factor, working as a mathematics-mechanics in the lower world, as celestial mathematics in the celestial world, and as angelic conjuration in the supercelestial world." There the matter-of-fact word "working" leaves no doubt as to her acceptance of the actual existence of magical operation, with perhaps even a suggestion of its efficacy.[26]

By this account, the method is similar not only in form but in purpose to that of the ley hunters.

If Yates's visionary methods seem peculiar and unacademic, this appearance is in part an artifact of academic rhetoric about itself. Jonathan Z. Smith noted the visionary quality of morphological discovery in Goethe, Lorenz Okken, and Eliade, from which as we saw he drew out the problem of comparison as more magical than scientific. The question that confronts us is not the preliminary vision or recognition; rather, we must ask what Yates *makes of* that discovery.

Not long after the publication of *Giordano Bruno and the Hermetic Tradition*,[27] unquestionably Yates's most influential book, there began a series of intermittent debates about the "Yates thesis," primarily within the history of science. In short, this "thesis," first described as such by Robert Westman and taken up by other critics, proposed that Hermeticism (and Hermetism) gave support to the nascent scientific revolution in three ways.[28] First, the

The Occult Mind

Hermetic worldview encouraged "man the operator," affecting nature rather than merely encountering and describing it. Second, the essentially Pythagorean numerological speculations promoted the mathematization of nature, which would come to fullest flowering in Newton's *Principia*. Third, Hermetic fascination with the sun lent credence to Copernican heliocentric cosmology. In her readings of Giordano Bruno, Yates argued that the Nolan philosopher, as a Hermeticist, fit all these criteria admirably, and she emphasized that "the history of science can explain and follow the various stages leading to the emergence of modern science in the seventeenth century, but it does not explain *why* this happened at this time."[29]

To contextualize, the twentieth century saw three rough phases in the historiography of early modern "occult and scientific mentalities," to borrow the title of an important volume edited by Vickers in 1984. First, the dismissive positivist perspective, in which science progressively develops alongside, but in despite of, various fanciful and fundamentally irrelevant occult theories; in this category may be placed Herbert Butterfield, for example, whose 1957 *The Origins of Modern Science* was for years used as a standard textbook introduction. Second, in a reaction inaugurated by Lynn Thorndike's magisterial eight-volume *History of Magic and Experimental Science* (1923–58), we see a shift toward a more positive evaluation of the relevance and influence of the occult on science, culminating in some of the more extreme statements of Yates and her followers: "[The] Hermetic attitude toward the cosmos was, I believe, the chief stimulus of that new turning toward the world and operating on the world which, appearing first as Renaissance magic, was to turn into seventeenth-century science."[30] Finally, the third phase—counterreaction—saw the debates over the Yates thesis, with major participants encompassing much of the best talent in early modern history of science of the 1970s and '80s.[31]

A reader coming fresh to these debates, who simply read through more or less in order, would likely conclude that Yates was mostly wrong about everything, a scholar of stunningly poor intellectual habits, and might indeed wonder why so much effort and ink had been expended to refute her apparently ludicrous claims. To be sure, a few fellow travelers extended or at least defended her arguments, but apparently they could be dismissed simply by reading the primary texts with some care.

And yet, as Cohen notes, there remains the disconcerting sense that she may have had secrets to impart. More soberly, I find that the most recent scholarship has quietly, tentatively, even slightly shamefacedly begun to revive Yates's arguments. One sees this clearly at conferences on early modern science and history: Yates is mentioned only in passing, but much of the spirit of her work continues to inform scholarship on occultism.

To understand this, to begin tracing what Yates did right and most interestingly how she did it, we need first to recognize the context of her work. The primary difficulty with the objections is that critics rarely seem to see Yates within her own historical context, so insistent are they to see Dee, Bruno, or whoever in theirs.[32] The problem of early modern magic was not new in Yates, after all—as already noted, Yates was part of an extensive response to earlier positivistic and overwhelmingly dismissive readings of occultism, a response she rightly situated in relation to the historiography of science. In the concluding pages of *Giordano Bruno and the Hermetic Tradition*, Yates attempts formally to distinguish between her project and that of the historian of science. For our own concerns with method and comparison in the study of the occult, it is worth pausing to consider these last ten pages in detail.

"With the history of genuine science leading up to Galileo's mechanics this book has had nothing whatever to do," she writes, a remark often misquoted by dropping the phrase "leading up to Galileo's mechanics." Yates continues, "That story belongs to the history of science proper. . . . The history of science can explain and follow the various stages leading to the emergence of modern science in the seventeenth century, but it does not explain *why* this happened at this time, why there was this intense new interest in the world of nature and its workings."[33]

The latent notion of following or tracking stages and lines becomes explicit throughout this conclusion: the Magus's "concentration on number as a road into nature's secrets," John Dee "in the line leading to the scientific advances," Giordano Bruno "as an important landmark"; Yates even concludes the whole book by remarking, "My chief aim has been to place Giordano Bruno within [a Hermetic] perspective, and it is my hope that this may of itself clear a road along which others will travel towards new solutions of old problems."[34] And in one of her most graceful and important comments here, the image of the hidden line dominates:

> Taking a very long view down the avenues of time a beautiful and coherent line of development suggests itself—perhaps too beautiful and coherent to be quite true. The late antique world, unable to carry Greek science forward any further, turned to the religious cult of the world and its accompanying occultisms and magics of which the writings of "Hermes Trismegistus" are an expression. The appearance of the Magus as an ideal . . . was . . .

The Occult Mind

a retreat from reason into the occult. . . . [The] appearance of the Magus ideal in the Renaissance [was] similarly a retreat from the intense rationalism of medieval scholasticism. . . . Hence, . . . when "Hermes Trismegistus" and all that he stood for is rediscovered in the Renaissance, the return to the occult this time stimulates the genuine science.[35]

If we take this image seriously, we soon note that Yates's lines are commonly *doubled*: Dee "on one level of his mind is a genuine mathematician, in the line leading to the scientific advances, and on another level is attempting to summon angels with practical Cabala." Leonardo too, in Eugenio Garin's reading cited with approval by Yates, "was able to co-ordinate his mathematical and mechanical studies with his work as an artist" because he was thinking "within the outlook of a Magus."[36] Yates lays out this conception as follows:

> Moreover, the mechanistic world view established by the seventeenth-century revolution has been in its turn superseded by the amazing latest developments of scientific knowledge. It may be illuminating to view the scientific revolution as in two phases, the first phase consisting of an animistic universe operated by magic, the second phase of a mathematical universe operated by mechanics. An enquiry into both phases, and their interactions, may be a more fruitful line of historical approach to the problems raised by the science of to-day than the line which concentrates only on the seventeenth-century triumph. Is not all science a gnosis, an insight into the nature of the All, which proceeds by successive revelations?[37]

Again:

> The basic difference between the attitude of the magician to the world and the attitude of the scientist to the world is that the former wants to draw the world into himself, whilst the scientist does just the opposite, he externalises and impersonalises the world by a movement of will in an entirely opposite direction to that described in the Hermetic writings, the whole emphasis of which is precisely on the reflection of the world in the *mens* [mind].[38]

Three points should immediately draw our attention. First, Yates's understanding of "genuine science" is at once traditionally positivistic and extremely peculiar. At base, modern science is *not* a gnostic procedure, nor does it seek "insight into the nature of the All." Indeed, the very externalization Yates perceives in science demands an epistemological absence: the new science had to prescind from such speculations and questions in order to achieve its phenomenal (in both senses) and relative ends. Thus a preliminary difficulty in understanding Yates's arguments is that she sees magic and science as having the same objectives, as asking the same questions—and the questions she perceives are rather more magical than scientific.

Second, the doubling of lines or tracks occurs not only within the material studied but also within the methods appropriate to their study. If the sixteenth century saw an increasing bifurcation into the magical and the scientific, in her account, modern historians too must divide their labors. Tracking the lines of science is proper to the historian of science, and at least implicitly Yates argues that their methods ought to be equally scientific and positivistic. By contrast the "line of approach" that seeks to understand the "Hermetic" worldview must, it seems, presume the validity and coherence of the object. For precisely this reason, Yates's method of tracing the Rosicrucian lines buried beneath the familiar landmarks of early modern history depends on conceptions of evidence, even an epistemology, more familiar to occultists and ley hunters than to historians. It is not, then, that Yates is an occultist; rather, she translates into an historical idiom that mode of thought and analysis she perceives within her materials. I doubt very much that she intended this effect, but it remains one of her greatest contributions to the historiography of the occult, and one as yet largely unexamined.

Finally, the insistence on lines and roads reflects a peculiar historicism. History here is a structure with meaning, a grand framework within which seemingly inchoate data gain transtemporal validity. Not that Yates is precisely a Hegelian or the like, but her historical methods *presume* such a meaning. Because she takes to extremes the reaction against older "bolt of lightning" approaches to the history of ideas, at times she appears to claim that there is really nothing whatever new in Bruno or Dee—or Newton for that matter. It all comes from earlier magical material. And in particular, it arises from the *Hermetica*, because they were supposed to be from Ægypt. Yet, strangely, she sets herself and her readers outside this perspective, opening her book on Bruno by revealing that "the return to a pure golden age of magic was based on a radical error in dating."[39]

This discontinuity is epistemic. The ordinary methods of the historian, to which Vickers and other critics quite reasonably advert, presume that validation of historical claims must lie in correct interpretation of sources. Yates too presumes this, of course, and by that logic fails in several cases. In place of historical method, she has tracked out a line in such a way as to be self-reinforcing; the ley so delineated would then be reconstituted, or more properly reactualized.

In effect, this is bricolage rather than history. But we must be clear: Lévi-Strauss's famous analogy in *La pensée sauvage* has come to apply broadly, among historians and scholars of all disciplines, to a vague sort of piecemeal construction, a formulation out of odds and ends, *bribes et morceaux*. This annuls the analytic, if not perhaps the poetic value of bricolage.[40]

In Lévi-Strauss's usage, bricolage refers analogically to an entire *episteme* radically alien to the historical. It reconstitutes the event as structure, such that diachrony is translated into synchrony, to use Saussure's categories, making history literally unthinkable. I shall return to this issue in greater depth in later chapters; for the moment, suffice it to say that bricolage, analogically applied, is a means of observing and classifying phenomena in order to put them to use. The interrelations of objects, particularly concrete objects of nature, become the categorical means by which to impose and also read meaning. That is, human events and structures are granted meaning by seeing them as in relation to natural formations. Events over time are similarly classified in terms of this extrahuman and fundamentally nontemporal (synchronic) structural formation, such that the event becomes structure and history—understood here as a meaning constructed diachronically, with respect to time and change as the dominant categorical form—has no place. History is, in such *pensées sauvages*, unthinkable, because there is no event that does not already have its place and meaning, and thus change over time is not a valid or meaningful relation.

Ironically, this suggests, at least by extension, that Eliade's reactualization amounts to bricolage, albeit Lévi-Strauss and Eliade had little common ground, personally or otherwise. But it would be more accurate to say that Eliade's *method* is that of the *bricoleur*: if he perhaps recognized this thinking within his many objects of study, could it be said that, like Lévi-Strauss, he had a neolithic—he would have preferred "archaic"—intelligence?[41] Whatever his methods analytically, it is nevertheless disconcerting just how accurate Eliade sometimes was. Even Lévi-Strauss would surely give him credit for his recognition of the "archaic ontology's" perception of time: the resumption of diachrony and event into synchronic structure manifests as the cyclical and heterogeneous nature of time, that is, *illud tempus*.[42]

Returning to Yates: whatever validity would remain in her arguments, as with Eliade it could not be evaluated on ordinary historical grounds. It could only receive proper critique under the auspices of analogy, or more properly *homology*. The question becomes whether the perspective she described matches that which she herself took. In other words, we must ask whether her *methods* were homologous to the theoretical positions she undertook to describe. If Yates's approach represents an uneasy tension between two *epistemes*, the historicist and the bricoleur, does that same conflict, and that same tension, arise in fact in the thought of Bruno?

To resolve the issue is no simple matter. Insofar as it can be thought, it requires that we too take the hypothetical proposed position. This is a danger: bricolage is not identifiable as that formation which self-reinforces through its procedures; the same applies in reverse to the historical. Thus in taking such a position we risk getting exactly the conclusion we hope to find. Practically, of course, such an invidious resolution is inescapable, and I shall examine the analytical problem in a later chapter. For the moment, it is by concerning ourselves with *science*, that most powerful of Western knowledge formations, that the issue may be deferred.

⁚⁚⁚

Yates argued that for Bruno, the Copernican universe represented a "Hermetic seal" rather than a scientific description of the universe, emphasizing Bruno's rejection of Copernicus's mathematical modeling. In particular, she argued that as his mathematical training was apparently weak, Bruno was "a reactionary who would push the Copernican diagram . . . back towards 'mathesis,' "[43] and on this basis she interpreted the Copernican discussions in *La Cena de le Ceneri* (The Ash-Wednesday Supper, 1584) and elsewhere in purely Hermetic-Neoplatonic terms.

Yates's claims have received powerful challenges from many sides. Robert S. Westman demonstrated clearly that many of Yates's favorite Hermeticists flatly rejected Copernican heliocentrism, in some cases preferring Tycho Brahe's compromise approach, but in others simply retaining the Ptolemaic geocentric system; at base, Hermetic-style sun worship did not entail a realist placement of the sun at the center of the universe.[44] In what is perhaps the most comprehensive and sophisticated treatment of Bruno's science, Hilary Gatti showed convincingly that Bruno was neither a Neoplatonist nor a Hermeticist; that his Copernicanism rested on a deep if occasionally imperfect reading of *De Revolutionibus*; and that his mathematics, while certainly weak in a number of respects (notably in his rejection of trigonometry, one of the most promising and powerful developments in early modern mathematics), nevertheless recognized the realist implications of Copernican theory in a way the Polish thinker had not, and in fact saw that Copernican heliocentrism would require not only a redescription of the cosmos but a radical and comprehensive rethinking of physics itself. Bruno's attacks on "merely mathematical" arguments must be read, in Gatti's account, as embedded within an important and even visionary understanding of the epistemological implications of the new science.[45]

In the wake of the various critiques of the Yates thesis, we are left with three crucial questions about Bruno's heliocentrism: Is there any remaining value in Yates's (mis)readings, in particular her claim that the Copernican universe represented a "Hermetic seal"? More generally, the question Westman concluded on, "What important contributions did Hermeticism make to the Scientific Revolution?"[46] remains pressing. Finally, how can Bruno's mnemotechnics, that is the art of memory (*ars memorativa*) on which he wrote so extensively, be linked to his physics and particularly his Copernicanism?

It is important that Bruno was not entirely consistent throughout his career, fully formed like Athena on bursting forth from the head of his Neapolitan monastery in 1576. As Edward Gosselin and others have shown, Bruno's thought was influenced by what he read and those he talked to, a process that continued until well into his trial in the 1590s.[47] Thus we cannot assume absolute coherence between Bruno's first surviving work, *De Umbris Idearum* (On the Shadows of Ideas, 1582), and his last, *De Imaginum, Signorum et Idearum Compositione* (On the Composition of Images, Signs, and Ideas, 1591). Furthermore, as Gatti shows, "Bruno never succeeded in creating a system of mnemonic images or signs capable of providing new answers about the infinite, atomically constructed universe he envisaged, thus obliging him, in the more scientific parts of his discourse, to fall back on a mythologized version of Euclidean geometry." That is, although "Bruno was attempting . . . in his art of memory . . . a philosophical investigation into the image-making properties of the mind added to an attempt to propose a picture-logic sufficiently flexible in its powers of association to act as a guide, in time and space, through the intricate finite vicissitudes of a newly atomic and infinite universe," nevertheless he did not entirely succeed.[48] Thus the modern interpreter faces a twofold difficulty with Bruno: no two works necessarily agree, and even in the final formulations the system does not achieve its own ends satisfactorily.

I suggest that we understand these problems as *intrinsic* to Bruno's project. That is, I propose that his aims were fundamentally unrealizable. Whatever incoherence or confusion we detect can be understood as an artifact not merely of Bruno's biography and his tragically shortened life, nor again of his mathematical or other deficiencies in training, but of the very impossibility of the project itself. A full understanding of Bruno, then, is an understanding of his grappling with problems, not solving them, and it requires us to recognize our own inabilities with respect to the same issues. The problem is thus to translate terms, such that we recognize in his intellectual agonies images and shadows of our own. As Lévi-Strauss put it with his usual eloquence, "Scientific explanation consists not in the passage from complexity to simplicity, but in the substitution of a more intelligible complexity for another which is less."[49]

As a first step toward fully grasping Bruno's project—a reading I will certainly not complete here—we may look to the debates over the Yates thesis. Within the epistemic comparative structure proposed, we may hypothesize that the inability of Yates and historians of science to agree on terms and issues, not to mention conclusions, may point toward a genuine difficulty in Bruno rather than a purely modern academic problem.

The divide in Bruno scholarship reflects that most enduring issue of the historian of science, the extent to which a thinker's ideas and work can or should be read within the context of science, modern or otherwise. With Bruno's Copernicanism in particular, the usual question is the degree to which his acceptance of heliocentrism can be ascribed to motivations and perspectives relevant to the trajectories of early modern science. Scholars also debate whether Bruno's treatises on memory have any significant bearing on this question; while it seems clear enough that Bruno himself did not imagine a radical divide between his cosmology and his memory arts, this does not entail that the two were inextricably entwined, such that his Copernicanism is incomprehensible or necessarily misread absent a simultaneous reading of his total oeuvre.

To be specific, Copernicus had proposed a mathematical description of the cosmos; it is still unclear the extent to which he considered this also a realist description. We do not entirely know, that is, whether Copernicus thought the sun was *actually* in the center with the earth in motion around it, or whether this was a *mathematical model* leading toward clarity in calculation, such that it is simplest and clearest to analyze the cosmos *as though* it were heliocentric. Certainly in the sixteenth century, the latter interpretation was the more common; it is equally clear that Bruno rejected it, and indeed may have been the first to recognize fully the implications of a realist Copernicanism. On the one hand, then, Bruno's rejection of mathematization was bound to his sense that the Copernican system had to be understood as more than a mathematical convenience, that it radically altered the nature of space, measurement, and physics itself. On the other hand, his dismissal of such mathematics appears "reactionary," to use Yates's term, a move away from the most promising developments in physics and astronomy in his day. Conversely, Bruno's memory theories appear to propose a symbolic and abstract language for analytical purposes. By this reading, Bruno's memory images are logical and structural tools, not Neoplatonic forms of transcendental ideas, implying that he did not reject the *reasons for* mathematization but only that particular *method* of symbolization; the memory images would then be an alternative to the mathematics and geometry he derided. If we take Gatti's comparisons to the epistemology of quantum theory seriously, as we should, we are faced at once with a Bruno who rejects the basis of Copernican heliocentrism and accepts only its conclusions, for symbolic, magical, and religious reasons; and another Bruno who seems to see far beyond the scientific revolution to recognize that the most rigorous mathematical accounts will ultimately be unable to generate realist descriptions of the universe. Such extreme disparity permits no reconciliation, for to explain Bruno is to choose a stance and follow its implications. The magus and the scientist cannot agree.[50]

I suggest that this disparity, indeed this incommensurability, is in fact central to the epistemic crisis Bruno wanted to resolve. To note that he ultimately failed is no criticism: the most recent scholarship on early modern magic and science has not succeeded either, and as I have already suggested—and shall explain toward the conclusion of the present book—the problem itself is insoluble. Bruno's genius in this area, then, manifests in his recognition that it *is* a problem, and that his own position straddles an unbridgeable divide.

Copernican heliocentrism presented the sixteenth century with many painful questions; for Bruno, among the most pressing was the epistemological status of mathematical description or modeling. Copernicus's mathematical formulations eliminated some of the more problematic structures of the Ptolemaic universe, especially the need for massive spheres upon or between which heavenly bodies moved and a number of the eccentrics and epicycles used to explain such phenomena as the retrograde motion of Mars. At the same time, the Copernican model could not eliminate all such structures; the retention of circular motion in particular necessitated some use of epicycles. Bruno saw here a serious problem: the simplicity of an infinite universe should not require structures whose sole function rested in mathematical explanation. He did not foresee Kepler's reevaluations, nor the ability of Gilbert's magnetic philosophy or the Newtonian analysis of gravitational force as the single force necessary to explain all planetary motion, but Bruno nevertheless saw that a mathematical model could not by itself describe the universe as it really is.

The question Bruno poses amounts to a consideration of the function of analogy. If a mathematical analogy accurately describes phenomena, is that then a sufficient account of reality? The problem, as Gatti points out with reference to Heisenberg, remains pressing: that a mathematical account of pseudoparticles in subatomic force interactions does indeed generate valid prediction does not entail that such pseudoparticles really exist. What then does such a model mean—that is, what epistemological status does it have?

Bruno's model, as presented in *The Ash-Wednesday Supper*, proposes that Copernicus's mathematical redescription of the cosmos entails a true infinity of space, such that it is impossible to call the sun, or the earth for that matter, the center. The sun is the center around which the earth revolves, just as the earth is the center around which the clouds revolve, but properly speaking the sun is not the absolute center, only a relative one. Indeed, an infinite cosmos cannot *have* a center: if we imagine an infinite line, its center would be halfway along, but each half would still be infinitely long. Extending the hypothesis, the stars may also be suns, around which other planets may revolve in the same fashion and by the same laws as in our solar system. To suppose that this cannot be, that space is finite, is to constrict the nature of God: an infinite God need not create a finite universe, and there is no reason to suppose that He did so; indeed, for Bruno, the possibility is ludicrous.

To analyze such a universe mathematically would require a completely different sense of mathematics itself. As far as Bruno understands it, at least, mathematics is bounded either by the finitude of number or by that of Euclidean geometry. Following from Cusanus's examinations of infinitude in geometry, Bruno points out that at the extreme, mathematics becomes incoherent and meaningless: an infinite circle is also an infinite line, such that the difference between zero sides and infinite sides is null. Because we are now dealing with an infinite universe, finite mathematics can only apply by weak and deceptive analogies. The only proper mathematics would be one capable of, and indeed founded on, the infinite. Such a mathematics appears impossible to Bruno, who thus rejects the tendency (in Copernicus, among others) to constrain thought by reference to mathematics.[51]

Gatti formulates Bruno's criticism of Copernicus very clearly:

[Bruno] centered his criticism on Copernicus's mathematical methodology and his lack of physical reasoning, because he thought that Coperni-

The Occult Mind

cus was confusing mathematical concepts and physical realities. . . . The sky in which thinking people lived at the end of the sixteenth century was still cluttered with eccentrics, epicycles, celestial orbs, and precessional anomalies which were clearly conceptual tools interfering, in Bruno's opinion, with a visualization of the real shape of the cosmos. Bruno wanted these concepts, which Copernicus had inherited from the traditional cosmology, to be recognized as purely mental tools. They should be flexible where they had to be used, and where possible be eliminated altogether.[52]

I have thus far emphasized Gatti's reading, the most sophisticated and comprehensive scientific account of Bruno. The question of Yates's Bruno remains largely untouched, except through implicit criticism. In formulating the other term of comparison, we must consider Yates's claim "that for Bruno the Copernican diagram is a hieroglyph, a Hermetic seal hiding potent divine mysteries of which he has penetrated the secret. . . . Bruno [reads] the Copernican diagram 'more Hermetico' [in a Hermetic manner], encouraged thereto by Copernicus' own reference to Hermes Trismegistus near the diagram in his book."[53]

Westman rightly draws attention to "a revealing piece of self-biography" in the preface to Yates's *Giordano Bruno and the Hermetic Tradition*. Yates originally planned an English translation of *The Ash-Wednesday Supper*, emphasizing in the introduction Bruno's "boldness" in accepting Copernicanism:

> But as I followed Bruno along the Strand to the house in Whitehall where he was to expound the Copernican theory to knights and doctors, doubts arose. . . . Was the Copernican theory really the subject of the debate or was there something else implied in it? . . . Some major clue was missing. . . . [After some years] it dawned on me, quite suddenly, that Renaissance Hermetism provides the long-sought-for major clue to Bruno. The right key was found at last; my former Bruno studies fell into place; and this book was written fairly quickly.[54]

In both *Giordano Bruno and the Hermetic Tradition* and *The Art of Memory*, Yates leans on the *ars memorativa* and the occult tradition of Ficino and Agrippa to explain Bruno's Copernicanism. In some sense, the "Copernican diagram," by which she means the diagram of the Copernican heliocentric system, operates as a compressed "key" to the mysteries of the cosmos itself. By internalizing this system through the locative memory arts described in

De Umbris Idearum and *De Imaginum*, the operative magus is enabled to manipulate the forces and powers of the universe. As Yates notes, "The procedures with which the Magus attempted to operate have nothing to do with genuine science. . . . The question is, did they stimulate the will towards genuine science and its operations?"[55]

Quite apart from the vexed question of Hermes Trismesgistus as a dominant influence on Bruno, Yates brings to bear several important pieces of evidence. First, these two texts are the first and last of Bruno's works to have survived, which at least suggests an enduring interest; although it is true that many of the works in between do not touch on the art of memory, at least overtly, it must be admitted that the total putative corpus, including the first and last works, two lost early works (*Arca di Noè* and *Clavis Magna*, as well as possibly *De' Segni de' Tempi*), and several in between (*Cantus Circaeus, Explicatio Triginta Sigillorum, Sigillum Sigillorum, Lampas Triginta Statuarum,* and so forth), demands some serious consideration of Bruno's mnemotechnics with respect to his other intellectual projects.[56] Where Gatti asks why, after some years of minimal involvement with memory, Bruno should have returned to it in *De Imaginum*, Yates suggests that he never left it at all: for her, *The Ash-Wednesday Supper* and other Copernican works represent simply another phase in Bruno's art of memory.

To oversimplify Yates's interpretations somewhat, she claims Bruno has recognized that Ficinian image-magic and the later Christian Kabbalistic (especially Agrippan) manipulations of letter and number require the mediation of imagination and the mind, and that powerful use of such techniques must therefore operate by drawing down celestial forces into the mind and transmitting them to other minds; Bruno's psychological magic in *De Magia* (On Magic, 1590–91) and especially *De Vinculis in Genere* (On Links in General, 1590–91) would seem to fit this account reasonably well.[57] For Bruno, then, the power of the art of memory is that it allows the deliberate construction of perfect, because ideal, images; instead of projecting them outward onto fallen nature, Bruno concretizes them as mental signs and operates from there. Thus the Copernican diagram of the heavens, which perfectly matches the metaphorical heliocentrism of Hermes and Bruno's own aesthetic sense of the infinite simplicity of the divine, becomes a hieroglyphic seal to be internalized. By thus reconstructing the mental space to match the real space outside, the magus empowers himself in a fashion far beyond the limited conceptions of a Ptolemaic finite universe.[58]

These readings of Bruno's Copernicanism are in many respects incommensurable. It is not a question of discerning to what extent either is true;

The Occult Mind

they understand Bruno to be doing fundamentally different things, having utterly different conversations. At base, what Gatti and Yates disagree about is Bruno's *question*. Gatti thinks his concern is primarily epistemological and deeply abstract; Yates thinks the matter operative and practical.

Granting that both Gatti and Yates are sensitive and careful readers, we cannot dismiss either position. Although the debate seems unresolvable, I suggest that we can nevertheless have it both ways. Let us suppose that Bruno's question, and indeed the thrust of his project, is both and neither. More clearly, his concern is to reconcile the various analytical and operational frameworks available to him, to subsume the abstract and the concrete under one all-embracing total method. If so, the whole interpretive problem turns inside out: Bruno can be read as mediating between Gatti and Yates, between science and magic.

For Bruno, as we have seen, the essential problem is that of infinity, and specifically how a finite mind can understand the infinite. To this old problem Bruno's rereading of Copernicus adds a new twist: if the universe is truly infinite, and thus has only a relative center, then the human ability to understand it is similarly limited to the finite and relative. There is no means by which to step outside and see the universe at a distance: the formulation of the mind and the constitution of the universe make the human subject purely incommensurable to its object of study. Thus understanding can only come through analogy, but analogies are always, as constructions of a finite mind, equally finite. Analogies can only approach the infinite universe asymptotically.

Bruno thus rejects any formally delimited and schematic system of analogy, such as mathematics. He suggests, I think, that such an intrinsically reductive system cannot but deflect us from understanding the infinite cosmos. In its stead, he proposes a radically expanded version of what William B. Ashworth Jr. has called "the emblematic world view," which Ashworth considers "the single most important factor in determining late Renaissance attitudes toward the natural world, and the contents of their treatises about it."[59] For example:

> To know the peacock, as [Conrad] Gesner wanted to know it, one must know not only what the peacock looks like but what its name means, in every language; what kind of proverbial associations it has; what it symbolizes to both pagans and Christians; what other animals it has sympathies or affinities with; and any other possible connection it might have with stars, plants, minerals, numbers, coins, or whatever. Gesner included

all this, not because he was uncritical or obtuse, but because knowledge of the peacock was incomplete without it. The notion that a peacock should be studied in isolation from the rest of the universe, and that inquiry should be limited to anatomy, physiology, and physical description, was a notion completely foreign to Renaissance thought.[60]

In the next two chapters, I shall take up the implications of this emblematic conception, better understood as hieroglyphic. For the moment, the issue is what Bruno does to such a conceit and how he connects it to the epistemological problem of an infinite universe.

Ashworth's point, which is well taken, is that the emblematic or hieroglyphic mode of natural history appears relatively unlimited. Beginning with the peacock, one can in theory come to every other object of the sensible universe through a vast web of correspondences. Every thing in the world, then, is like a word in a dictionary, coming to its full meaning only by reference to the entirety of the lexicon. But for Bruno, such a system remains utterly limited by comparison to a true infinity: vastly large and infinite remain incommensurable. A web of correspondences so large as to be notionally analogous to infinitude would have to escape the very mind that tried to use it, would need in fact to depend on a kind of forgetting, an inability to grasp the scale of the construction. What is missing from the emblematic conception Ashworth describes, then, is the ability not only to discern—through study, analysis, thought—the connections already present but hidden (occult) within the world and within history, but actually to *construct* such connections. Only invention decouples the emblem from its history, the hieroglyph from Ægypt.

We might recall the bad reasons fallacy: because proposition p is derived from reasoning R, and analysis shows that R is invalid, we claim that p must be untrue. Logically, however, it is possible that p could be true; the validity of the proposition is not determined by the reasons proposed for it. Frances Yates's argument that the Copernican heliocentric system was for Bruno a "hieroglyph, a Hermetic seal hiding potent divine mysteries," is of this sort: the proposition seems to me entirely valid, but not for the reasons proposed.

At base, Bruno recognizes an aspect of Ægypt that Yates does not: it is lost, and always has been. Ægypt's nature is precisely such that we can no longer read Hermes as prophet but only as nostalgic. Fully to understand him prophetically, in his own voice, would require that we not read the text in a fallen language but perceive it by linguistic means utterly alien to us, that is, in its original perfect hieroglyphs. As we cannot reconstruct this except by analogy, the crucial question in understanding a vision like Hermes' is the

The Occult Mind

epistemological status of hieroglyphic analogies and the means of evaluating their adequacy.

I do not think Bruno should be read as a Hermeticist in Yates's sense, but there is no reason not to take seriously his references to the *Hermetica*. Following up from some famous remarks by Copernicus himself, Bruno gestures toward Hermes' sun worship. But Bruno and Copernicus mean fundamentally different things by this. Copernicus primarily wishes to show that his ideas are not quite so radical or new as they might seem, having classical precedents of a most legitimate sort. Bruno, however, means something quite other, for he suggests a genuine parallel between the Hermetic vision and the Copernican. Thus far, Yates would agree. But she has misunderstood the nature of this parallel, which is abstract and epistemological, properly epistemic, rather than operative or derivative.

Bruno's point, I suggest, is that when he reads either Copernicus or Hermes, he encounters a brilliant mind attempting to formulate an analogy to the universe as it really is. Both analogies are entirely legitimate, yet they disagree utterly; I see no reason to think that Bruno had not noticed this relatively obvious fact, something Yates had to go to some trouble to suppress. Both cosmologies are fundamentally centered and finite: Hermes' is geocentric, Copernicus's heliocentric, but in either case beyond the ultimate distance there is always an end or limit. This Bruno could not accept as anything other than a convenience of the finite mind. For him, then, Hermes was a prophet in the same sense as Copernicus—or vice versa.

Bruno attempts to reconcile an uneasy blend of several types of cosmological analogies—mathematics, classical mythological imagery, the art of memory, atomism, Copernicanism— into a single nearly infinite analogy. Such a model would not accurately describe the universe as it really is, but it would be much more adequate. It would also be utterly unlimited, not susceptible to reification or fixing. Its very nature would reflect the radical otherness of the cosmic infinity.

For example, Bruno seems in his atomism to translate the Hermetic principle of the microcosm into wildly different terms. If Hermes suggests that "as it is above, so it is below," Bruno proposes that as the cosmos is infinite, so too is the atom properly infinitesimal. However "Hermetic" the conception, this is surely a different Hermes.

Thus it is fair to say that Bruno does perceive the Copernican model as a hieroglyph and a Hermetic seal. But that for him is yet another analogy, as pregnant with meaning—and yet as insufficient and meaningless—as all the others.

It is not unreasonable to compare Bruno's epistemology to structural linguistics; I put off for the moment comparison to Lévi-Strauss's structural anthropology. Bruno is indeed proposing a system under which all signs and symbols are deeply and intricately interwoven, yet in themselves essentially meaningless, incapable of grasping the meanings they seek. That he did not succeed is hardly grounds for criticism. Bruno himself sees that his "mathesis," his metamathematics appropriate to an understanding of what Gatti has called a "crisis epistemology"— understanding the infinite and the infinitesimal through a language of abstract logical signs (*entia rationis*)—was in *De Triplici Minimo* "to be seen as an expression of a desire to reach the truth rather than an entirely successful project."[61] On this point Gatti corrects Yates: "The [mnemotechnical] temples [of Apollo, Minerva, and Venus, in which all figures, numbers, and measures are at once implicit and explicit] are thus neither abstract entities nor magical seals. They are rather the intellectual coordinates or the measuring devices through which the mind approaches the physical world."[62] Gatti's insistence that Bruno's formulation recognizes "the innate quality of epistemological discourse," that is, the sense in which one cannot interpret ideas or approach truth except through the structures already embedded within the finite mind, seems to me persuasive. At the same time, she underestimates the potential of a "magical seal": for Bruno, such seals represent precisely the mode of developed and constructed thought that can, if stripped of the problematic and unnecessary traditional limitations on memory arts, reach an approximation of the maximum and minimum.

In the end, Bruno continued to grapple with the art of memory, in *De Imaginum*. As we have seen, Yates sees this as no change at all; for Gatti, it is a claim for the incapacity of not only mathematics but also mathesis. Here I think Yates has it right—again, for somewhat the wrong reasons. Bruno has come to realize that constructing anew, on a purely logical basis, cannot generate a system larger than that from which it was constructed. The culmination of his system would be the fullest possible account of the nature of meaning and epistemology framed in nonschematic terms. To put it differently, it would be a system in which the logical entities of thought would be actual things and not hypothetical reductions, concrete rather than abstract objects. Because the mind is embedded fully within the world it wishes to understand—as Bruno puts it, "the painter could not examine the portrait from those aspects and distances to which artists are accustomed; since . . . it was not possible to take the least step backward"[63]—the infinity apprehensible to the mind is the plenitude that surrounds it—the world itself.

The Occult Mind

In order to effect this analysis, I have postulated an epistemic divide to which I shall return more explicitly in later chapters. I have proposed also that two modern analytical approaches, those of Yates and Gatti, can be taken to represent the two poles of Bruno's dilemma—a dilemma he was unable to resolve. It remains to consider, briefly, the implications of such a reading for the methodology of scholarship on magical and occult thought.

Yates's exceptional success in reading Bruno has a kind of visionary quality. She describes her realization of the Hermetic connection as a sudden movement of the mind, and her prose rings with the conviction of the convert. Like Alfred Watkins on his Herefordshire hill, it seems she saw the whole thing laid before her in an instant. Thereafter, it was a matter of tracking out hidden lines.

As a matter of methodological reflection, I should like to suggest that Yates, like Eliade in a sense, cannot properly be read as a historian. It is striking and worth deep consideration that both chose this particular term for their disciplinary affiliations: Yates the historian of ideas, Eliade the historian of religion. By ordinary historical standards, both must stand convicted of innumerable bad habits and faulty readings, as their many critics have noted mercilessly. But if we read Yates otherwise, as a reactualizer rather than a historian, her best qualities regain luster.

The comparison to Bruno should be taken seriously. Like him, Yates immersed herself in texts and a personal, idiosyncratic way of reading them. She too worked from a vision: having seen the whole before her, she tried to emulate the traditional historians she admired in piecing together the puzzle, never losing sight of the thread, the image, the line she was tracing. As a rule, her major conclusions and what amount to intuitions are stronger than her logical and critical analyses, though she often showed great perspicacity there as well. But it is best to read Yates's failings as arising from a weak sense of distance: she cannot step outside what she analyzes, cannot "take the least step backward" from the picture. It is no surprise that she never quite understood what Bruno meant by this metaphor in *La Cena de le Ceneri*: she was simply too close to the canvas.

Where does that leave the post-Yatesian scholar of magic? Imbued with a kind of theory she apparently never read, assailed by critical and epistemological doubt, we cannot simply step into what we study as she did. Given her considerable misreadings, it is not at all clear that we would wish to do so if we could. And the method thus far examined requires above all a peculiar sort of object of study, one disconcertingly aware of his own position within an historic epistemic shift. Bruno indeed recognizes that in his time, the already irrecoverable loss of Ægypt will be trumped by a loss of the very nostalgia for it, and he attempts to formulate, explicate, and resolve the epistemological problem that entails. Yet we can hardly expect this of everyone; indeed, Bruno may very well be unique in this sense.

At base, Bruno is "doing theory," and to refuse to treat him in the same fashion as one treats twentieth-century theorists is to assert that Bruno has nothing to say to us, or alternatively that recent thinking is intrinsically inapplicable historically. The scandal of Yates and Eliade, in effect, is that they want to engage in dialogue with those whom they study, and they attempt to do so by projecting themselves mentally backward: Eliade wants to view the "archaic ontology" from within, "experientially," and Yates wants to interpret Bruno on his own terms. By contrast many more recent scholars implicitly or explicitly project an absolute break between themselves and those whom they study, allowing them to apply modern analytical perspectives without permitting Dee or Bruno to apply theirs. If the reactualizing technique of Eliade and Yates succumbs to Evans-Pritchard's criticism of the "if I were a horse" mentality, of naively imagining oneself as something one is not, these more recent approaches assert too strongly that those we study are radically other.[64]

Comparative methods, which always uncomfortably mingle the synchronic and the diachronic, are thus not only useful but necessary. There is no way to avoid them. When we study people of other cultures or times, we ipso facto make comparison to ourselves, if only negatively or under the aegis of translation. To be sure, the claim that comparison implies identity, the Eliade-Yates reactualization, annuls important difference. But the pseudohistorical claim against comparison as intrinsically bad method is bigotry masquerading as rigor.[65]

The proper difficulty is that comparison entails a deep epistemological problem, rooted in a deeper epistemic divide, the same divide we have seen arising in Bruno as well as in Yates and the ley hunters. In his famous lecture "Structure, Sign and Play in the Discourse of the Human Sciences," Jacques Derrida noted that the epistemological systems of both the bricoleur and the *ingénieur*—the latter perspective including that of the historian—have in common a *centered* formulation of truth itself, albeit a center that is differently placed. Against this, Derrida juxtaposes the Nietzschean *play*, a radically decentered mode of thought and understanding. And yet, Derrida says, "I do not believe that today there is any question of *choosing*."[66] For him, the differ-

The Occult Mind

ance (avoiding protective accents or italics) underlying *both* epistemes—play and center—requires analysis and consideration, but *not* because one should then select among options.

Might it be said that Bruno too recognized this? At the least, we might see in him one who recognized a crisis in European intellectual history, a point at which it seemed things might turn, might choose between options. In the end, a choice was indeed made, and the epistemology of the bricoleur receded ever further. But might we have chosen otherwise? Or was it always already not a matter of choosing?

Consider writing, for Derrida a manifestation of the "differance" underlying this epistemic conflict between historian and bricoleur, and perhaps between scientist and magician. Is bricolage then comparable to history in the same way as play would be to writing—or the reverse? For Derrida, generally the reverse, but at the same time the disjuncture is not prestructured, for in that case it would always already have announced itself within. In short, differance prevents our knowing which way the analogy properly works, for if it did, the analogy would be structured and formulated within the realm of historical/bricoleur formations, not beneath it, generatively and in labor.

If we have read Ægypt as a land of shifting sands upon which synchrony and diachrony meet, can one in fact inscribe and then read her hieroglyphics at all? To what might such hieroglyphs be compared?

3 ⠿ THE THEATER OF HIEROGLYPHS

No matter how loudly we clamor for magic in our lives, we are really afraid of pursuing an existence entirely under its influence and sign. . . .

Like all magic cultures expressed by appropriate hieroglyphs, the true theater has its shadows too, and of all languages and all arts, the theater is the only one left whose shadows have shattered their limitations. From the beginning, one might say its shadows did not tolerate limitations.

Antonin Artaud, *The Theater and Its Double*

In 1564, having been "pregnant" with it for seven years,[1] the Elizabethan magician, philosopher, mathematician, courtier, and sometime prophet John Dee (1527–1608) gave birth to *Monas Hieroglyphica* in twelve days of frenzied labor.[2] The work describes a perfect written character, the hieroglyphic monad, and presents terse arguments on the model of mathematical proofs for its allegorical, alchemical, astrological, and graphic completeness.

In essence, the monad figure begins with the astronomical symbol ("hieroglyph," in Dee's terms) for Mercury (☿) placed atop that for Aries (♈). A dot is placed in the center of the circle, such that it parallels the symbol for the sun (☉), and the semicircle at the top shifts downward halfway to the dot in the circle. Dee explains that within this base, every astronomical symbol appears: to find the figure for Mars (♂), for example, remove the top semicircle and the dot, trim the Aries horns slightly, and rotate the symbol 135 degrees counterclockwise. This is not merely an orthographical game:

> Or is it not rare, I ask, that the common astronomical symbols of the planets (instead of being dead, dumb, or, up to the present hour at least, quasi-barbaric signs) should have become characters imbued with immortal life and should now be able to express their especial meanings most eloquently in any tongue and to any nation? Yet a further great rareness is also added, namely that (by very good hieroglyphical arguments) their external bodies have been reduced or restored to their mystical proportions.[3]

And in the series of twenty-four "theorems," Dee argues explicitly that each line, curve, or mark in the monad not only derives from such symbols but actually expresses their deeper hieroglyphic reality. For example, the first, eighth, and last theorems:

Theorem I. The first and most simple manifestation and representation of things, non-existent as well as latent in the folds of Nature, happened by means of straight line and circle. . . .

Theorem VIII. Besides, a cabbalistic expansion of the quaternary, in accordance with the customary style of numeration (when we say, one, two, three, four), produces in sum, the denary, as Pythagoras himself used to say; for 1, 2, 3, and 4, add up to ten. Therefore, the rectilinear cross (which is the twenty-first letter of the Roman alphabet) and which was considered to be formed of four straight lines, was not without reason chosen by the oldest Latin philosophers to signify the number Ten. Its place in the alphabet, too, is [thus] determined; for the ternary, multiplying its strength by the septenary, establishes that letter [as the twenty-first]. . . .

Theorem XXIIII. As we made this little book take its beginning from point, straight line, and circle, so also we have made the last linear effluxion [issuing] from our monadic point describe a circle which is almost analogous to the equinoctial completing its circuit in 24 hours. Thus we shall now at last, in this our twenty-fourth speculation, consummate and terminate the permutations (defined by the number 24) and the metamorphosis of the quaternary, to the honour and glory of Him who (as John, the arch-priest of the divine mysteries, witnesses in the fourth and last part of the fourth chapter of the Apocalypse) sits on the throne and around Whom four animals (each having six wings) speak day and night without rest: Holy, holy, holy [is the] Lord God the Almighty, Who was, Who is, and Who will come; Whom also 24 elders, (having cast off their golden crowns) [and] falling prostrate from 24 seats placed in a circle, adore, speaking: Thou art worthy, O Lord, to receive the glory, and the honour, and the power, for Thou hast created all things. Because of Thy will they are, and have been created.

Amen, says the fourth letter.[4]

Even within Dee's lifetime, his magical work resisted cohesive interpretation. He wrote extensively on a wide range of topics, from mathematics and navigation to political tracts, but the brief *Monas Hieroglyphica* has probably prompted more speculation than any other of his works. Recently, scholars have also turned their attention to what Dee called his *Libri Mysteriorum*

(Books of Mystery), partly published in a hostile edition in 1659, which narrated and transcribed his conversations with angels.[5] All told, Dee's more obviously magical works constitute a considerable library of arcana, interpretation of which has occasioned wide controversy, and one hopes that the approaching anniversary of his death will prompt additional scholarship.[6] In the next few pages, I can hardly reformulate Dee scholarship, even if I wished to do so. But study of early modern intellectual magic has tended to eschew theoretical approaches, and thus by inserting my concerns with comparison and writing I hope to offer some new avenues for analysis.

There are six essential studies of Dee, all recent: Nicholas Clulee's *John Dee's Natural Philosophy: Between Science and Religion* laid the foundations for future scholarly study, on which William Sherman, Deborah Harkness, Håkan Håkansson, and Györgi Szőnyi have built; Bernard Woolley's semipopular biography completes the list.[7] These works are, in their own terms, entirely satisfactory. Of course, being the oldest, Clulee's book has the most gaps, but as the others primarily build on him we have now an imposing and at last solid edifice of scholarship.

In most scholarship before Frances Yates, Dee appeared wildly incoherent: a serious scientist and mathematician on Mondays, Wednesdays, and Fridays, he turned into a superstitious madman on Tuesdays, Thursdays, and Saturdays. On Sundays, of course, he rested. Since Clulee's work in particular, we can now see that in a broad sense at least Dee's total oeuvre had some sort of conceptual continuity. At the same time, scholars have struggled to understand several questions:

1. If the magical project was consistent, what was that project? That is, if both the *Monas* and the angelic conversations (i.e., the *Libri Mysteriorum*) sought a particular end, we do not yet fully understand that aim.
2. Why was the *Monas* unsatisfactory? After all, if these two magical operations were indeed consistent, the earlier *Monas* must not have achieved Dee's goals, but we do not clearly understand why.
3. Why do we see a drastic shift of frame, from explicitly mathematical with alchemical undertones in the *Monas*, to linguistic, cryptographic, and visionary in the *Libri Mysteriorum*?

At least implicitly, we might note a further problem:

4. Are these two projects consistent with Dee's political aims, so well explicated by Sherman, be they grandly "cosmopolitical" or part of the ordinary world of patronage at the Elizabethan court? Can we read the *Monas Hieroglyphica* politically, or must we return to the pre-Yates notion of Dee as a deeply inconsistent thinker?[8]

The Occult Mind

In order to approach these questions in the *Monad*, let me begin by summarizing the state of our understanding of Dee's magical thought. Like so many other early modern philosophers, Dee struggled with a semiotic problem: How can mankind communicate with God? More specifically, how can we *read* the writing of God upon the world, conditioned by His writing within the world of Scripture? This, of course, is an old chestnut, to which early modern thinkers added distinctive and influential fillips. First, the skeptical revival forced the recognition that knowledge founded on the phenomenal world could only be relative to that world; this went hand in hand with increasingly sophisticated understandings of Aristotle, such that scholars had to recognize an absolute division between the experiential and the metaphysical or divine.[9] Second, the period saw a tremendous rise of various kinds of *philosophia perennis*, or *prisca magia et philosophia*, notably Hermeticism, Kabbalah, alchemy (in many forms), and so on—the movements discussed by Frances Yates. Third, ever-increasing access to texts had both the advantage of enabling clearer understanding and the disadvantage of revealing conflicts and disagreements where they were not supposed to occur, as between scriptural and Aristotelian warrant.[10] Fourth, Europe's political and institutional-religious situation was clearly under strain, to say the least, and for some, such as Dee, the world was obviously approaching its last days.

Responding to all this, the monad grounds all writing, linking every character to a system of knowledge and reason that unifies the Book of Scripture, the Book of Nature, and relative human knowledge. Further, following Cornelius Agrippa's move to link the divine and the natural in writing, and arguably Johannes Trithemius's use of ciphers to effect meaning-ful contact between distant communicants, Dee sees the monad as not only grounding writing *within* knowledge but also as grounding *knowledge*, making it a master key to interpretation—what he called a "real Cabala."[11] As James Bono argues, Dee moved beyond Agrippa in seeking a "real Cabala" that manipulates *things*, not merely language; the monad not only *refers* to things, in however motivated a fashion, but is itself *constituted of things*.[12] Thus the "real Cabala" transforms and rotates the "letters" of nature and at the same time performs more traditional operations on letters in scripture. In the monad, Dee found his resolution to the problem that nature and scripture must coilluminate and not contradict. It thus provided a place to stand between God and man, scripture and nature, alchemy and astrology, word and thing, Protestant and Catholic, thought and action.

There is general agreement that the changes from the *Monas* to the angelic conversations are less drastic than they appear.[13] Nevertheless, we must account for a shift from mathematical construction of a figure to ritual-magical summoning of angels into a glass. As with Agrippa and Trithemius, the answer lies between two opposed poles, poles that Dee himself sought to bring together. First of all, Dee did indeed find the *Monas* unsatisfactory, in that it did not achieve his personal or professional goals. Thus the changes from the *Monas* to the angelic conversations reflect Dee's increasing discontent with his situation, accomplishments, and prospects for satisfactory resolution of various projects.[14]

But this very human solution is also only half the answer. The other parallels a number of dichotomies of concern throughout this book: prophecy and nostalgia, synchrony and diachrony, history and structure, science and magic. I suggest that Dee understood the *Monas* and the angelic actions as similar not only in purpose but in *method*, as *activity*. To make a long story short, the book *Monas Hieroglyphica* does not *construct* a perfect character but *explicates* a vision vouchsafed by God. The book is an account of Dee's attempt, by ratiocination and application of a range of knowledges, to interpret, as is also obviously true of the angelic conversations, in which Dee struggled desperately to make sense of peculiar and often contradictory messages.[15] Methodologically, it is all emphasis: the conversations emphasize acquisition of visionary knowledge, though interpretive elements have increasingly come to light; *Monas Hieroglyphica* emphasizes interpretation, which I would insist is the flip side of the same magical coin. For Dee, thought and action are conjoined here.

Theoretically at least, there is nothing especially new about this summary of Dee's later thought. Unfortunately, the aftermath of the "Yates thesis" debates described in chapter 2 entailed a certain inability or hesitation in reading Yates's favorite figures, Dee and Bruno, and thus perhaps blocked recognition of progress made in understanding them. If we may take this cursory overview as given, however, a few major problems remain, having to do with the apparent incoherence or at least multiplicity of Dee's projects. In particular, we do not yet understand the relationship between the *Monas* and the angelic conversations or *Libri Mysteriorum*, nor do we have a clear sense of how these magical projects intersected with his worldly political aims. The latter problem is especially difficult in reference to the *Monas*: the work has clear mystical and magical aims, but Dee remarked in his dedication that "if your Majesty will look at it with attention, still greater mysteries will present themselves (to your consideration) such as we have described in our cosmopolitical theories."[16]

The problem lies with us, not with Dee. As we have already seen with

Bruno, magical thought often undermines, challenges, or even ignores common divisions among fields of knowledge or practice. This is true both in early modern terms and our own: Bruno certainly recognized that the *ars memorativa* was not usually understood as intertwined with astronomy or mathematics, and the difficulty of our understanding the links he sought to forge is exacerbated by far more absolute disciplinary divisions in our own time. Just so, if modern scholars have difficulty understanding how the *Monas* could be both political and mystical, that is not to say Dee's contemporaries grasped the meaning readily. In that Dee clearly saw the monad figure as something of a key to the mysteries, I believe that a synthetic reading will provide groundwork for a fuller understanding of the *Libri Mysteriorum* and, more broadly, of Dee's intellectual trajectory. To put the problem succinctly, we no longer see Dee as half a scientist and half a magician, as did earlier scholars. We now confront a Dee who was half private mystic, half political actor. We require a political understanding of private mystical ritual.

::::

If we examine the *Monas* in terms of modern performative theories of ritual, the political levels of which are to the fore, the text manifests an amazingly self-conscious, self-referential form of what Catherine Bell has called "ritualization."[17] Simply, Bell argues that the division between "ritual" and other forms of behavior is necessarily an arbitrary, cultural one—a point already implicit in Émile Durkheim's *Elementary Forms*. Methodologically, this entails that one can study how such a division is constructed and reinforced; in short, one can study the processes and strategies by which people construct particular dimensions of human behavior as in some way *other*, oriented toward metaphysical absolutes of one kind or another, such that the very division can become invisible, "natural," occult.

Considering such issues in the *Monas*, it seems Dee knows that formulating an experiential mode of practice centered outside the physical entails projection of ontological certainty. He has no objection to that move, unlike ourselves, as for him it is a matter of faith, not self-criticism. But he also knows that this projection will require that the object so constructed be reified as a thing unto itself, divorced from its creator in both senses, both God and Dee. Here Dee follows Agrippa in emphasizing that the strange ontological status of the written word must provide the link between God and man, and by taking this skeptical-fideist move to its logical conclusion in self-consciousness, Dee formulates a master key of the written character in the hieroglyphic monad.[18]

Dee believed the monad had revealed itself to him, and he spent many later years trying to understand what he had written. In a strangely Derridean fashion, the monad seemed always already to have been written, to have written itself, such that Dee as its writer was distanced from the writing even as, and before, he had himself written it down. Like Antonin Artaud, he had his words stolen from him before he could write them.[19]

I have elsewhere argued that Agrippa failed with a similar project because he could not find a complete bridge between spheres: the Incarnation gave structure, but this single data point could never provide the *experiential* knowledge to ground the system in the world. Agrippa's system is Neoplatonic in that sense; it is systematic, cosmic, and synthetic, but also distanced from experiential support.[20] Dee faced the same problem, and given his mathematical genius also recognized its insolubility: formal mathematics can apply analogically to the physical, as a model, but one can never absolutely demonstrate their *real* contiguity. Until Newton found a way to support the connection, mathematical knowledge and prediction could only logically describe and could not itself be granted status as physical reality. As we saw with Bruno, Dee was not alone in perceiving mathematical analogy as a fundamental epistemological problem.

What Dee does is to discover a sign that supports the Agrippan structure, thereby revising the project. Insofar as he combines all signification into the monad, he seems to continue from Agrippa, building a super-sign by means of what I have elsewhere called "analog signification," such that it refers to everything at once in every sphere.[21] But if we read it so, we must acknowledge that Dee failed: as with Agrippa's system, the monad cannot actually bridge spheres, because all we have is a mathematical analogue of what it *might* be like *if* there were actually such a bridge. But Dee claims quite the reverse: he sees the monad as it is, itself, and then discovers within it all these modes of signifying *already present*. He has recognized that insofar as he is the author of the system, that system is locked out of the divine; realizing instead that as *written sign* the monad already stands apart, Dee can analyze its existence and properties scientifically and dispassionately, and ask how it is that this sign constitutes the needed bridge between spheres.

Thus far, we have only translated Dee's thought into our own terminologies. The monad is a self-aware example of ritualization. Dee constructs an experiential object that has a special status outside the world. He even grants it sacred status, quite literally. Because the practice of thinking and analyzing the monad is itself a performance of and encounter with the universe of signs standing outside the monad, what we see in the book *Monas Hieroglyphica* is a kind of formal laboratory notebook of ritual practice, Dee's collated, pol-

The Occult Mind

ished notes of ritual encounters with the divine through the monad. If he had lived long enough, he might one day have distilled his angelic conversations into a similar form, explaining the Enochian revelations in the mathematical language of proofs.

Yet this reading of the *Monas* as within Dee's world of practice, though it implies the political in some sense (following Pierre Bourdieu, Sherry Ortner, and Catherine Bell), still fails to explain concretely how Dee could have thought the monad a political object.[22] We know that he did so; his dedication of the book to Maximilian II (1527–76), emperor of Germany and Holy Roman emperor-elect makes this explicit, beginning with a "hieroglyphic figure . . . after the manner (called) Pythagorean" demonstrating the extreme rarity of the monad and the "still greater mysteries . . . such as we have described in our cosmopolitical theories."[23]

Josten remarks that these "cosmopolitical theories" refer to an unidentified work, but with the notable exception of Sherman, who considers the cosmopolitics to have nothing to do with magic or occultism, recent scholarship on Dee has accepted that while there may not have been a single such work his cosmopolitics runs throughout his writing. Later in the same dedication, Dee argues that the monad has a transformative power that implies a strongly political dimension:

This our hieroglyphic monad possesses, hidden away in its innermost centre, a terrestrial body. It [*sc.* the monad] teaches without words, by what divine force that [terrestrial body] should be actuated. When it has been actuated, it [*sc.* the terrestrial centre of the monad] is to be united (in a perpetual marriage) to a generative influence which is lunar and solar, even if previously, in heaven or elsewhere, they [*sc.* the lunar and solar influences] were widely separated from that [terrestrial] body [at the centre of the monad]. When this *Gamaea*[24] has (by God's will) been concluded (which [word] to the Parisians, I have interpreted as Τῆς γαμῆς αἶαν, i.e. as the earth of marriage, or as the terrestrial sign of a union performed in the realm of [astral] influences), the monad can no longer be fed or watered on its native soil, until the fourth, great, and truly metaphysical, revolution be completed. When that advance has been made, he who fed [the monad] will first himself go away into a metamorphosis and will afterwards very rarely be held by mortal eye. This, O very good King, is the true invisibility of the *magi* which has so often (and without sin) been spoken of, and which (as all future *magi* will own) has been granted to the theories of our monad.[25]

On one level, Dee argues, in line with his other statements here and else-where on adeptship (*adeptivus*), that the mystical transformation or trans-mutation of the adept repositions him outside and above the ordinary world, as indicated by the shift from the terrestrial to the celestial. But at the same time Dee's choice of the phrase "native land" (Nativa Terra), in a dedi-cation addressed to a king and emperor who had only recently (1562) as-sumed one throne and would shortly (1564) assume another, we can hardly dismiss as accidental. Indeed, if we have learned anything from Sherman's work on Dee's reading and writing it is that they were eminently worldly. In short, we find Dee claiming that his metaphysical and private-mystical monad, the foundation of a proposed epistemological revolution in the ab-stract sciences as well as in orthographic or typographic arts, is simultane-ously a powerful instrument of political change.

Insofar as this problem has been addressed by previous scholarship, the usual reading appears to depend on a causal link: if wise kings read the book and are transformed by the monad, this will trickle down to the common people. But this reading seems at odds with Dee's own formulations; if such were his aim, it is hard to understand why he went to such trouble to make the text so cryptic and difficult—Maximilian's son Rudolph II, for example, "commended the book *Monas*, but said it was too hard for his Majesties ca-pacity."[26] Dee was hardly so foolish as to presume that his addressee would necessarily read and interpret this strange text accurately—surely that would require the very unworldly magus imagined by Yates that Sherman so vi-ciously dismisses. I suggest instead that for Dee no categorical distinction separates political action from mystical meditation. Just as earlier scholars struggled to understand how science and magic could be indistinguishable in the sixteenth century, so now we must grapple with the possibility that a hypercompressed ritual object, a mandala in Szőnyi's formulation, can be-come a political *actor* and not merely an instrument.

⁘

As we saw in chapter 1, comparison depends on a double gesture. First, one identifies, abstracts, and constructs the object of study; this procedure can in general be termed morphological or structural, depending on one's methods and presuppositions. Second, one situates and contextualizes the object with respect to some larger class; in traditional comparative work this operates ahistorically, while in more recent formulations (especially those of Jonathan Z. Smith) it becomes historical. To use some of Smith's terminol-ogy, the first step *defamiliarizes* the object, dislodging it from an obscuring background so that its distinctive features become apparent, while the second *familiarizes*, making the object an instance of something known.[27]

With the notion of Ægypt, I tried to defamiliarize the magical nostalgia for Egypt, leading to a somewhat inside-out reading of the *Asclepius*. The justification for the move is the seeming familiarity of Egypt: because we think we know about Egypt, we miss the peculiarities of Ægypt.

The problem with Dee is quite the reverse. It is not that Dee is too familiar, too normal. On the contrary, as the many studies of Dee have revealed, the difficulty lies in his unfamiliarity. Thus the familiarizing procedure has dominated Dee studies, with each new work seeking an appropriate context into which to place him. Yet this process has failed, not only because it has not achieved consensus or even comprehension but because historians have undermined familiarization with defamiliarizing presuppositions.

Yates dropped Dee into the "Hermetic Tradition," following up from her student I. R. F. Calder's work on Dee "as an English Neoplatonist."[28] Of course, Yates had in some sense to *invent* this context, making the historical value of her study questionable. Thus Clulee moves to the history of science and places Dee "between science and religion," to use the subtitle of his book. More recently, Sherman places Dee within the world of intellectuals and court patronage. One could continue in this vein, but it should already be clear that none of these moves has resolved the problem. Before Yates, Dee seemed simply incoherent, unfamiliar because incomprehensible. From Yates onward, we see Dee in a series of flickering images, like a badly drawn flip book.

The crucial difficulty arises from disciplinary presuppositions. Because these studies situate themselves within early modern intellectual, cultural, or science history, they insist on the otherness, the unfamiliarity, of their object. For the historian, after all, the purpose of familiarizing Dee by historical context is ultimately to defamiliarize the context, to understand late sixteenth-century intellectual and science culture as a distinct, unique object. In this sense the historian's procedures are not structurally different from the comparativist's. Indeed, it is long past time to recognize that history is intrinsically comparative.

Traditional historians resist cross-cultural (so-called "ahistorical") comparison but rarely present the logical and methodological reasons for such resistance accurately. Most commonly, they argue simply that historians cannot accept ahistorical analyses. But apart from the fact that to define cross-cultural comparison as ahistorical entails a specific and narrow sense of "history" as endeavor, this argument presumes a necessary contiguity of the historian's own position with that of the object studied. Taken seriously, this objection requires historians to study only their ancestral roots, such that all historians of China should be Chinese.

Of course, anticomparativist historians do not intend this racist conclusion. Rather—and with considerable justification—they worry that cross-cultural comparison will lead to the annulling of difference. That is, if we familiarize one historical object by classifying it with another from a different culture, there is a grave danger that we will come to ignore the necessarily many differences. To say that medieval Japanese society had a feudal system could, if taken too strongly, lead one to disregard the many factors that made this society unlike the European prototype. And indeed, precisely this objection can and should be (and has been) leveled at a great many of our early predecessors in the comparative study of culture.

Practically speaking, however, comparative methods have developed considerably since the middle of the last century; to say that all comparative study has fallen prey to this tendency to annul difference is simply to express ignorance. More important, by denying its own comparative basis, historical scholarship becomes assailable on precisely the same grounds.

On the one hand, radical familiarization through historical context risks making particular people into effects of history. Some work in the history of science, for example, has gone so far toward social contextualization that Newtonian mechanics becomes little more than an expression of seventeenth-century English society. This is structurally equivalent to old-fashioned "bad" comparison, annulling difference in the name of familiarity.

On the other hand, the recently more popular radical defamiliarization, which insists on the uniqueness of its objects, risks incomprehensibility. If the other is *simply* other, we have no way to understand. Setting aside obvious moral concerns about dehumanizing those we study, the practical difficulty is that this procedure destroys the possibility of interpretation. Furthermore, because it dislodges the scholar from the analysis, such defamiliarization ends up denying everything we ought to have learned from the theoretical revolutions of the last few decades.

These difficulties manifest clearly in the study of John Dee. As we have seen, early interpreters in effect refused interpretation, seeing Dee as incoherent. Yates and her successors have worked to familiarize, to make Dee an instance of the known, but have ultimately foundered on both his undeniable peculiarities—peculiarities, let us note, seen as such in his own time—and the historian's methodological insistence on difference.[29]

Consider William Sherman's *John Dee: The Politics of Reading and Writing*

The Occult Mind

in the English Renaissance, which Anthony Grafton called a "model mono-graph."[30] Sherman describes his project as set against Yates's "myth of the magus," that is, the notion that John Dee "was a philosopher-magician who aspired through study of the arcane sciences to understand the fabric of the cosmos and to achieve union with the divine."[31] He makes his broad point strongly:

> [One] of Yates's enduring legacies is a myth of the magus that has without doubt become part of our historical unconscious. Although some of Dee's twentieth-century manifestations have owed little to historical verisimilitude, I use the word *myth* not in the sense of an imaginary con-struction, to deny the reality that Yates describes; rather, I use it in the sense of a narrative and rhetorical construction, to highlight Yates's story as an interpretive strategy imposed on Dee—in order not simply to make sense of him, but also to fashion him into something useful for her larger purposes.[32]

Specifically, Sherman argues that "the myth of the magus . . . essentializes Dee by isolating him from his social and spatial circumstances." This essen-tialization is effected by

> two historiographical operations. . . . First, in constructing a narrative so compelling that it has easily won its battle with unruly and often contra-dictory evidence, Yates and her students have ignored many records of Dee's activities and works that are incompatible with the myth of the magus. Second, they have identified him with historiographical cate-gories that have more to do with twentieth-century academic concerns than sixteenth-century cultural phenomena.[33]

In other words, the unitary picture of Dee as magus becomes a framework imposed on all Dee data, and documents that do not match are passed over or at least deemphasized. This is the classical objection to comparative famil-iarization. In Sherman's view, Dee scholars work this way because of funda-mentally anachronistic (i.e., ahistorical) academic concerns. In short, the modern academic construct—the magus—receives higher priority than do contemporary categories, documents, and evidence.

Similarly, Sherman asserts that scholars have constructed Dee as an iso-lated, eccentric "magus," disconnected from the intellectual and political dis-course of his environment—yet only in an endnote does he reveal that the single most important study of Dee, Nicholas Clulee's, does not fall into this trap. Nor, let us note, does Deborah Harkness's exceptional study of Dee's angelic conversations, on which Sherman does not remark here. Sherman thus conveys the impression that the Yates interpretation of the Elizabethan "magus" was entirely dominant until Sherman himself recognized Dee's position within his intellectual and political environment; yet in order to do so, he must both disregard the context in which Yates wrote and suppress the weight of scholarship since her time.

I do not intend by this to undermine or challenge Sherman's basic approach, nor his main conclusions. The issue is *why* Sherman makes these claims: he insists that Dee cannot be "essentialized" as a figure of total cohesion, a disembodied mind that never changed, a participant in one intellectual discipline (Yates's Hermeticism) only indirectly linked to other scholarly and political endeavors. These points are well taken, and if they were already made by both Clulee and Harkness that does not invalidate their repetition. Yet Sherman by this particular *rhetorical strategy*—something to which he would have us pay close attention in early modern thinkers and writers— contrives to essentialize and divide into rigid formal categories the *modern* thinkers and scholars with whom he engages. That is, Sherman applies an excellent method of *adversaria* in reading texts from the early modern period, but confines that method to historical documents. Modern scholars, by contrast, he may treat in much the same manner he deplores when used by Yates.

Lacking here is a recognition that the texts we study are not really so different as all that. In a lengthy and valuable discussion of early modern reading practice and library construction, Sherman, like his colleagues in the sociology of reading, draws attention to annotation methods and cataloging practice. Dee's library appears to have been organized quite haphazardly, with books shoved in more or less wherever they would fit, albeit under general headings. The marginalia of Dee, like those of his contemporaries Isaac Casaubon and Thomas Smith, indicate important points and graceful passages in the text under review, and Sherman justly contends that these denote bits of the texts intended by the reader for later appropriation into his own writings.[34]

All fascinating, but surely rather familiar? I have organized my own modest collection under three rubrics—fiction, occult, nonfiction—and then alphabetically by author. Friends sometimes complain about this system, because unless they remember who wrote a given work, they have no way of finding anything on the shelves, nor can they browse within a topical heading to find works of interest. True, of course, but the fact is that, like Dee, I know what I have, and I do know the authors; when (as certainly happens) I

The Occult Mind

forget, I have the pleasure of rediscovering texts, and after all if I remember the title and perhaps the color of the volume I can simply browse the area: I know it was just up there on the top right, maybe the second shelf down, which again brings to my attention the odd volume that has slipped from memory. If Lévi-Strauss claimed he had a neolithic intelligence, should I claim an early modern one? Or is Dee's methodology really a great deal more familiar than Sherman recognizes?[35]

Similarly, the annotation practices Sherman describes, common among working scholars and students in the early modern period, seem eminently familiar. Perusing my copy of a favorite work or one with which I have engaged at length, one will generally find running annotations in a cryptic scrawl meaningful solely to myself. For example, where a volume discusses issues of textuality that particularly interest me (assuming these are not the central focus of the book), I usually put the Chinese character *wen*, meaning "writing," because it fits neatly into a small margin and has for me a clear meaning. Is this really so peculiar? One suspects that Sherman's books will offer little purchase to future historians.

Sherman's criticisms neatly sum up much of the post-Yates responses, in both their strength and their weakness. The primary difficulty, as we saw in the last chapter, is that these recent critics rarely seem to see Yates within her own historical context, so insistent are they to see Dee, Bruno, or whomever in theirs. In other words, Sherman—and I choose his work as a particularly clear example of a constant dynamic—has, by denying the comparative basis of historical work, fallen into many of the traps usually associated with comparison.

If we are to make coherent sense of Dee's *Monas*, we must begin with familiarization, as scholars since Yates have seen. We now know enough about the work and its various contexts to do this with precision; a preliminary de-familiarizing construction, in other words, is the laudable result of decades of historical study. But if we are to avoid falling back into circularity, to evade the historian's overinsistence on difference, this familiarization must be cross-cultural, ahistorical in the sense that the context must not arise from early modern historical trends. Of course, the purpose of such comparison must be constrained: it is not that Dee's work *is the same as* the object of the comparison, but rather that it *is similar in specific ways*, which then illuminate Dee. We need a new perspective.

No is a Japanese dramatic form that developed in the Muromachi period (1333–1573) and by the late Edo period (1603–1867) had achieved the fixed, crystallized form seen today. The dramas, which have a relatively consistent structure and are performed exclusively by male actors, employ music, chant, dance, masks, elaborate costumes, and highly stylized movement and stage design to produce dramatic and arguably mystical effects. Perhaps most remarkable to the new viewer are the almost glacial pace, the non-melodic and seemingly arrhythmic music, and the famous masks that have become icons of traditional Japan, though the nearly plotless focus on Buddhist emancipation from worldly desire also sharply distinguishes Nō from most theatrical forms familiar in the West.[36]

It is common to emphasize the theoretical genius of Zeami Motokiyo (1363–1433) and his successor Komparu Ujinobu Zenchiku (ca. 1405–70), who exercised powerful shaping influences on the development of Nō. As the story is usually told, Zeami and his father Kan'ami Kiyotsugu (1333–84) developed Nō out of the older *sarugaku* and *sangaku* entertainment forms. Kan'ami linked *monomane* (mimetic imitation) with *yū* (mysterious elegance) in his performances and his plays, laying the foundation for the aesthetic and dramatic synthesis of Nō itself. Zeami, a brilliant performer, playwright, and theorist, acquired the patronage of the shogun Ashikaga Yoshimitsu (1368–1408), who also became his lover, and this high elite interest helped raise the drama out of the murky world of nomadic troupes (*za*) playing to rustics and philistines. After Zeami's exile on the death in 1428 of Yoshimitsu's successor Yoshimochi, he continued to write and theorize the nature of his art in a series of secret texts that have only in the last century been made available outside the Nō schools descended from him.[37] In these treatises, Zeami draws increasingly heavily on Buddhist terminology to develop a comprehensive aesthetic of Nō[38]; he also argues for Nō as a *geidō*, an artistic "way" like tea ceremony (*chanoyu*, *chadō*) or calligraphy (*shodō*), proposing stages of an actor's artistic development parallel to stages of spiritual progress. Zenchiku continued the development, both theoretical and practical, and put elite patronage on a firm basis, not dependent on particular personal relationships. As a playwright and theorist, Zenchiku is usually seen as conservative with respect to Zeami's focus on depth and elegance, and in his writings he drew ever more deeply on religious conceptions to refine the sacred unity of his art. Over the next several centuries, aristocratic and perhaps ecclesiastical interest and support permitted Nō to grow and bloom, preserving and formalizing the tradition in order to further refine its aesthetic purity. Despite the historical and intellectual intricacies of this art and its theory, one commentator and former practitioner noted that

The Occult Mind

Noh is not meant to be comprehended by the intellect. It is theater of the heart, predicated on direct experience through feelings. In order to appreciate Noh, . . . all that are required are the most basic understanding of the play and a delicate and rich sensibility that allows one to take in directly and respond sympathetically to the variety of sentiments of the hero, educed through the medium of dramatic events evolving on the stage. Noh is the very essence of "the Japanese soul."[39]

Of course, this conception of Nō also expresses and reproduces many of the ideological tropes of Japanese nativist (*kokugaku* and *nihonjinron*) discourse.[40] The intersections of religious definition and terminology, class, nationalism, performative antiquity, traditionalism, and assertions of aesthetic difference clearly mark the discourse on Nō as within the nativist mode. Although these tropes appear consistently, it is striking that modern Japanese insider discussions of Nō, on the one hand, and Zeami's theoretical work (which precedes the rise of kokugaku), on the other, formulate such different views of the dramatic form, and that neither is obviously concordant with the ideas of Motoori Norinaga and Hirata Atsutane, the two most dominant thinkers of Tokugawa nativism. By using nativist thought to pry apart these various conceptions of Nō and set them into dialogue with our concerns about politics, ritual, and writing, I hope to open possibilities for understanding *Monas Hieroglyphica* and to suggest challenges for regnant theories of performance in ritual.

The details of each Nō are laid down in a *yōkyoku* or text, which prescribes not only lines in the sense of an ordinary play but also rhythmic and chant structures. The dramas are divided into five major types, based on the central figure (*shite*)[41]: God plays, in which the shite is a *kami* (god or spirit) who bestows blessings; Warrior plays, in which the shite is a warrior, often from the *Tales of Heikei* (Heikei monogatari), who reexperiences his last battles; Woman or wig plays, in which the shite is a woman who examines the relationship between her past beauty and her present age, ugliness, or death; Madness plays, in which the shite is someone who has gone mad and explains his or her trauma;[42] and Demon plays, in which the shite is, or becomes possessed by, a demon, whose exorcism or departure constitutes the primary dramatic thrust.[43]

Nō plays usually have two structuring acts (*ba*). In the first, the secondary or side character (*waki*), most often a traveling priest or monk, encounters the shite as an old or otherwise unremarkable person. As the two converse, the shite hints at or reveals a spiritual nature: the shite is really a ghost, for example, or a god in disguise, or possessed by a demon. This revelation concludes the first act with the departure of the shite from the stage. As an entr'acte, comic actors perform an *ai-kyōgen* (usually abbreviated *ai*) during which a local peasant retells the story thus far. In the second act, the shite returns, now costumed in a fashion appropriate to his or her true nature, and through explication of the situation (usually from the past) is persuaded to come into accord with the true nature of things, usually through some form of enlightenment resulting from the elimination of desire. In the most representative Nō, the shite is a ghost who has remained trapped in the world by desire; over the course of the play the shite comes to terms with this and is enabled to give up attachments to the world and move onward toward enlightenment.

Komparu Kunio elegantly describes the experiential impression of Nō:

> The chorus chants in unison in a way that seems to reach into one's soul. This contrasts with the sharp vibrations of the drums and the eerie calls of the drummers. The melody of the flute seems to represent the state of mind of the character [*shite*], and the character's heart reveals itself through a mask that seems to have an infinite number of expressions and through beautifully choreographed movements. The rich brocade costumes harmonize in a mysterious way with the bare, unpolished wooden stage. In the play, a character appears, something happens to the character, and through this happening many emotions are evoked in the audience.[44]

As Paul Claudel remarked, "Le drame, c'est quelque chose qui arrive, le Nō, c'est quelqu'un qui arrive."[45]

Considered as ritual in a simple sense, this type of Nō drama enacts the spiritual transformation of the shite through the offices of the *waki*. In Eliadean terms, this is a reactualization of the sacred acts of gods or culture heroes. What is perhaps somewhat unusual is that, because the ritual is staged theatrically, the audience must become participants through a kind of empathic connection to the shite; Zeami's theories formulate means by which the actor can evoke this identification on the part of the viewers. To make the comparison to Dee's monad explicit, we can read the shite, or better the total performance of the Nō, as a dynamic symbol into which the meditating audience enters. This reading is confirmed by the many discussions of Nō that emphasize the dreamy half trance of the audience, the purely symbolic and structural nature of the mise-en-scène, and the sacred character of the dances and chants.

The Occult Mind

An important dimension of such interpretations of Nō is its often-claimed historical connection to ancient *kagura*, read as shamanic possession rituals. In this understanding, the actor is actually possessed by the shite, which in some sense resides within the mask. This accounts for the elaborate ritual character of the costuming process, which concludes with explicit reverence toward and meditation on the mask, itself finally donned at the end of a private ritual that is solely the actor's. The possession-ritual theory is most powerfully supported by the clearly ancient drama *Okina* in which, uniquely, the actor dons his mask onstage; the process culminates in his transformation into or possession by the kami Okina himself, who then bestows blessings on the assembled multitude.[46] This special play is usually only performed at festivals such as the New Year, often to open a full program of five dramas, one of each type in order (God, Warrior, Woman, Madness, Demon). Such a full program takes the single-play transformation to the metastructural level, where the entire day of performances manifests the structure of a single play. *Okina* begins this process by seeking the blessings of this god, who then witnesses and guides the complete event.[47]

A full program follows a structure that runs throughout Nō aesthetics: *jo* (beginning, slow), *ha* (development, faster), *kyū* (climax, fast). This triplicity dictates rhythm and emotional or dramatic intensity in each small piece of a play (*dan*), in each act (*ba*), and across the whole. In a full program, the God play is *jo*, beginning the event in a stately and minimally dramatic fashion; the Woman play (*ha*) expresses the height of the mysterious (*yūgen*) power of the event, when the maximal energy is developed but remains coiled up like a spring; and the Demon play (*kyū*) releases this energy in a burst of excitement. If *Okina* is the appropriate beginning to this process, preceding the God play, it is because the possession of the actor in that special play invokes the magical power that will underlie and sanctify the whole structure.

Attractive though the possession theory is in a number of respects, reminiscent of Jane Harrison's famous theory of Greek theater's development from ritual, it cannot be taken as complete.[48] Zeami was insistent that the actor is not the shite but rather stands at a remove *behind* the shite, which he then manipulates like a marionette:

"Indeed, when we come to face death, our life might be likened to a puppet on a cart [decorated for a great festival]. As soon as one string is cut, the creature crumbles and fades." Such is the image given of the existence of man, caught in the perpetual flow of life and death. This constructed puppet, on a cart, shows various aspects of himself but cannot come to life of itself. It represents a deed performed by moving strings. At the moment when the strings are cut, the figure falls and crumbles. *Sarugaku* [i.e., Nō] too is an art that makes use of just such artifice. What supports these illusions and gives them life is the intensity of mind of the actor. Yet the existence of this intensity must not be shown directly to the audience. Should they see it, it would be as though they could see the strings of a puppet. Let me repeat again: the actor must make his spirit the strings, and without letting his audience become aware of them, he will draw together the forces of his art. In that way, true life will reside in his *nō*.[49]

Zeami's view is more concordant with Dee's monad than with possession: the glyph is not divine in a simple sense but rather an instrument through which the divine may manifest itself in a structured and controlling manner to transform the meditating scholar. Just so, the art of the Nō actor is that of the ultimate puppeteer, who must not only make his masked and costumed body into a marionette but also induce the viewer's spirit to enter the hollow shell of the puppet, thereby forcing the audience to experience the spiritual transformation of the shite. If there is possession here, one might almost say it is the *audience* who experience it.

Historically, early ritual forms and explicitly religious dramas have no clear relationship to the development of Nō. Important works emphasize family connections to a wide range of Heian arts, some explicitly religious, some apparently secular.[50] Akima Toshio, arguing that Kan'ami's family were Asobi-be outcastes specializing in funeral rites, suggests that this accounts for the frequent use of ghosts as shite. Matsumoto Shinhachirō's Marxist-informed studies emphasize the outcaste status of all such performers and argue that Nō was a deliberate reformulation of *sarugaku* aimed to capture the patronage of the samurai class and thereby lift the actors out of their low social position. Honda Yasuji focuses on *Okina* as a link between Nō and early *shushi* (exorcistic) and *kagura* possession. Gotō Hajime, examining the relationship between *sangaku* and *sarugaku*, stresses connections to both *kagura* and *wazaogi* (comic pantomime), arguing for a shift from the "circus-like spectacle" of *sangaku*, with its origins in Chinese court entertainments, to the "indigenous" mimetic (*monomane*) mode of *wazaogi*; he reads the synthesis with *kagura* as "a triumph of the 'indigenous' genius for *wazaogi* over the 'imported' skills" of *sangaku*.[51]

Rather than battle with these problematic technical distinctions on historical grounds, let us examine the ideological content of the discourse on and embedded within Nō today. Over centuries of formalization and pa-

The Occult Mind

tronage, this art has been strategically manipulated to become an instrument of state and national ideologies. Without simply discarding the formative theories of Zeami and Zenchiku, Nō practitioners and their patrons, as well as modern scholars, built upon the form in a new ideological framework to make it serve political ends, ends best understood in the context of nativism (*kokugaku*).

First, some account of the Tokugawa formalization of Nō is necessary, in order to distinguish later Nō from what Zeami performed and theorized. Sometime shortly after Zeami's death, Nō became allied to the contemporary (fourteenth-century) comic art *kyōgen*, which provided the forms and structures for the *ai* between Nō acts; in full programs, freestanding *kyōgen* plays would be performed between Nō plays themselves. During the seventeenth to nineteenth centuries, *Nōgaku* (i.e., Nō in conjunction with *kyōgen*) became increasingly associated with the elite patronage of the shogun, daimyo (feudal lords), samurai, and commoners who were—or wished to appear—sophisticated; other forms (such as Kabuki) served more popular, middle-class audiences. This separation led to an emphasis on preservation rather than innovation, greater formal reverence accorded to Nō masters "and, in general, to a slow, ceremonial tempo which favored the creation of an aura of loftiness aimed more at the approval of the upper class initiates and connoisseurs than at the pleasure of the general public";[52] the decrease in pacing is most striking when we recognize that whereas modern Nō take about two hours to perform, Zeami refers to a full-day program of as many as sixteen dramas, suggesting that in his time Nō lasted perhaps forty minutes.

The Tokugawa regime championed Nō to such a degree that it offered official recognition to the five long-established schools (*za*) organized on a family structure. These schools deliberately detached themselves from ordinary contemporary life in order to emphasize better the traditional nature and antiquity of their art, one effect of which was the growing treatment of the masters as revered teachers by both samurai and the nouveau riche. In the eighteenth century, the heads of the schools were known as *iemoto*, masters of "families" or schools in much the same sense as masters of tea ceremony or certain martial arts, a classification that helped affirm their role as preservers and transmitters of an orthodox "way"; ironically, this also resulted in the selection from a total corpus of some three thousand plays a nearly fixed canon of only about 240. By the nineteenth century, the *iemoto* of Nō were often treated as arbiters of aesthetic tradition; as Ortolani notes, "It is no wonder that the *iemoto* began to feel as if they belonged to the highest strata of society, since, in fact, they had the means to associate with the rich and the powerful—thus becoming oblivious to their outcaste beginnings."[53] What is most important for us is that the social rise of Nō and its masters progressed in lockstep with the formalization and deceleration of the art, and that these performative changes were constructed as cleaving ever more strongly to tradition and antiquity.

The kokugaku movement may be said to begin in earnest with Kamo no Mabuchi (1697–1769) and Motoori Norinaga (1730–1801). To simplify wildly, these nativists (*kokugakusha*) considered that contemporary Edo society had fallen away from its traditional values, and they sought traces of earlier and superior ways submerged under the surfaces of poetry, the arts, labor, and religion. This project led to the formulation of a number of typical binaries: ancient/modern, simple/elegant, rural/urban, peasant/elite, Japanese/Chinese, Shinto/Buddhist, indigenous/imported, real/imitation, spontaneous/deliberate, poetry/prose, emotion/reason, speech/writing.[54] Motoori is most famous for his massive work *Kojiki-den* (1798; pub. 1822), a close study of the eighth-century legendary history *Kojiki*, in which he not only tried to bring to light the hidden truths of its mythological content but also to discern beneath its early uses of Chinese characters the phonetic structures of archaic Japanese spoken language.[55] He is also strongly associated with what has often been called the "Shinto revival," the very term suggesting immediately a core principle of nativism: that a return to or resurrection of antiquity, on whatever basis, was revival rather than reinvention.

Given that Nō was a relatively recent art, primarily patronized by urban elites, whose aesthetics depended heavily on elegance and on Buddhist cosmology, emphasizing mimesis (*monomane*), elaborately fixed in strong textual forms (*yōkyoku*) and anything but spontaneous, it would appear to be precisely the sort of thing nativists would denounce. Indeed, Ōkuma Kotomichi (1798–1868) attacked theories of the restoration or mere recapitulation of ancient ways and forms as "imitative," "like looking at the Kabuki."[56] How then could *Nōgaku* be assimilated to nativist purposes, be taken as emblematic of the "essence of the Japanese soul"?

To give a partial answer, we must note Motoori's extremely influential rethinking of the aesthetic concept *mono no aware*, literally something like "pathos-response to things"; *mono* (thing) here is the same as in *monomane*, the loosely mimetic mode in *Nōgaku* perhaps arising from *wazaogi*. Although already in the opening of *The Tale of Genji* (early eleventh century) *mono no aware* had a strong element of pathos, in that it is an emotional response to beautiful things recognizing that they are fleeting and will pass

The Occult Mind

away, Motoori focuses rather on its spontaneous quality as a spiritual person's naturally elegant poetic response to real things, as opposed to a reasoned response couched in self-conscious elegance that imitates Chinese standards. We can understand *mono no aware* as relevant to Nō if we emphasize *audience* rather than performer, reversing without exactly opposing most of Zeami's theorizing: the point is not that the *performance* of Nō fits desirable categories, but rather that it is constructed to *evoke* the desired responses in its audience. Here we return to Zeami's marionette: the object is to distance the audience from their quotidian existence as urban elites and project them spiritually into the world of the shite, the real world of the kami—the illud tempus of sacred *gesta*, as Eliade would have it. In a very Eliadean mode, we might read Nō as a ritual form in which the performers are not really the participants at all, for the actors are only instruments by means of which the real participants—the elite audience members—experience reactualization of archaic yet hauntingly present spiritual transformations that occurred in the time of the kami.[57] For Motoori, as for many of the nativists, we might say that the time of creation, the time of the creator-gods Izanami and Izanagi, was a kind of Ægypt in Japan.

Hirata Atsutane (1776–1843) departed most obviously from "the master," as he referred to Motoori, in that he did not consider the *Kojiki* the most reliable source for the archaic way of the kami. He granted considerably higher value to prose, and indeed strung together the poetic accounts in *Kojiki* into a kind of narrative. For Hirata, "a continuation of the creation was impossible without [his audience's] constant involvement in making the land habitable. [Thus] Hirata's method itself prefigured the crucial element of his narrative by 'returning' to a time before the contemporary division of labor that correlated the social structure with a separation between mental and manual work."[58] Not unlike Hermes read nostalgically, Hirata viewed the distinction between thought and action as a negative effect of historical time, in that the Japanese people—especially elites—had come to divide their work from their thought through acceptance of "rational" Chinese characters. We shall return to the "rationality" of Chinese writing in chapter 4, but for the moment let us note that the emphasis on actively spoken words provoked Hirata to stress the "historical facts of the 'prayers' (*norito*) [as] superior [to] and more correct than the accounts of the *Kojiki* and its record of the godly age."[59]

To use Harootunian's term (borrowed from Bakhtin), Hirata's "chronotope" was explicated from a range of early texts and formed into a single cosmological narrative. This chronotope—a sort of space-time continuum of the "folk" *imaginaire*—was the illud tempus to which the nativists wished in some sense to return. But Hirata, recognizing that simple restorationism would lead to false imitation, sought a means to bridge the divide between contemporary alienation from and archaic unity with the way of the kami. Where Motoori believed that only poetry could bridge this gap—and that weakly—Hirata shifted toward bodily activity in the form of labor. For him, everyday life in the traditional village was a seamless web of bodily practices, all homologized to worship of the kami. If the *norito* prayers and the ancient tales and poems from the *Kojiki* and elsewhere were thus representations of the ancient forms of worship, bodily everyday life (sexuality, eating, labor) were that worship itself.[60]

We are once more faced with a difficulty: whatever else Nō might be, it is hardly everyday life. Let us return to Zeami for a moment, this time focusing on the performer as much as the audience; by examining Nō's function as a "way" we may clarify its strategic utility to the late nativist project.

In his justly celebrated book *The Karma of Words*, William LaFleur demonstrates a striking concordance between the five-play structure of a full Nō program and the Mahayana Buddhist cycle of realms of beings (Sanskrit *gati*, Japanese *rokudō*). Further, he suggests that the greatest Nō plays also demonstrate this progression through the karmic cycle by positioning the shite such that the roles or levels are in conflict. For example, "The passion of a woman for a man long absent will drive her to frenzy—representing a clear example of what was regarded by the classical Buddhists as passion's deepening of delusion—but also provide her with an unparalleled capacity for fidelity and single-mindedness. What seems right according to one code is wrong according to another."[61] Although this disparity has often been read as between Buddhist and Shintō or Confucian ethics, LaFleur argues that it actually makes sense within a Buddhist context, particularly one informed by Japanese thought. He quotes Dōgen: "In the Buddha dharma, practice and realization are identical."[62] In other words, Zeami's Nō is a theatrical form in which the very attempt to recognize, understand, and potentially overcome this disjunction is itself to complete it; like Austin's speech-acts, the plays are their own realization. By this reading, Zeami's insistence on the actor's progress as parallel to monastic development is literal: the actor, by striving to overcome the disjuncture within the play through its perfect performance *as* disjuncture, achieves the end that the play had seemed only to represent.[63]

In the context of Hirata's nativism, this understanding of Nō would have great power. The unity achieved here through performance and identifica-

The Occult Mind

tion is an assertion of identity, a denial of difference. The act is the end, the self is the other, the actor is the shite, the performer is the audience—and these equivalences are bidirectional, such that the total performance of Nō asserts the reciprocal unity of all beings within the way of the kami. Taking this still further, such an understanding would entail that the symbolic anti-realism of Nō manifests awareness of its own nature as representation, admission of which avoids the problem of restorationist imitation. Through Zeami's doctrine of the emptied-out marionette, we might say that Nō, recognizing its inability to progress beyond representation into the real, achieves that impossible end because of its self-consciousness. In other words, because the elegance, fixity, self-conscious archaism, and—in a sense—falsity of Nō are both central to the form at every level and recognized for their inadequacy to represent the truth of the unseen, Nō's very honesty enables it to transcend its limitations insofar as it is a living form to which and through which human beings respond transcendently.

I must emphasize that these are hypothetical readings. Within the vast literature of kokugaku, there must somewhere be a great many excurses on Nō, its virtues and its flaws. My claim is not that I have read as Motoori or Hirata did, nor that my reconstruction fits any particular nativist view. Rather, I want to suggest that Nō offered valuable possibilities to the nativist project, and that its rereadings in this vein did not require distortion of Nō's "true meaning" any more than they could simply find in Nō an already-perfected expression of "the Japanese soul."

To conclude this brief examination of nativism in the discourse on Nō, we may consider the work of Yanagita Kunio (1875–1962), a folklorist whose influence on the modern American study of religion has yet to be explored fully.[64] This may clarify the means by which ideology can be embedded in the nondiscursive elements of ritual, even while it reminds us that the nativist project lent itself to complicity in the darkest chapters of Japanese history.

Harootunian lists a number of the essential tenets of nativism throughout its long duration:

> its massive displacement of the political for the religious (the social); its consistent rejection of history for a pre-class, folk chronotype and a privileging of place; its disciplining of the body in the service of work, which rescued the body from the blandishments of pleasure announced by the [Edo] culture of play (gesakuron); its noninstrumental conception of language, which insisted on communication not between men and other

men but between a community and the world and the gods who made and gave it; and its intense conviction in human reciprocity and self-sufficiency.[65]

He emphasizes also that "they were able to overcome the opposition between mental and manual, theory and practice, because the body now brought separate experiences together,"[66] a point worth emphasizing in the context of Zeami's bodily-practice-as-realization theory of transmigration. In the wake of the extreme disillusionment occasioned by the Meiji Restoration, which had appeared to offer a return to the way of the kami but actually only appropriated rhetorical tropes of nativism to serve an ever-stronger state ideology, nativism largely declined as a political mode.[67] Yanagita sought to develop a "new nativism" founded in folk ethnography (*minzoku-gaku*), appropriate to the new century's concerns about Westernization, industrialism, and modernity.

Like Hirata, Yanagita emphasized the importance of place, specifically the rural village, with its shrines, fields, and other scenes of everyday life. But where Hirata had envisioned a utopian ideal-type of the village, existing literally "no-place," Yanagita situated the ideal place in real geographic space; traveling from village to village in the rural countryside, he sought to recover surviving traces of the archaic submerged under and threatened by modern industrial exploitation.[68] This shift from u-topos to topos, however, necessitated a move from Hirata's language of difference to a rhetoric of homogeneity. We might read these moves as sophisticated expressions of the two halves of Eliade's theory of sacred space: Hirata had formulated sacred space as radically other, to which the ordinary, profane space of the village existed in a reciprocal relationship. But like Eliade, Yanagita asserted that this sacred space could actually be entered simply by crossing the threshold of a shrine or temple. To make this congruent with Hirata's vision, Yanagita asserted that the space thus entered was somehow homogeneous with all such spaces, in contrast to the heterogeneous space of the profane world outside. The result was that all villages and shrines were at a deep level ontologically the same, and thus all Japanese people were united by their ties not only to local spaces but to the "land" of their birth.

By shifting the site of difference from village/kami to urban/rural or modern/archaic, Yanagita also erased the radical distinction between the ordinary folk (*aohitogusa*) and the kami. Although this might seem like the culmination of Hirata's project, in the sense that it completed the move toward divinization of people and humanization of gods, it also annulled the reciprocal relationship that had supported Hirata's theory of labor. For Hirata, the gods created good things, and through labor-as-worship the people expressed gratitude. In Yanagita's rethinking, this relation could in effect be taken for granted, for so long as village life was active and functional, the cycle of creation and worship necessarily went on: the "footprint of the life of the peoples' past has never stopped," he wrote.[69] Thus a ruralization movement, such as had arisen in the mid-nineteenth century, was an unnecessary reassertion in the form of practical politics of what was always already true.

Hirata's sophisticated structure necessitated an other, which Yanagita located in the state. Where Hirata had seen the self-other relation as reciprocal, Yanagita probably saw it, rather simplistically, as mildly antagonistic. But by making the state into the other, he also made it a *necessary* part of Japanese life, as against the nativists' increasing opposition to the Tokugawa centralized bureaucracy (*bakufu*). Further, Hirata's notion of reciprocity haunted Yanagita's work, to the point that although he thought his project antiauthoritarian, he had constructed a system in which everyday labor amounted to worshipful gratitude offered to the state; residual antagonism was reduced to criticism "directed less toward political policy than toward conserving the true content of cultural form by defining it."[70] In this discourse of a timeless and irreducible Japaneseness in a reciprocal—if conflictual—relationship of worship and gratitude with the imperial state's unending generosity, one readily sees materials for fascist appropriation.

We have seen that tropes of the various nativisms appear throughout late discourse on Nō, but here I would emphasize the postwar era. With the Occupation available as a present other, it was easy enough for conservatives to claim Japanese unity by way of contrast. In asserting the unbroken continuity of Nō back to ancient *kagura* and formulating its aesthetic experience as irreducibly Japanese, such discourse would surely have found support in the obsequious willingness of Westerners—perhaps especially Americans—to accept anything so obviously different as evidence of depth and truth. In short, the wild proliferation of Japan-centered Orientalism in the last several decades—Zen, martial arts, samurai, ninja—offered assurance to right-wing traditionalists that "the Japanese soul" possessed something special and different. As the 2003 film *The Last Samurai* demonstrates, neither this wide-eyed Orientalism nor its fascistic implications has yet subsided to any great degree. And even a skimming of the literature about Nō aimed at Western audiences reveals an emblematic trope: the difficulty, confusion, otherness, and even tedium experienced by Western viewers demonstrate the depth and perfection of the art as an ideal expression of the ineffable uniqueness of the Japanese soul.[71]

⁘

Before returning to *Monas Hieroglyphica*, it is worth reflecting on what this comparative detour into Nō and nativism has revealed. In particular, we must consider whether these historical reflections on admittedly peculiar ritual forms entail anything beyond their assistance in resolving the immediate analytical problem.

The study of ritual is conspicuously dominated by the allied forms known as "ritual studies" and "performance studies," respectively associated most strongly with Ronald L. Grimes and Richard Schechner, and in both cases powerfully guided by the ghostly voice of Victor W. Turner. Simply put, ritual studies draws on theatrical arts and ideas to understand ritual, and performance studies on ritual to understand theater. I find these approaches unsatisfactory because of a naïveté that seems always to inhere in the analyses.

In his important early work, *Beginnings in Ritual Studies*, Grimes devotes two chapters to analysis of *zazen*, the Zen ritual practice of seated meditation.[72] Here he formulates and demonstrates his methodology, known as "ritology," and differentiates it from other, more "traditional" scholarly modes. In particular, Grimes insists that ritology should not privilege texts or even discourse in the ordinary sense, and he deploys the silence of zazen to argue that discourse may be so superfluous to a given ritual that emphasis on it will necessarily distort the object of analysis and even destroy the possibility of understanding. By briefly elucidating the similarity of this ritology to the discourse on Nō, I shall argue that Grimes's well-intentioned method is in principle incapable of avoiding complicity in the ideologies of institutionally powerful voices.[73]

Grimes's ritology is in essence a phenomenology of the external. It displaces the discursive and the intellectual, arguing that a ritual is complete unto itself. This acontextual strategy appears clearly in his choice to examine the ritology not of zazen in general but of zazen as it is practiced in American Zen centers. "If I were considering Zen ceremony in Japan or Korea," he writes, "I would have to say something about its political and civic functions. . . . Zen, of course, does not serve these functions so obviously as Shinto and other forms of Buddhism in Japan." He continues, "North American Zen centers are just beginning to be established in their respective local communities; so community, not nation, is their major civic focus."[74] In other words, the fact that we are talking about American Zen makes the specifically Japanese or Korean national functions and implications irrelevant; besides, Zen does not have such functions.

In this brief example, we can already see a potential problem, in that the logic is faulty. If Zen has minimal "political and civic functions" in Japan, why would it be necessary to discuss them if the object of study were zazen in Japan? And if, conversely, there are very strong nationalistic and nativist ties, as there most certainly are, how do we know they are irrelevant simply because the ritual has been transplanted to North America?[75]

These questions, once raised, haunt the whole ritology. In Grimes's account:

> Decorum tends to be culture-specific. So bowing, like eye decorum, which rules that the eyes not wander but remain directed toward the floor, may be felt by North American practitioners to be more "Japanese" than "Zen." . . . [Bowing] can serve as a gesture of humility, as well as one of greeting or conclusion. And for those with Western kinesthetic heritages, it may also suggest piety, since the position of the hands . . . is associated with Christian acts of piety.[76]

Here we have a clear indication that zazen means something different, or means differently, in North America than it does in Japan. Presumably Japanese practitioners do not mark their bowing as "Japanese" in the same way as do American ones; if they have the same feeling, the "Japaneseness" in question would be quite differently constructed in relation to the practitioner. And when "those with Western kinesthetic heritages" interpret bowing as pious, Grimes's text suggests that they impose a theistic conception of piety on the nontheistic Zen. Apparently the context matters very much, since Grimes also tells us that "the meaning of a gesture is not identical with what is said about it by people who do it."[77]

Grimes's point with all this is put clearly enough:

> My fieldstudy, visits, and practice in five [North American] Zen centers . . . lead me to think that such notions as "ritual as symbol system," as useful as they are in the study of Western and tribal rites, may miss an essential point about Zen ritual, namely, that many of its gestures do not "mean," refer to, or point to, anything. . . . A commonplace of ritual studies is the discovery that people who practice rituals often cannot say what a specific gesture or object means. . . . In Zen centers one meets what I call "exegetical silence." There is nothing to say about what is done, no story, no exposition. But the silence is not of ignorance, mystifi-

cation, or forgetfulness. The silence is intentional. Sometimes there really is nothing to say.[78]

He notes that practitioners "seldom speak of Zen 'ritual' or 'ceremony'; they speak of 'practice.' . . . The whole point of Zen practice is to eliminate the split between . . . preparation and execution, symbol and referent. In Zen a gesture is just a gesture; the mistake lies in looking for more."[79]

But in the flow of Grimes's prose, it is easy to lose track of the implications. Zen ritual and its various parts "mean" nothing, in the sense that they do not refer to something else. The "whole point"—which is to say, the *theological point*—of Zen ritual is to deny such reference and see gesture or ritual as nothing but itself: "*Zazen* is not a preparation for anything, even enlightenment. There is to be no difference between practice and goal. In fact, to practice sitting with a goal in mind is to subvert *zazen*. One's goal is to sit without goals."[80] In short, a ritology on Grimes's model demonstrates perfect adequacy between ritual form and theological conception. Everything in zazen means exactly what Zen masters have always said. By a mysterious act of imagination, Grimes claims, his method can induct this meaning from the external physical facts of the ritual itself.

But zazen has not "always" meant this. It is not even clear that zazen means this, or works like this, in modern Japanese Zen temples and monasteries. Indeed, this formulation of Zen practice fits smoothly with late nativist discourse, while it does not with much earlier Zen. We have already seen glimpses of the range of possibility of Zen thought on physical practice and its relation to transcendence in Zeami—not that Zeami was a Zen master or exclusively influenced by Zen thought, but certainly Zen practice in his day was not univocal. We have also seen that in the long duration of kokugaku, the notion of "ordinary" behavior as itself worship in the sense of being attuned to the "way" became dominant. There can be little question also that the Zen of D. T. Suzuki and Suzuki Shunryō was deeply, even overwhelmingly, determined by such reformulations of "Japanese" tradition, thought, and aesthetics—I use quotes because the notion of Japanese identity is so contested within these discourses.[81] And while it is true that Grimes's analyses predate Bernard Faure's radical rewriting of Zen and Chan orthodoxies, Grimes's fundamental claim is that ritology does not require such extensive intellectual-historical support. Thus a "ritology" of zazen which concludes that the practice can only be interpreted—without reference to historical, theological, or political discourse—in terms formulated in

The Occult Mind

recent centuries under complex ideological circumstances, is deluded or dishonest.

I do not believe that Grimes is dishonest, promoting a worrisome ideology under mystifying camouflage. But his method appears incapable of discerning that these many forces are always at work within the practice. On that ground alone, we must question the utility of ritology, as it cannot but serve as a mouthpiece for the institutionally most dominant ideology among those studied.

Unfortunately, we must push farther. These last criticisms would apply equally if Grimes had done his field study among Japanese practitioners in Japan. But in fact those studied were North Americans "with Western kinesthetic heritages," that is, they grew up in homes where the gestures of mainstream American Christian piety predominated or, more likely, were exclusively available. Let us return for a moment to bowing, which "felt" "more 'Japanese' than Zen." Grimes says, "In North American zendos [Zen centers] bowing is one of the first gestures learned by practitioners. It is also the one most likely to lead people quickly to discover the 'physiology of faith'. Christians and Jews who practice Zen sometimes confess that, even though they are no longer theists, they find themselves resisting bowing."[82] If we recall that respectful bowing is still an ordinary gesture among Japanese people—with gradations akin to a slight smile at a passing stranger, a wider smile at a colleague in the office, a quick handshake for the acquaintance not seen for a while, and a nervous grin and formal handshake for the boss—we must ask *why* bowing is taught to new *zendo* members so soon? Why is it important to express respect *in a Japanese manner*?

The same practice appears in many martial arts schools, again strongly influenced by forms and modes of Zen that combine such nativist discourses as *bushidō* with the discourses on Japanese traditional identity often promoted in the West.[83] In short, the ideologies and discourses embedded in North American Zen practice are complex, tightly interwoven, and most certainly not univocal. Furthermore, these layers are inseparable from the gestural or kinesthetic; one cannot simply view and practice ritual without imbibing other modes of discourse and symbol. If, as Grimes seems adamant to assert, ritology is uninterested in these layers and meanings, preferring to present as univocal true interpretation the watered-down ideological formations sold by national-identity industries, then ritology is in principle incapable of achieving anything worth the time and effort required.

When ritology encounters the extraordinarily powerful and sophisticated industries of Japanese nativism, national identity, and self-promotion, it finds only silence: "There is nothing to say about what is done, no story, no exposition. . . . Sometimes there really is nothing to say." For the responsible scholar of ritual, such silence is an unacceptable option.

⁙

John Dee recalled that in 1546 he mounted a production of Aristophanes' *Peace*, and noted that "many vain reports" arose about the methods behind the flying brass scarab he constructed.[84] But perhaps his most daring theatrical experiment was the series of angelic conversations he conducted over the course of his later life, which constituted an extension of the dramatic ritual performance that is *Monas Hieroglyphica*.

To understand simultaneously the mystical and political dimensions of Dee's magical works, we must recognize in them a conception not unlike Motoori's *mono no aware*. For Dee, the power of the monad and the Enochian language lay in their ability to evoke from "sensitive" people an immediate and natural response to things as they really are. Because they were constructed on linguistic principles from before the falls from Eden and Babel, these powerful hieroglyphs could pierce the veil of contemporary history and allow access to truth.

Where Motoori developed his analyses in reference to a history that, if it required interpretation, was at least partly accessible through such texts as *Kojiki*, Dee had both the advantage and the disadvantage of a total inability to encounter his own Ægypt in a scholarly fashion. Motoori could read *Kojiki*, but Dee had to seek oracular and visionary means to find a text at all. On the one hand, this meant that Dee could probably never have developed his linguistic theories in as much depth and sophistication as did the great nativists; on the other, the political implications already latent in a project such as Motoori's, which took several generations of *kokugakusha* to bring fully to light, were clearly present to Dee.

I noted earlier that Dee's *Monas* should be understood as extraordinarily self-conscious with respect to ritualization, founded on the recognition that the monad had to be alienated from Dee to be liberated to its metaphysical and ontological possibility. That is, by grounding the monad in the differential absence of the written word, Dee was able to encounter it as exterior to himself. Considered in light of the nativist project, Dee would seem to have perceived that by seeking in archaic tradition an absolute reality divorced from the contemporary political and religious situation, and then explicating that tradition in powerful signs, the archaic and divine reality could become

The Occult Mind

a political agent. Certainly individual meditation on the monad could effect transformation, but in some sense the very fact that at least one person had been so transformed enabled the ontological clarity of the monad to spread as though by itself. No recapitulation or restoration was necessary or appropriate; Dee might well have seen such projects as "imitation," as did Ōkuma.

By this reading, the monad itself was like a shite. Empty itself, perfectly formed in the divine image but somehow spiritually hollow, the monad had an actor who stood behind it and who was in a sense constituted graphically by it: an angel, or God himself. This Actor pulled the marionette's strings, forcing the sensitive viewer to inhabit the shell and be projected into the higher spiritual realms of absolute ontological reality. For Dee, the transmutation of the viewer by this process made him a kind of shite himself; those who encountered him in the proper vein might themselves be transformed, or at least prepared for a deeper encounter with the monad. It is stretching a point to compare the transformed magician to a warrior-shite and the monad to a wig role, infinitely pregnant with *yūgen*, but it is not unfaithful to Dee to see in the monad a coiled mysterious energy that he believed would lead to the coming climactic, culminating, apocalyptic moment of the true theater of the world.

The transformation in question Dee called "the fourth, great, and truly metaphysical, revolution," and he remarked that the monad "can no longer be fed or watered on its native soil" until this revolution "is completed."[85] On the one hand, as Clulee, Håkansson, and Szőnyi indicate, this revolution referred to the alchemical transmutation of the adept—Dee himself—and its completion would have made him a kind of new Adam capable of effecting "the restitution of nature and the redemption of man."[86] Our reading of Nō suggests that he would then become the monad, serving as a vehicle for this same revolution, now returned to its "native soil"—meaning simultaneously Britain and the human, microcosmic body—and thus the "great, and truly metaphysical revolution" would necessarily play out on the European political stage.

The fact remains that Dee was disappointed of his hopes. The *Monas* did not produce the desired revolution, in Dee or elsewhere. Yet he did not entirely despair: in particular, he did not turn away from the fundamental vision he had received, the vision that gave birth to the monad. Instead, he asked for—and received—divine license to converse with angels, and so became a kind of prophet of the revolution he had hoped to lead:

I have sought . . . to fynde or get some ynckling, glyms, or beame of such the foresaid radicall truthes: But after all my foresaid endevor I could fynde no other way, to such true wisdom atteyning, but by thy Extraordinary Gift. . . . I have read in thy bokes & records, how Enoch enjoyed thy favour and conversation, with Moyses thou wast familier: and also that to Abraham, Isaac, and Jacob, Josua, Gedeon, Esdras, Daniel, Tobias, and sundry other, thy good Angels were sent, by thy disposition to instruct them, informe them, help them, yea in worldly and domesticall affaires, yea, and sometimes to satisfy theyr desyres, doutes & questions of thy Secrets. And furdermore considering the Shew stone which the high preists did use, by thy owne ordering.[87]

Thus Dee turned to angelic summoning as a continuation of the *Monas* project by other means.

Antonin Artaud said that "without an element of cruelty at the root of every spectacle, the theater is not possible. In our present state of degeneration it is through the skin that metaphysics must be made to re–enter our minds,"[88] the second sentence of which Grimes used as the epigraph to *Beginnings in Ritual Studies*. Might it be said that the hieroglyphic monad failed because it did not enter through the skin? If so, we might need to seek cruelty in the *Libri Mysteriorum*.

Cross-cultural comparison has revealed a discontinuity within Ægyptian discourse. If on the one hand magicians such as Dee sought to revitalize the *philosophia perennis*, working historically to sieve the sands of time, on the other they projected their certainties and knowledge into graphic forms such as the monad—importantly the *hieroglyphic* monad, despite its visual incongruity to hieroglyphs as inscribed on Ægyptian remnants. For us, the problem only gains force: if Grimes's purely synchronic analyses fail because of their divorce from history, then to impose a historical dimension on Ægypt—a land precisely without history or time—can only eventuate in misreading.

What Dee and Nō and kokugaku all show, however, is that these theoretical problems do not lie solely with us; they are not only artifacts of our late modern intellectual histories. Indeed, in their various ways these thinkers and discourses all grappled with the same fundamental methodological difficulties as we do: synchrony and diachrony, structure and history, and (in every sense) the writing of the past. To move forward, then, it behooves us to examine their struggles in our own terms as well as theirs. In short, the problem of Ægypt manifests as a problem of reading history, or of historical reading.

The Occult Mind

The historical methodologies of Ægyptian magic require consideration. Seekers and mystics have sought that land for millennia and have developed means by which to track its contours. Sometimes these are not so distant as we might think, or like to think; at times, the line dividing "serious" scholarship from "wild speculation" is far thinner and straighter than we might wish to admit. Without discerning methods of magical historical reconstruction, of relating history to the time out of time that is Ægypt, we cannot understand magic itself, nor be certain that we ourselves do not stand in the shadow of the pyramids.

These ambiguities, redundancies and deficiencies remind us of those which doctor Franz Kuhn attributes to a certain Chinese encyclopedia entitled "Celestial Empire of Benevolent Knowledge." In its remote pages it is written that the animals are divided into: (a) belonging to the Emperor, (b) embalmed, (c) tame, (d) sucking pigs, (e) sirens, (f) fabulous, (g) stray dogs, (h) included in the present classification, (i) frenzied, (j) innumerable, (k) drawn with a very fine camelhair brush, (l) et cetera, (m) having just broken the water pitcher, (n) that from a long way off look like flies.

Jorge Luis Borges

Carlo Ginzburg, in an important essay on method, remarks:

The relationship between typological (or formal) connections and historical connections . . . [has] to be confronted even in its theoretical implications. . . . In the case of my current work . . . the integration of morphology and history is only an aspiration which may be impossible to realize.[1]

In one of his most recent meditations on morphology and history, Jonathan Z. Smith quotes this remark and comments that "an integration of the morphological and the historical . . . Ginzburg rightly judges to be an urgent *desideratum*." Smith, as we have seen, argues that such an integration must rest upon the morphology of Goethe; for him, an applied structuralism cannot succeed, and he judges it a virtue to conceive "of the morphological and the historical as two ways of interpreting the *same* data analogous to synchrony and diachrony in Saussure's formulation (unlike Lévi-Strauss, who all but mythologizes them as opposing forces)."[2]

Although I grant Smith's concern that Lévi-Strauss overstated the case, I am nevertheless persuaded of the impossibility of such an integration as Ginzburg seeks. Smith's distinction between modes of interpretation, while heuristically valuable, cannot fulfill larger synthetic hopes.

This epistemic problem is at base not solely methodological, lying within the scholar's frame of reference and hence manipulable there. Rather, it manifests continually in historical data; to use Smith's terms, it is a *first-order* problem.

In "Trading Places," Smith formulates this distinction with reference to magic:

Abstention, "just say 'no'," will not settle "magic." For, unlike a word such as "religion," "magic" is not only a second-order term, located in academic discourse. It is as well, cross-culturally, a native, first-order category, occurring in ordinary usage which has deeply influenced the evaluative language of the scholar.[3]

To put this differently:

In academic discourse "magic" has almost always been treated as a *contrast* term, a shadow reality known only by looking at the reflection of its opposite ("religion," "science") in a distorting fun-house mirror. Or, to put this another way, within the academy, "magic" has been made to play the role of an evaluative rather than an interpretative term and, as such, usually bears a negative valence. . . . As is the case with the majority of our most disturbing and mischievous hegemonic formulations, the negative valence attributed to "magic" has been, and continues to be, an element in our commonsense—and, therefore, apparently unmotivated—way of viewing cultural affairs.[4]

Smith's points are well taken. In his inimitable fashion, he has cleared out the underbrush and identified the cracked idols that had lain hidden there. These contrast definitions, when applied as substantives, necessarily lend credence to triumphal positivism or progress of some sort or another, commonly a triumph of rationality and spiritual freedom. One is immediately reminded of Frazer's worrying argument: "The old notion that the savage is the freest of mankind is the reverse of the truth. He is a slave, not indeed to a visible master, but to the past, to the spirits of his dead forefathers, who haunt his steps from birth to death, and rule him with a rod of iron."[5]

Yet if we set these points beside Smith's remarks about comparison as typically more magical than scientific, discussed in chapter 1 above, we have an interesting puzzle. Might we say that comparison is indeed typically magical? (Usually magical, typical of magic, of a type with magic. . . .) We should then expect to find Smith not the first to formulate comparison and magic together. Even more, we may find that the very "first-order" usages that have most "deeply influenced the evaluative language of the scholar" are those that recognize and emphasize the comparative dimension of the problem.

In short, the methodological problem of morphological and historical integration is linked, both historically and morphologically, not only to the problem of comparison but also to that of magic, a problem in either case manifesting both from within and at an exterior remove. The programmatic integration of morphology and history is in this sense not so much impossible as mythological: it is the mode of understanding of the sages of Ægypt. To overcome the difference and the distance would demand a spell.

###

As a beginning, consider once more Bruno's *De Imaginum, Signorum, et Idearum Compositione* (On the Composition of Images, Signs, and Ideas: 1591). We have already seen this text in reference to Bruno's Copernicanism and the problems of a new science; it remains to take up linguistic and classificatory issues. Bruno's title is perhaps too clear, ironically leading to confusion about the text, for the book treats nothing more nor less than the composition—both formation and formulation—of images, signs, and ideas, meant in something extraordinarily close to modern semiotic senses.

The 1991 translation of the work by Charles Doria and Dick Higgins includes an exceptionally important discussion of the text in their introduction:

> Bruno seems to be approaching something like modern semiotics, the study of signs and codes (though of course he does not call it that). But semiotics also considers how things acquire meaning, and how such meanings are conveyed. Thus, the centrality in semiotics of the distinction between sign and word, the "signifier" and "signified," the thing it refers to or means. In the following passage from Book One, Part One, Chapter Ten, Bruno discusses the importance of both:
>
> > Images do not receive their names from the explanations of the things they signify, but rather from the condition of those things that do the signifying. For in a text we are not able to explicate passages and words adequately by signs like those we trace out on paper, unless we think of the forms of sensible things, since they are images of things which exist either in nature or by art and present themselves to the eyes. Therefore images are named not for those things they signify in intention, but for those things from which they have been gathered.
>
> One wonders if Ferdinand de Saussure, the father of modern semiotics, who did his researches in the 1890s just after the first collected volumes of Bruno's Latin texts appeared, read it. Saussure published nothing about this; in fact most of what we have comes via his and his

students' notes. But it is not inconceivable that he knew Bruno's Latin texts, since the 1890s were a time when Bruno was very well known, at least as a martyr figure. But this, of course, is only speculation.[6]

Perhaps to follow up the speculation, they use as an epigraph the following partial sentence from Lévi-Strauss: "Images cannot be ideas, but they can play the part of signs."[7]

Doria and Higgins have seen that Bruno's last completed work is at base a meditation on signification, and furthermore one that already recognizes the essentially relational function served by the sign. Reading *De Imaginum*, especially the abstract and theoretical book 1, part 1, we find that *image* is more or less equivalent to *percept*, *idea* to *concept*, and that like Saussure Bruno understands the sign to mediate between these.

But if Bruno has in some sense invented semiotics—rather an overstatement, given the considerable and complex literature on signification in the sixteenth century—that is not to say he has the same purposes in mind as do Saussure or Charles Sanders Peirce, or Lévi-Strauss for that matter.[8] As we saw in chapter 2, Bruno's interest is not at heart linguistic: his interest in language and signification serves practical, applied ends in developing and stabilizing knowledge in the face of an infinite universe of infinitesimals. For him, semiotics replaces the mathematics he disdains.

Examination of both the theoretical preliminaries and the seemingly repetitive applications in *De Imaginum* reveals a fascination, almost an obsession, with classification. The constructed mental system of the memory artist must have rigid and constant rules to allow rapid navigation, a point well known since Yates's *The Art of Memory*. Yet in Bruno, there is an important flexibility: once the stabilizing classificatory images are in place, threaded like charms on a bracelet, we discern meaning through the interrelations. While the procedure can thus illuminate a text or a sequence of facts, it can also be used to legitimate an interpretation unconnected to the text or sequence itself. Bruno warns against this but offers no real guardrail to prevent it.

For example, consider the unusually lengthy fifth chapter of book 3, "Proteus in the House of Mnemosyne." Here Bruno takes the opening of Virgil's *Aeneid* and uses the words and images to expound philosophically, demonstrating the protean mutability of the words. For our purposes, the first line—"Arma virumque cano Troiae qui primus ab oris" [I sing of arms and the man, who first from the shores of Troy]—must suffice:

{Let us suppose} I have decided in my spirit to argue about the immortality of the world. I must seize upon some means by which THE UNIVERSE, that is, this event's UNENDINGNESS may be separated from its subject. I make the customary choice, and pick Proteus and parts of a very famous and widely published poem, or rather simple words from it, and these words change by metamorphosis into the same number of middle terms as those by which I assemble arguments for the form of my proposed object. { . . . }

[I.] First from *arms*, which signify powers and instruments which last forever, I deduce the eternal universe.

II. From *man* I deduce the act of being able to maintain existence forever.

III. From *cano* [song], which refers to the harmony of things and their indissoluble co-temperament, and which must suitably persevere, that which exists in mutations and alterations.

IV. From *city* {i.e. Troy}, which signifies the commonwealth of the universe (for let nothing oppose it) up to decay and passing away; for what are contraries in the universe are not contrary to the universe, for they are the universe's parts and members.

V. From the *primacy* of him who always acts and perseveres; first, since the efficient is he who is his immediate cause, he should be the eternal efficient cause, since an original cause can not be an efficient cause, unless proceeding from another first beginning, in which case that one would then be the truer first principle. But if it should exist in the prime to which it is not, all in all it ought to exist likewise when there is no other later successive cause and there is always cause, which, when the first beginning has been removed, would not be a principle. Therefore, by a necessary duration the caused universe accompanies the universal cause.

VI. From the *shores* (because of the similarity of the word there may be a middle term as well according to the signified, which we won't quickly pass by), it must be that the word of the divine mouth, that is, the work of god's omnipotent effect remains forever. Since it is true in the highest degree and obviously is good, obviously it is right that it should exist, obviously it is not right that it should not exist. { . . . }

Generally the same series of termini will reveal the cosmos (taken in another sense) as earth and moon, which are distinguishable by us from the universe, just as corruptible in its means.

First, from arms, that is from the means by which they exist as variable.

Secondly, because of the strengths of the cause particular and immediate, which are finite, just as effect, subject and subject's power are finite.

The Occult Mind

For matter, form and strength of the earth are finite; quality is variable and composition decomposable.

Thirdly, because of its symmetry and alterable contemperament, because it does not offer such things as were formerly alive. Or according to the song of those who prophesy: "I shall move heaven and earth," that is, I shall change; "one day I will consign earth and sky to destruction."

Fourthly, because of the dissonance of its commonwealth's members.

Fifthly, because it is an efficient cause and conserves and forms itself in a secondary and dependent manner, not a prime one.

Sixthly, because it has shores beyond itself, to which and from which they recognize a dependence.[9]

As we saw in chapter 2, part of the difficulty in interpreting Bruno here arises from the project's incomplete success. Nevertheless, this lighthearted argument, or serious game, shows much about Bruno's art of memory in its latest phase.

Gatti explains the problem posed by *De Imaginum* succinctly:

What interested Yates . . . was Bruno's use of images of the signs of the zodiac and his Lullian memory wheels composed of numbers and letters from the ancient alphabets. She believed such images and icons were constructed to contain magical energies and powers that could be manipulated to call down into the mind the higher grades of being and knowledge contained in the stars. Through the influence of these "superior agents," the Magus could learn about the nature of the things in the lower world or earth. The difficulty is that Bruno, from the beginning, refused to contemplate the neo-Platonic concept of hierarchical grades of being in the natural universe on which such an interpretation . . . depends. . . . The question remains: What use did he contemplate for the classical and renaissance art of memory within the newly infinite spaces of the post-Copernican universe?[10]

Gatti also points to the more recent discoveries of Rita Sturlese, who finds "that the constructions of memory places . . . are designed in very complex ways so that they function similarly to calculatory tables: that is, they can be used for the formation of words, or even phrases, linked to images designed to help memorize them." Even so, "Sturlese has been unable to answer this question [of what the memory wheels and tables were for]."[11]

Gatti's own interpretation is also worth quoting:

Bruno's purpose, in my opinion, in his works on memory is to formulate an account of the processes of thought which is different from an abstract logic. He attempts to illustrate the ways in which the primal chaos of impressions is reduced to order by principles innate to the mind; at the same time he takes into account the historical and social processes through which languages, both of words and images, have developed organically through the course of civilization. The image of the tree to signify the mode of growth of languages, derived from Raymond Lull, acquires in Bruno a historical dimension. The social consensus is seen to be an important part of what is considered truth, for the ways in which, at any time, words and images are used depend not only on the power of imagination of the individual but also on the shared conventions of the society in which he lives. This awareness of the historical growth of languages and imagery tends to limit the possibility of applying his works on memory to the dramatic needs of the new science to develop a new logic of inquiry.[12]

In the playful demonstration of Proteus in the house of Mnemosyne quoted above, we see support for Gatti's interpretation, but the very "protean" nature of the argumentation still baffles. With both Yates's and Sturlese's views, we would be unable to account for the willful inconsistency of these textual manipulations: If this is all memorization, as Sturlese suggests, what is memorized? The Virgilian text? The outline of a planned debate or discourse on the infinite universe? Does it not matter that one of these is used as a model for the other? And the talismanic reading of Yates certainly fails to explain this passage, which Yates would presumably read, as she had an unfortunate habit of doing, as a disguise or blind set up by Bruno to deceive.[13]

Yet Gatti has, I think, lost a crucial point of agreement between Yates and Sturlese, one she otherwise accepts: this art of memory is practical, not purely theoretical. In Gatti's view, Bruno here gives "an account of the processes of thought"; the plays on Virgil are descriptive, not prescriptive. Here she has just slightly dropped Bruno's thread.

My own reading is tentative, offered for speculation and criticism by specialists more versed in Bruniana. I begin with several hypotheses that seem in keeping with those scholars' conclusions. First, *De Imaginum* is at heart practical; the descriptive and theoretical preamble serves a prescriptive and operative end. Second, both the elaborate formation of "atria" and the plays upon Virgil and the infinite universe have equal, if not identical, status as ap-

The Occult Mind

plications. Third, Bruno is never so serious as when he is at play: as in such works as *Candelaio* and *La Cena de le Ceneri*, it is often the most obviously playful and stylish passages that incorporate the deepest meanings.[14] Fourth, as discussed in chapter 2, the art of memory is not in *De Imaginum* a turning back, an intellectual retreat, but a way forward with real intellectual problems of great weight.

A final quotation, describing "the places of species" in book 1, chapter 2 of *De Imaginum*, will permit us to put these disparate pieces into some sort of order:

> Just as a category, when it is distinguished as a subaltern in the most particular and individual character of other characters, so too do we proceed purposefully by a certain order, as it were, of nature that designates the characteristics of that category and of art that explains all discovery and research. First we recognize some sort of immense and endless object, then a space and receptacle, then a body in that receptacle and space, then a multitude of species coalescing out of such material or matter. In the same way among the infinite and countless species we recognize one space cast before the power of our senses as the sky, which most people perceive because of the change of diurnal motion, and the species of stars as finite. We leave to them those distinctions and numbers of the heavens, the distribution of each in various spheres, likewise the scale and boundaries of the elemental zone, and the universal parts of this round world represented in a way as if fashioned out of earth and water, the two elements predominating in the great composition of the earth. We descend to places that are special and common, wherein the operation of the external sense as handmaiden of internal sense aids their cooperation, for this reason, so that we will not be disturbed either by their absence or their multiplication, as if we were limping along on shorter legs or else with more added on than is right.[15]

Here Bruno begins to describe setting up atria, special rooms constructed in the mind and containing rigidly ordered images linked to letters and notions. Each of the twenty-four atria has its own name and image: *Altar*, *Basilica*, *Carcer* (prison), and so on, such that they spell out the alphabet. They are each filled with a further twenty-four images around the exterior, and these in turn lead to further subjoined openings or rooms. In the course of a number of bewildering chapters with minimal explanation, Bruno lays out a vast network of mental spaces mapped by a consistent scheme and keyed to the arbitrary sequence of twenty-four letters.[16]

Without delving into minutiae, it seems clear that any given object can be positioned in this system under numerous headings. Further, any sequence of objects or terms can be so positioned, but here the combinatorial factor would appear to make use intractable. That is, if the "operator" must skip around wildly and without any absolute certainty from atrium to atrium, image to image, how is he to avoid losing his way?

First of all, Ariadne's thread appears in the form of light, upon which Bruno discourses at length. This light of phantasy emanates from the mind and also from images, casting shadows that are the signs of ideas.[17] Strikingly, Bruno uses the metaphor of light in a rather traditional al-Kindī–inspired sense of rays,[18] but with a typically Brunian twist: discussing motions among the "archetypal or original, physical, and umbral" three worlds, Bruno says that "from the third through the middle an ascent is available to the first, in the same way that we descend from the sun to the aspect of the moon's light, . . . or as in a mirror, notwithstanding the fact that the light can be sent directly into the mirror from the sun, and that from the mirror light can be turned back toward the sun on a direct and immediate track."[19] Here we see strongly Bruno's notion that light leaves tracks, imprints or impressions like seals in wax; these are the shadows of ideas (*umbrae idearum*) and the shadows of things. Thus navigation within the palatial storehouse of memory is made possible by the very illumination of the causative images and phantasy themselves.

Second, "We are deliberately proposing a method which by no means concerns things but which treats, rather, the significance of things, a method in which may be easily ascertained that there exists beyond a doubt a productive power of all things, by those . . . who will . . . describe the species of things."[20] Here the epistemology of *De Imaginum* moves quite stunningly outside of what we expect. The art of memory, it seems, is not locked to things themselves, but rather manipulates and examines their significance at a remove from the things. And yet for those who "describe the species of things," this art demonstrates "a productive power of all things."

I have now moved backward, from the book 3 discussion of Virgil to the opening chapter of the whole text (setting aside the crucial dedicatory epistle). As with the title, the basic solution to our difficulties with this text lies in nothing more (and nothing less) than taking Bruno at his word. To understand how a method that does not concern things but only their significance can nevertheless demonstrate something absolute and certain about the things themselves, we must presume that all those atria and images, and their application to Virgil, are intended at least in part to prove the point.

The Occult Mind

The semiotic and structural proposal mentioned at the outset now comes to the fore. The Virgil manipulation shows that there can be no absolute correlation between images and ideas, because their connection is always mediated by signs, which are entirely relational. At the same time, Bruno's *atria* formulate an essential principle: while signs are free (or unstable) by comparison to things themselves, they are relatively constrained by comparison to ideas. Further, system may be imposed on signification in order to impress a shadowy systematicity on ideas, and thus on thought itself. But whence would this system arise? It cannot be the free invention of the mind, because that mind is already relatively constrained by signification. Therefore, Bruno suggests, the fact that system can be imposed on signs implies the possibility of a *structural* analogy between the systems of nature and the systems of thought. The purpose of the art of memory is thus to use the phantasy to induce exterior things to impress their shadows on our minds in order that we may then build from this a structural analogy in thought.

Lévi-Strauss famously remarked that among "savage" peoples, "the animal and vegetable species are not known as a result of their being useful: they are deemed useful or interesting because they are first of all known."[21] Giordano Bruno would surely have agreed.

⁞⁞⁞

We have seen that the early modern magical discourse on classification—for that in the end is what the art of memory certainly accomplishes—grappled with the problem of a synchronic understanding of historical objects: the change of languages over time, for example, had to be systematized in order to be made useful. In Bruno's art of memory this had a practical purpose, albeit a somewhat unclear one, but in tandem with the development of scientific classification would arise an equally occult complement. To move further toward clarifying the initial problem posed by Ginzburg and Smith, of an analytical method at once synchronic and diachronic, we need to examine this later formation. I thus turn to one of the less-acknowledged ancestors of the comparative study of culture.

Father Athanasius Kircher (1602–80), Jesuit "master of a hundred arts," wrote thirty-one major texts, generally lavishly illustrated folios, covering an extraordinary range of topics: astronomy, magnetism, geology, music, numerology, Egyptology, cryptography, and Sinology, to name only major interests. Though ill-treated by Enlightenment historians, Kircher's work is experiencing a revival, partly sparked by the fourth centennial of his birth.[22]

A synthetic picture of this amazing man has yet to emerge. As a beginning, I suggest that we understand his intellectual project in light of yet another of his achievements, the museum at the Collegio Romano, of which Kircher's own collection was the core, and for which he was the curator (figure 1). In identifying him as a collector of the extraordinary and unusual, we are also led to interpret his work constructively, formulating a vision of the world and of antiquity.[23] This assumption of coherence emphasizes a linguistic reading, not only because of Kircher's many discussions of languages in general but also because his last and culminating book *Turris Babel* (1679) deployed all his massive erudition to reconstruct the origins of language. Indeed, Kircher presents a striking constellation of ideas about perfect languages and knowledge. In *Polygraphia Nova* (1663), he offers cryptographic writing as the basis for perfect language. In the extravagant three-volume *Oedipus Aegyptiacus* (1652–54), he uses allegory to decipher hieroglyphic inscriptions in bizarre but fascinating ways. And in *China Illustrata* (1667), he examines Chinese writing allegorically, arguing that it descended from Egyptian via the lineage of Noah.[24]

In his own time, Kircher was a controversial figure. Although he received lavish praise, no one seems to have known quite what he was doing. Opinions varied considerably by region, intellectual stance, and religious affiliation. Henry Oldenburg, secretary of the Royal Society, remarked that Kircher's work provided "rather Collections, as his custom is, of what is already extant and known, yn any new Discoveryes," although he assiduously collected Kircher's many publications.[25] Other contemporaries, as well as more recent scholars, also considered Kircher too gullible, relying on dubious sources to provide exotica.[26] And yet, for example, Kircher's *China Illustrata* announced its "purpose and occasion" as resolving a long-standing scholarly controversy, the problem of the Sino-Syrian monument that attested to Christianity in Tang dynasty China. Importantly, Kircher's loudest critic on this matter, Georg Horn, was a Protestant, and in defending the monument and its interpretation Kircher also defended Catholicism and the Society of Jesus.[27]

Even within the Catholic world, where Kircher received most of his accolades, he did not go unchallenged. In a recent dissertation on Kircher's hieroglyphics, Daniel Stolzenberg carefully tracks the fortunes of a mysterious Arabic manuscript by one Rabbi Barachias Nephi, "concerning the manner of interpreting and deciphering the hieroglyphic letters of the Egyptian obelisks."[28] When the great antiquarian Nicolas-Claude Fabri de Peiresc (1580–1637) first met Kircher in 1632 and discussed this manuscript, he wrote to Gassendi that it "makes me much more hopeful than I once was about the

The Occult Mind

Figure 1. The main hall of the museum at the Collegio Romano. Frontispiece, Georgius de Sepibus, Romani Collegii Societatus *[sic]* Jesu Musæum Celeberrimum . . . *Amsterdam: ex Officina Janssonio–Waesbergiana, 1678. f GC6 K6323 678r. Houghton Library, Harvard University.*

discovery of things that have been so unknown to Christendom for nearly two thousand years," and anxiously sought to purchase a copy of any works by Nephi.[29] By the time of his death in June 1637, however, Peiresc had become increasingly disillusioned with Kircher's abilities as an interpreter, suspicious of his vaunted breadth of knowledge, and dubious about the worth of this manuscript: "I always suspected," he wrote to Kircher, "what you never dared to confess until now, that there was some jest or weakness of the author's mind, and maybe even some squalid material and falsity, as well as this dismal magic."[30] This story of progressive disillusionment, in which those learned men who at first expected the greatest revelations from Kircher increasingly suspected inability, exaggeration, or even dishonesty on the Jesuit's part, was repeated many times throughout Kircher's long career. Yet even so, it is striking that with each new promised book, the old excitement never quite dissipated, never quite gave way to cynicism.[31]

On the face of it, Kircher's contemporaries accepted the validity of his project but disagreed about his methods and analytical achievements. Yet even a cursory examination of contemporary remarks reveals that not everyone agreed what Kircher's project actually *was*. Clearly the *Ars Magna Sciendi* (Great Art of Knowing), as his 1669 book title had it, lay at its heart, but it was less clear in what such an art might consist.

Relatively recently, Kircher has seen something of a comeback in scholarship. Anthony Grafton is noteworthy in having described Kircher as "just about the coolest guy ever" on National Public Radio, a sentiment that would surely not have been shared by intellectual historians a generation or so past.[32] Despite several volumes of work, however, the problem Kircher's contemporaries faced, of understanding exactly what his project *was*, remains unresolved.

For the historian, as Antonella Romano notes, the basic problem with Kircher is to situate him in some sort of context. But which? Consider for a moment what those who followed Michel Foucault tried to do: they wanted to explain a complete universe of discourse with respect to one more familiar to us, and from this implicit comparison—and it is always implicit—to draw conclusions about how discourse works.[33] But as Romano remarks, "Kircher's life, world, and work belong, without a doubt, to a universe to which we have lost the key."[34]

In the epigraph that opens this chapter, made famous by its partial, acontextual use in Foucault's *Les mots et les choses*, Borges, writing about the perfect language scheme of the seventeenth-century English thinker John Wilkins, draws a comparison between such languages and Chinese encyclopedism.[35] Foucault drew attention to the seeming incoherence of such classification systems, thereby to suggest that classification is a culturally specific discursive practice that has a tendency toward naturalization, a tendency to be absorbed by discourse circles as normative and, thereby, to become a basis on which to exclude other discursive practices as silly or incoherent.

Unfortunately, Foucault's analysis of developments in seventeenth-century encyclopedism and categorization, however stimulating, was ill-informed, poorly researched, and at times factually wrong, a point made brutally clear in the preface to the second edition of Paolo Rossi's *Clavis Universalis*.[36] Rossi emphasizes that the analysis was historically inaccurate, which is certainly the case, but it is also worth noting that despite the use of a quotation that signals the possibility of a comparative, cross-cultural understanding of classification and discourse, Foucault eschewed such a move in his book. Jonathan Z. Smith too, discussing the possibilities of structuralism, remarked that if Lévi-Strauss is comparative without being historical, where structuralism "has been interestingly historical (e.g. M. Foucault), the comparative has been largely eschewed."[37]

Kircher too is a classifier and comparison-maker, locating his many collections within complex frameworks of synchronic and diachronic relations. Indeed, the many contributors to Paula Findlen's *Athanasius Kircher: The Last Man Who Knew Everything* use the word "connections," as in Kircher's interest in the connections among things or ideas, until it almost seems a mantra—and yet there is little discussion of what "connections" *in general* might have meant to Kircher or his readers. At a distance, one can see why Kircher wanted to find such connections, but when we get down to details the whole picture becomes blurred, as though, as Bruno remarked, we were too close to the canvas. Indeed, Romano refers to Kircher's "blurring" of disciplines as a fundamental problem in understanding his work.[38] To examine Kircher is to examine classification or categorization—and yet to recognize that Kircher's aims and methods in the "great art of knowing" vary considerably from what we now see as normative to the classificatory enterprise.

A recent volume of essays on Kircher bears the subtitle "The Baroque Encyclopedia of Athanasius Kircher," and indeed the encyclopedic mode is commonly ascribed to him; we may note that Rossi's discussion in *Clavis Universalis* occurs in a chapter on "Encyclopaedism and Pansophia."[39] Here "encyclopedia" refers to Diderot, as well as to the tradition of Corneille, Bayle, and Alsted. Kircher's works can be located here, given his disparate interests, voluminous publications, and collections of oddities from all over. But one cannot extend this historical contiguity to a modern conception of encyclopedism. If an encyclopedia strives for totality and even universality, its principle is *organizational* rather than *analytical*. Thus, while Antoine Court de Gébelin's nine royally subscribed folios on *Le Monde Primitif* (1777–96) claim to cover the totality of the intellectual and cultural world, it is not usually situated within the encyclopedic tradition, in part because the author *has an argument*: he thinks that allegorical analysis of everything under the sun reveals the ancient Ægyptian, superior understanding of the world. The connection to Kircher is not fortuitous: Kircher has in many respects the same objective, and his methods, though more coherent, also take allegorism as primary. In short, outside of a literary history already thoroughly examined, it may be more valuable to read Kircher as a precursor of the *comparative and structural* tradition than of the encyclopedic.

In Kircher, cryptography, perfect language, the origins of language, hieroglyphics, and Chinese characters are not separate issues but part of a grand attempt to develop a perfect system of knowledge—the *ars magna sciendi*. As to what these disparate linguistic objects have in common, they all focus on written rather than spoken language, and concern deciphering as a way to discern meaning.

Consider Egyptian hieroglyphs, Kircher's interpretations of which are relatively well known. Following the Renaissance tradition of Egyptology, Kircher presumed that hieroglyphs represented ideas through allegorical pictography, as described for example by Horapollo:

> When they wish to depict the Universe, they draw a serpent devouring its own tail, marked with variegated scales. By the scales they suggest the stars in the heavens. This beast is the heaviest of animals, as the earth is heaviest [of elements]. It is the smoothest, like water. And, as each year it sheds its skin, it [represents] old age. But as each season of the year returns successively, it grows young again. But the fact that it uses its own body for food signifies that whatever things are generated in the world by Divine Providence are received back into it by [a gradual process of] diminution.[40]

And the Ægyptian priest, immensely expert in all things sacred, would simply look at the glyph and understand at once this complex notion of the universe. Even if he did not already know the particular hieroglyph, he could derive its meaning from his knowledge of allegorical interpretation, animals, divinity, and so forth.

For Kircher, this mode of interpretation can be reversed: by increasing one's knowledge of particular hieroglyphs in reference to both the totality of known facts and the contexts in which glyphs appear, one reconstructs the mental and cultural universe of Ægypt. This is rather like Erwin Panofsky's "iconology," in which analysis of art objects, from both physical representations (pre-iconography) and cultural symbols (iconography), can discern the Weltanschauung of the artist and his or her culture; note also that Panofsky's object of study, like his method, was firmly rooted in the humanistic tradition.[41]

Kircher's comparisons among such compressed signs depend on an allegorical theory of homology: he presumes that similarity in structure must stem from similarity of origin, thus Chinese characters have a hieroglyphic structure because they descend from Egyptian. Although shifts in sense occur—a given character may have no analogue among hieroglyphs—the *structure* remains constant. In particular, the signs interrelate at a deeper level than sense: circular characters are linked not by meaning or shape, but by reference to *concepts* of circularity, as in the *ouroboros* figure Horapollo described.

This is not unlike the semistructuralism we saw in Bruno. Signs do not inherently mean anything definite but develop meaning by horizontal reference to one another and vertical connection to a deep system of abstract principles. For example, each character of later alphabets derives, according to Kircher, from progressive orthographic manipulation of a hieroglyphic base, in itself iconic (figure 2).

Despite such universal semiosis, Kircher's increasing focus on the Tower of Babel directs our attention to the historically degraded nature of the sign, even in its relatively idealized forms. Before Babel, signs pointed to referents by divine fiat; after Babel, this connection was broken, and both spoken and written signs began their progressive drift away from perfection. But written signs retain a structural relation to perfection because of the same exteriority Dee saw in the monad; thus the importance of hieroglyphics for perfect language and knowledge. In short, Kircher proposes a diachronic classification in historical terms: pre-Babel Adamic language descends into hieroglyphs, then to Chinese, then to mere transcription of sound; to reverse the direction, he discovers the underlying principles, builds a new cryptography that factors out culture, then moves to align that "real character" system with the ever-expanding world of true knowledge. As a result, he finds himself able to decipher historical hieroglyphic inscriptions, albeit his conclusions differ fairly dramatically from those of modern Egyptologists (figure 3).

We have seen something not unlike this "real character" theory in John Dee, whose "real Cabala" manipulated objects as much as graphic signs. Kircher too emphasizes objects, but these have a tangibility quite unlike the

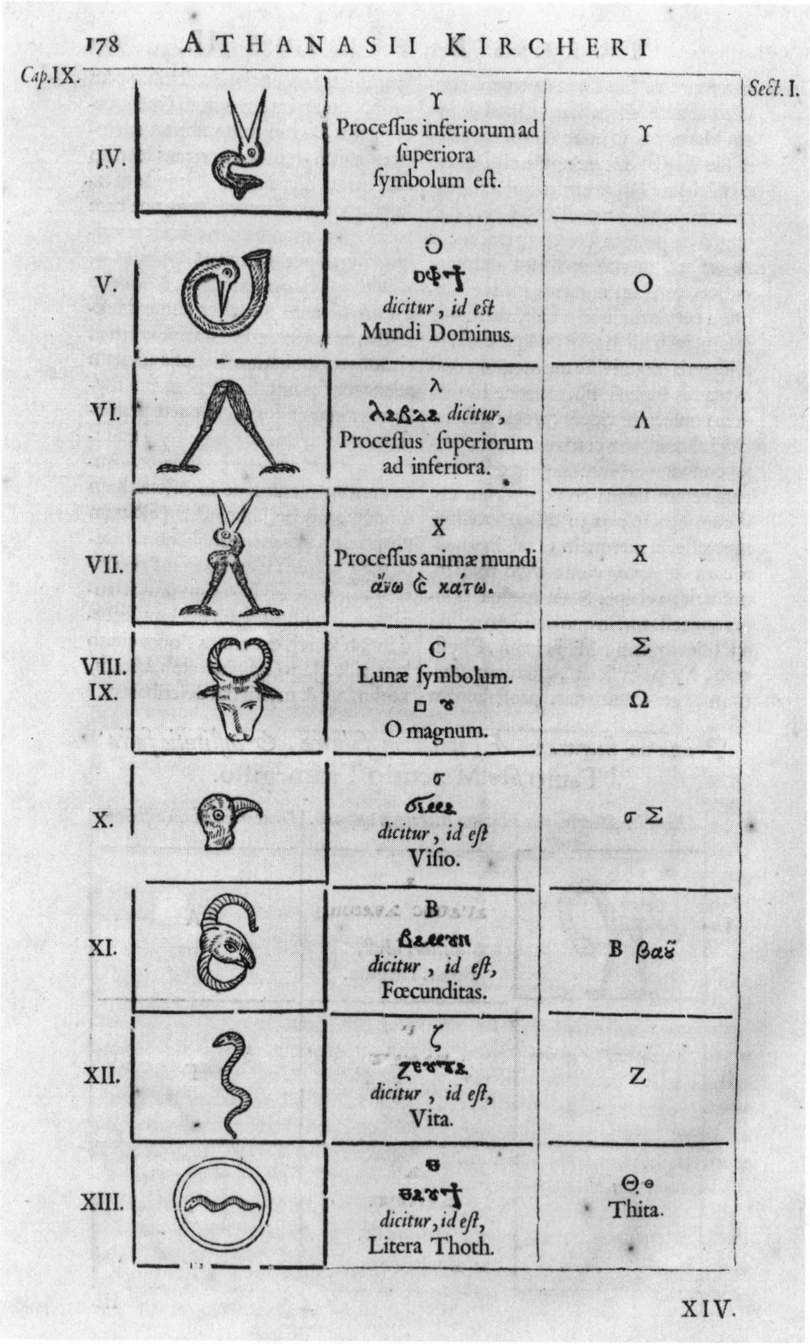

IV.		Υ Proceſſus inferiorum ad ſuperiora ſymbolum eſt.	Υ
V.		O ϖΦϯ *dicitur, id eſt* Mundi Dominus.	O
VI.		λ λзβзз *dicitur,* Proceſſus ſuperiorum ad inferiora.	Λ
VII.		X Proceſſus animæ mundi ἄνω & κάτω.	X
VIII. IX.		C Lunæ ſymbolum. □ ʼϛ O magnum.	Σ Ω
X.		σ σιεεз *dicitur, id eſt* Viſio.	σ Σ
XI.		B βзεεʼϡι *dicitur, id eſt,* Fœcunditas.	B βαῦ
XII.		ζ ζεʼϡτз *dicitur, id eſt,* Vita.	Z
XIII.		ϑ ϑзʼϛϯ *dicitur, id eſt,* Litera Thoth.	Θ θ Thita.

XIV.

Figure 2. Hieroglyphs and their alphabetic derivations. Page 178, Athanasii Kircheri e
Soc. Jesu Turris Babel, sive Archontologia . . . *Amsterdam: ex officina Janssonio–*
Waesbergiana, 1679. f GC6 K6323 679t2. Houghton Library, Harvard University.

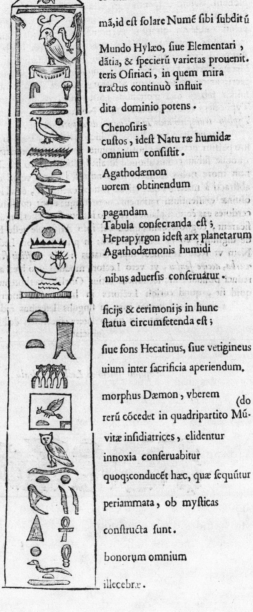

Hemphta Numen supre-
influit virtutem

in siderei Mundi ani-

vnde vitalis motus in
omniumque rerum abun-
ex vbertate Cra-
quadam sympathia

duplici in sibi sub

Vigilantissimus
sacrorum canalium
in qua vita rerum

Ophionius
ad cuius sa-

vitamque pro-
Sacra hæc ei
cuius beneficio cæleste
diuini Osiridis

assistentia ab om-

Præterea in sacri-
finem eiusdem

Eparisterium Naturæ
id est Naturæ efflu-

Quo allectus Poly-
varietatem

Typhonis technæ

Vnde vita rerum
ad quod plurimum

pentacula, siue

rationes, quibus

sunt enim viæ

acquirendorum potentes

mum & Archetypon
& munera sua

mã, id est solare Numé sibi subdit ú

Mundo Hylæo, siue Elementari,
dãtia, & specierũ varietas prouenit.
teris Osiriaci, in quem mira
tractus continuò influit

dita dominio potens.

Chenosiris
custos, idest Natu ræ humidæ
omnium consistit.

Agathodæmon
uorem obtinendum

pagandam
Tabula consecranda est;
Heptapyrgon idest arx planetarum
Agathodæmonis humidi

nibus aduersis conseruatur.

ficijs & cerimonijs in hunc
statua circumsetenda est;

siue fons Hecatinus, siue vetigineus
uium inter sacrificia aperiendum.

morphus Dæmon, vberem
(do
rerũ cõcedet in quadripartito Mú-
vitæ insidiatrices, elidentur
innoxia conseruabitur
quoq;conducét hæc, quæ sequũtur
periammata, ob mysticas
constructa sunt.
bonorum omnium
illecebræ.

Figure 3. Egyptian hieroglyphics on an obelisk, as translated by Kircher. Page 78, Obelisci
Ægyptiaci . . . *Rome: ex typographia Varesij, 1666. The Burndy Library, Cambridge,
Massachusetts.*

hieroglyphic monad. In Kircher's museum we again encounter an attempt to think through objects, a "science of the concrete." Paula Findlen has examined an important bifurcation in the procedures of collecting over the course of the sixteenth and seventeenth centuries, with one direction moving increasingly toward classification and natural science, and the other shifting to become a dilettantish hobby that emphasized the marvelous over the typical.[42] If we are to understand Kircher cohesively, we must read his objects and collections as signs, and recognize that his linguistics is often rooted in collecting. This places signs in a difficult, potentially intractable position among structure, signification, and the historical.

Kircher's discussions of Chinese characters provide concrete examples of this interconnection of objects, graphic signs, and history. In *China Illustrata*, we read:

> About 300 years after the flood, in the time that the sons of Noah dominated the earth and spread their empire all over the earth, the first inventor of writing [according to the Chinese] was the emperor Fu Xi. I can scarcely doubt that he learned this from the sons of Noah. . . . [in particular] Ham [who] first came from Egypt to Persia and then planted colonies in Bactria. We understand that he was the same as Zoroaster. . . . At the same time the elements of writing were instituted by Father Ham and Mercurius [or Hermes] Trismegistus. . . . The old Chinese characters are a very strong argument for this [history], for they completely imitate the hieroglyphic writings. First, the Chinese constructed the characters from things of the world. Then, the chronicles teach, and the form of the characters amply demonstrate, like the Egyptians they formed their writing from pictures of animals, birds, reptiles, fishes, herbs, branches of trees, ropes, threads, points, then later developed a more abbreviated system, which they use right down to the present date. Their number today is so large that every learned man must know 80,000 at a minimum. . . . Moreover, the Chinese letters are not arranged as an alphabet . . . nor do they have words written with letters and syllables. Particular characters do show a particular syllable or pronunciation, but each character has a specific sound and meaning, and so there are as many characters as there are concepts which the mind wishes to express.[43]

Specifically:

> When they are describing things with a fiery nature, they use serpents, asps, and dragons which by their particular arrangement indicate a partic-

The Occult Mind

ular word. For describing airy things they use pictures of birds, and for watery, fish. . . . So, the original characters were based on the drawings of animals [for example]. Posterity did not follow this pattern, but substituted lines and dots for the drawings. . . . One can see in the figures . . . how the original branches, leaves, and fish gave way to the modern form.[44]

He continues by explaining sixteen different types of characters, of which the seventh may serve as an example (figure 4):

The seventh form of characters, made from turtles, are indicated by the letters H, I, K, L, and M, and were invented by King Yao. These are explained by the Chinese words written as: *Yao yin gui chu zuo*, that is, King Yao wrote this letter with turtle shells.[45]

Kircher now concludes the body of his discussion with an important explanation of the differences between Chinese and Egyptian writing:

The Egyptians did not use the characters in common conversation with each other, nor was it legal to teach one unless he had been legally and po-

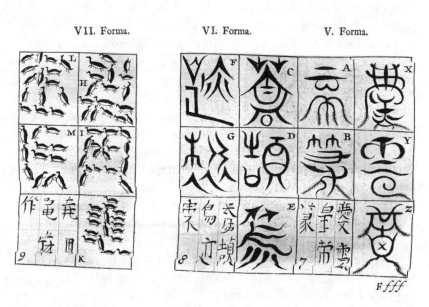

Figure 4. The origins of Chinese script: an alphabet of turtles. Page 229, Athanasii Kircheri e Soc. Jesu China Monumentis . . . illustrata. *Amsterdam: apud Joannem Janssonium à Waesberge and Elizeum Weyerstraet, 1667. Brown University Library.*

The Magic Museum 〔 101

litically delegated to learn it. Nor did they use these figures of animals casually or in an unlearned way, but they used them to express hidden powers and functions, and they signify the greatest mysteries in nature. . . .

Moreover, the hieroglyphic figures do not show simple syllables or names, but whole concepts, so that if you look at a scarab, it does not refer just to the animal, or to the physical sun, but the occult operations which its archetype causes in the intelligible world. All of these things are completely lacking in the Chinese characters. . . . I do not deny, however, that the Chinese have so adapted the significance of many of their characters that an ingenious allusion is possible, which, however, is not the same as the subtle significations of the hieroglyphs. . . . [For example, a given] character C signifies "to be afflicted" and it is made from the two characters B and A. B means heart and A means gate, which [together] means "the gate of the heart (is) closed." A man in a state of affliction feels that all his breaths are concentrated within the gate of his heart, and so he feels fear, terror, and affliction.[46]

As we shall see, this insistence on the differences between systems has considerable importance in Kircher's thinking. For him, such differentiation marks the possibility of classification and ordering, both synchronic and diachronic. At the same time, this passage also indicates the common absence of a systematic approach to classification: the differences are marked in a piecemeal fashion and tend quickly to slip into interesting trivia of uncertain categorical value.

Some of Kircher's sources have been discovered: Knud Lundbaek has published a facsimile and translation of seventeen manuscript pages from the *Confucius Sinarum Philosophus* (1689), probably written by the Sicilian Jesuit Prosper Intorcetta (1625–96), who arrived in China in 1659 and returned to Rome in 1671. In Rome he met with Kircher at the Collegio and had in hand the manuscript pages in question, which contains Chinese originals of Kircher's tortoise writing. Lundbaek has also given some explanation of what Chinese sources must have been used here, as has Haun Saussy.[47]

At this preliminary stage, we see where Kircher got his information, and we have some immediate context within which to place his readings. But to situate Kircher's work within larger intellectual contexts such as encyclopedism and comparison, to make sense of what he thought all this Chinese and Egyptian information meant, and thereby to see his project and its relevance for our own historical and methodological concerns, we must make a detour into the structural dimensions of comparison.

The Occult Mind

The epistemological status of what amount to analogies has become an ever larger question in these comparative explorations. With the tentative formulation of occult and historical perspectives as representing an epistemic divide, I have argued that such analogies not only arise within the works we study but also, when we compare among them, between our own and their positions and concerns. Some historians of science have examined such analogical thinking, usually with negative results: scientific (and historical) analogies and models are not equivalent or properly homologous to those occurring in occult systems. To challenge this argument, supported as it is by much the same ideologies and structures as prop up the blanket refusal of comparison, will help clarify the stakes that Kircher has in effect put on the table.

I shall focus on an influential article by Brian Vickers, whom we last saw mercilessly but justly revealing Frances Yates's ley-hunting methods. In 1982, at a seminal conference on "Hermeticism and the Renaissance," Vickers presented a paper titled "On the Function of Analogy in the Occult," in which he attempted an overview and critique of analogical thinking in magical systems in general.[48] As well as taking on board occult material from the early Greeks to the early modern West, Vickers touched on Chinese systems and those of nonliterate tribal peoples; unlike most of his colleagues, he also used theoretical models from a range of disciplines, notably classics, intellectual history, anthropology, and the sciences.

In a powerfully destructive criticism of occult thought, Vickers argues that the scientific "reaction against the occult" constitutes "not so much . . . the destruction of analogy but . . . the reassertion of its true function." Analogy, he argues, has real value "as a descriptive or heuristic tool," but in thought such as Kircher's it becomes "a matrix into which reality had to be assimilated." In short, occult analogy amounts to a systematic formulation of correspondences and classifications upon arbitrary cultural bases. Occultists such as Kircher mapped and interpreted the world solely through cultural parallels, and thus their systems analyze not nature but their own intellectual society.[49]

Reading this article, one is assailed by a disturbing sense of déja vu. Although the particular objects under analysis certainly differ historically, has this not been said before? Two moments in the text especially leap out:

Armchair anthropology used to be a term of scorn used by field-workers for those of their colleagues who stayed at home and theorized without visiting primitive tribes. This [astrological ethnography in Ptolemy] may be called armchair geography, since to describe the inhabitants of the world it is not necessary to leave one's room; all that is needed is a scheme. The result here is wholly theoretical—*abstract*, one might be tempted to say, were it not for the concrete details.[50]

And in reference to D. P. Walker's consideration of Ficinian correspondence magic as not unlike language, Vickers writes:

It seems to me that in describing the correspondence system as a language, Walker is giving just as misleading a judgment of language as [S. K.] Heninger did of metaphor. The correspondence system is based on resemblances, similarities, often heterogeneous and superficial, yet it claims to represent real, purposeful connections. The linguistic sign, as defined by Saussure, is known to be arbitrary and is based not on likeness but on difference, the crucial element being the line that separates the sign and the concept signified.[51]

Analogies in magical thought, theoretical versus fieldwork anthropology, abstract thought with concrete objects, structural linguistics . . . surely Vickers is responding to *The Savage Mind*?

Apparently not. No reference to Lévi-Strauss appears, despite the twenty years between *La pensée sauvage* and Vickers's article. In a follow-up article the same year, Lévi-Strauss's book is mentioned in a list of relevant works, in a footnote, but there is no evidence that Vickers read or at least absorbed much from it. The only anthropologist mentioned in any detail is Stanley Jeyaraja Tambiah, whose peculiarly Austinian speech-act theory directly opposes structural interpretations of magical action.[52] I prefer to think that Vickers— like (apparently) his interlocutors in intellectual history and the history of science—is simply ignorant. I have no reason to think him one of those tediously gleeful pronouncers of the death of structuralism, few of whom have understood it well enough to comment. For at base most of Vickers's article amounts to a meandering, fascinating but confused restatement of Lévi-Strauss's initial *question*—formulated as a negative answer:

[Instead] of deriving their methods from the physical world by processes of observation, experiment, quantification, theory, and so forth, the occult imposed traditional thought categories onto the world and "read" nature in the light of them. Obviously some of the occult sciences— alchemy and astrology, for example—made a partial use of observational techniques, but the results were then subordinated to some preformed interpretative model, often magical or mystical, which was neither derived from reality nor testable by it.[53]

Twenty years earlier, Lévi-Strauss wrote:

It may be objected that science of this kind can scarcely be of much practical effect. The answer to this is that its main purpose is not a practical one. It meets intellectual requirements before or instead of satisfying needs.

The real question is not whether the touch of a woodpecker's beak does in fact cure toothache, but rather whether one can, from some point of view, see a woodpecker's beak and a man's tooth as "going together" . . . and whether by means of these groupings some initial order can be introduced into the universe. Classifying, of whatever sort, as opposed to not classifying, has a value of its own.[54]

Using Western occult sources, Vickers raises a double question: (1) how, logically, does all this analogizing thought operate? (2) to what extent can this mode of thought be compared to the scientific? Lévi-Strauss, having set up exactly this double question—with the additional point that such peculiarly nonscientific science both produced extraordinary results and mysteriously did not lead to ordinary scientific thought (a mystery he calls the "Neolithic Paradox")—proposes his famous bricolage analogy as a first approximation. Vickers's article should thus be read as a preface to a translation of *La pensée sauvage* into the worlds of Western occultism.

If this account appears dismissive, I do not intend it so. It is indeed unfortunate that scholarship on magic in literate societies has missed this crucial theoretical shift, but the hypothetical translation proposed would be no simple matter. Early modern European occult uses of analogy have deep affinities to the "savage thought" Lévi-Strauss describes, but as we have continually seen they are conditioned by historical sensibilities at odds with what Lévi-Strauss sees in tribal societies. On the other hand, this critical disjuncture is in part an artifact of Lévi-Strauss's methods, a crucial analytical slippage to which Derrida long ago called our attention.

A comparatively positive scientific assessment of Kircher comes in a revealing article by Stephen Jay Gould on Kircher's paleontology. Gould primarily wishes to demonstrate that Kircher recognized the organic origin of fossils; indeed, Gould suggests "that no Stage One of inorganic darkness ever existed," that is, that not only Kircher but in fact the whole early modern discourse on fossils accepted their organic (as opposed to spontaneous) generation.[55] For our present discussion, the most striking point is "that Kircher's limited categories for inorganic origin of some fossils lie embedded within a broader taxonomy that does not utilize organic *versus* inorganic as a basic, or even an important, criterion for a *fundamentum divisionis*."[56] Kircher writes that he "will not speak here of the innumerable oysters, clams, snails, fungi, algae and other denizens of the sea that have been converted to stone, because these are obviously found everywhere in such a state, *and hardly merit any attention*."[57] In other words, Kircher's intricate attempts to classify and make sense of fossils emphasize only that which remains problematic. His interest in exotica here manifests an earnest endeavor at inclusion, at ordering what had not been ordered. Thus his search for analogies turns out be properly a hunt for homologies, for underlying constancy to classify the exotic. Far from simply imposing preexisting thought categories on sensory data, as Vickers would have it, Kircher, like Bruno, hoped to discern unknown categories latent in a mass of seemingly disparate materials. The frontispiece of his 1641 *Magnes; sive, De Arte Magnetica* demonstrates admirably the vast range of data sets, of those "disciplines" Romano considers him to "blur" (figure 5); in this image, we see also that Kircher sought to connect such data with rigid chains.

In part, Vickers's criticism of Kircher's parallel hunting amounts to a restatement of one of Lévi-Strauss's more devastating criticisms:

> This supposed association [among systems] is the result of a *petitio principii*. If totemism is defined as the joint presence of animal and plant names, prohibitions applied to the corresponding species, and the forbidding of marriage between people sharing the same name and the same prohibition, then clearly a problem arises about the connection of these customs. It has however long been known that any one of these features can be found without the others and any two of them without the third.[58]

To generalize, one must be exceedingly wary of presupposing coherence and constancy, lest one reify assumptions as known facts against which to evaluate data.

The application of this valuable stricture to Kircher is clear enough: he sought exactly such connections as these in his somewhat magpielike collecting work. But at the same time, as we have seen with Bruno, the fact that Kircher sought cohesion does not entail that he achieved it, and conversely does not ensure that we understand the *mode* of cohesion sought.

Figure 5. Magnetic links connecting knowledge. Frontispiece, Athanasii Kircheri . . .
Magnes; sive, De Arte Magnetica opvs Tripartitvm . . . *Rome: ex typographia
Ludouici Grignani, sumptibus Hermanni Scheus, 1641. The Burndy Library,
Cambridge, Massachusetts.*

In her fascinating meditations *On Longing*, Susan Stewart explicates the coherence of collection:

> In contrast to the souvenir, the collection offers example rather than sample, metaphor rather than metonymy. The collection does not displace attention to the past; rather, the past is at the service of the collection. . . . The collection seeks a form of self-enclosure which is possible because of its ahistoricism. The collection replaces history with *classification*, with order beyond the realm of temporality. In the collection, time is not something to be restored to an origin; rather, all time is made simultaneous or synchronous within the collection's world. . . . The collection presents a hermetic world: to have a representative collection is to have both the minimum and the complete number of elements necessary for an autonomous world—a world which is both full and singular, which has banished repetition and achieved authority.[59]

By this logic, what we must study in Kircher is not the total collection, the autonomous "hermetic" world of the museum and the written oeuvre, but rather the *logic* of the system. It is not unreasonable to question the extraordinary grandeur, even arrogance, of Kircher's totalizing goal. But to criticize methodologically and analytically, as Vickers wishes to do, we must focus on the means by which he sought to annul time and absorb history.

Lévi-Strauss's criticism was, of course, directed at modern scholars who, he claimed, had first defined totemism as an institution founded on three systems, and who then analyzed the ways in which particular cultures did or did not possess this institution. Lévi-Strauss notes that this begs the question (*petitio principii*): the method presupposes the real existence of such an institution. If instead these three systems (naming by natural species, prohibitions with respect to eponymous species, exogamy by species) are independent modes of classification that use nature to structure culture, then the institution of totemism itself disappears: "I believe that the anthropologists of former times fell prey to an illusion," he writes in summary of his book *Le totémisme aujourd'hui*.[60]

The same criticism, though it may apply to Kircher, certainly hits home with scholars of Western occultism. Vickers, for example, uses Kircher as a battleground on which to criticize the work of S. K. Heninger Jr. on early modern poetics and the use of what he "deplorably loosely" (as Vickers rightly notes) calls "Pythagorean cosmology."[61] Heninger provides a table from Kircher's *Musurgia Universalis* (Universal Music-making,[62] 1650), and explains that it lays out a "9-fold correspondence between ten distinct cate-

The Occult Mind

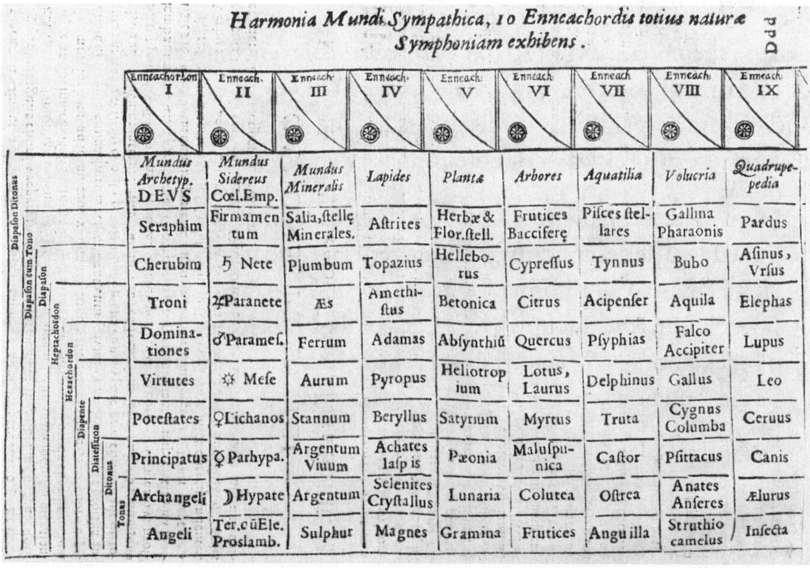

Harmonia Mundi Sympathica, 10 Enneachordis totius naturæ Symphoniam exhibens.

Ddd

Enneachordon I	Enneach. II	Enneach. III	Enneach. IV	Enneach. V	Enneach. VI	Enneach. VII	Enneach. VIII	Enneach. IX
Mundus Archetyp. DEVS	Mundus Sidereus Cœl.Emp.	Mundus Mineralis	Lapides	Plantæ	Arbores	Aquatilia	Volucria	Quadrupedia
Seraphim	Firmamentum	Salia,ſtellę Minerales.	Aſtrites	Herbæ & Flor.ſtell.	Frutices Bacciferę	Piſces ſtellares	Gallina Pharaonis	Pardus
Cherubim	♄ Nete	Plumbum	Topazius	Helleborus	Cypreſſus	Tynnus	Bubo	Aſinus, Vrſus
Troni	♃Paranete	Æs	Amethiſtus	Betonica	Citrus	Acipenſer	Aquila	Elephas
Dominationes	♂Parameſ.	Ferrum	Adamas	Abſynthiũ	Quercus	Pſyphias	Falco Accipiter	Lupus
Virtutes	☼ Meſe	Aurum	Pyropus	Heliotropium	Lotus, Laurus	Delphinus	Gallus	Leo
Poteſtates	♀Lichanos	Stannum	Beryllus	Satyrium	Myrtus	Truta	Cygnus Columba	Ceruus
Principatus	☿ Parhypa.	Argentum Viuum	Achates Iaſpis	Pæonia	Maluſpunica	Caſtor	Pſittacus	Canis
Archangeli	☽ Hypate	Argentum	Selenites Cryſtallus	Lunaria	Colutea	Oſtrea	Anates Anſeres	Ælurus
Angeli	Ter.cũEle. Proslamb.	Sulphur	Magnes	Gramina	Frutices	Anguilla	Struthiocamelus	Inſecta

Figure 6. Classification of objects and qualities ascribed to the scale of the ennead. Page 393, lib. 2, Athanasius Kircher, Musurgia Universalis, sive, Ars Magna Consoni et Dissoni . . . *Rome: ex typographia hæredum Francisci Corbelletti, 1650. From the Archives at New England Conservatory of Music, Boston.*

gories of existence: angels, heavenly spheres, metals, stones, plants, trees, water creatures, winged creatures, four-legged animals, and colors" (figure 6). The vertical lines indicate "the hierarchical stratification within any given category"; meanwhile,

> when read across, the diagram designates the items which are correspondent in each of the ten categories. For example, cherubim are correspondent to lead, the topaz, the hellebore, the cypress, the tunny-fish, the bittern, the ass and the bear, and black. Kircher sees the whole as a unified, harmonious system which reconciles opposites in musical terms of the diapason.[63]

Of this diagram and of Heninger's reading, Vickers asks, "What do those items have in common? If one were given them outside this grid, how could they be connected? Do they have any real correspondence, either of structure or of function? Apart from providing ten categories (arbitrarily), and arranging the items in each, does the grid, in fact, connect anything?"[64]

Heninger argues that these correspondences amount to poetic metaphors used for reading the book of nature: "The job of 'making' [such correspondences] then becomes not so much a creation of something new, but rather a discovering of something already prescribed in God's book of nature." For Vickers, however, this is a misunderstanding—whether on Heninger's or Kircher's part is unclear—of both discovery and of metaphor:

> Here there is neither creation nor discovery, since the form is predetermined and self-duplicating. Heninger claims that the juxtaposition creates a "transfer of information from one level to another," by which "the poet explains the unknown by means of the known and fulfils the purpose of metaphor." Yet, since all is known, how can information be transferred, and how can the unknown be known?[65]

In fact,

> The items in the correspondence grid are not metaphors at all. Whereas metaphors suggest resemblances between two discrete entities or levels of existence—resemblances that are perceived by the imagination, and assented to or not—the correspondences are claimed to be not just resemblances but actual identities, in the realm of objects or essences. They are not perceived by the imagination but by the rational mind, and *must* be assented to—otherwise the whole system risks being abandoned. Again, where metaphors and models, in indicating similarities, also insist on differences—my love is like a red, red rose only in some respects, thank goodness!—correspondences assert similarity or identity and are not interested in differences. . . . The ingredients of the correspondence grid, then, are not metaphors but things, which, it is claimed, represent patterns of connection within reality. But can one connect them horizontally?[66]

Therefore,

> The correspondences in fact constitute a classification system, not a mode of discovery. . . . In the experimental tradition, metaphors are used as models that attempt to describe some observable process or relationship in the physical world, the body, or the brain. One fundamental criterion for the model is that it be based on similarity, but also on difference, in the sense that the model must be different from the reality it is used to describe. If the two are fused, the operative distinction collapses. In the experimental tradition, analogies are used to comprehend parts of reality; in the occult tradition, reality can only be understood by being turned into analogy.[67]

The Occult Mind

I do not challenge Vickers's general critique of Heninger, who certainly falls into the kind of triumphal celebration of occult syncretism as poetry emblematic of immediately post-Yates literary scholarship in this field. But Vickers has in the analytical process fallen into exactly the sort of analogy-as-identity fallacy (technically the fallacy of false or weak analogy) he perceives in occult thought: Vickers apparently takes for granted that Heninger has Kircher right, and that therefore criticism of Heninger's dubious analysis may stand as equivalent to a criticism of Kircher's thinking. Interestingly, this reveals the basis of Vickers's argument: by reading this analogy (Heninger/Kircher) as an identity, Vickers implies that scholarship on occult thought has already fully understood it, in which case all that remains is evaluation.[68]

Here Vickers has fallen prey to an illusion: like the "anthropologists of former times," he has assumed that we already recognize the systems of thought lying behind the object of study. He finds that "many of the basic operations of occult science"—note the assumption of singularity and cohesion here—"take the form of grading reality in terms of a limited number of categories. . . . These are mental categories, self-generated to create system, not derived from observation from reality. Occult science first constitutes a matrix, then assimilates experience to this matrix." As a result, "instead of deriving their methods from the physical world by processes of observation, experiment, quantification, theory, and so forth, the occult imposed traditional thought categories onto the world and 'read' nature in the light of them."[69] In other words, occult thought formulates categorical structures on the basis of "tradition" and then imposes them on the world; because it then reads nature through these lenses, it is tautological, bound always to find in nature what it itself put there.

Setting aside the point that, as Lévi-Strauss, Foucault, Derrida, Bourdieu, and others have all demonstrated in their various fields and fashions, this procedure is intrinsic to the interpretation of nature, we may recall that Bruno was already aware of the problem. As we have seen, he did not entirely succeed in resolving it; indeed, these various structuralist and poststructuralist thinkers have convincingly shown that it is insoluble. But Bruno also sees what Vickers does not: the categorical structures imposed on the world must come from somewhere; they cannot arise ex nihilo, but must have a source at least partly outside the mind.

Furthermore, the aforementioned discussion of the ennead scale in Kircher's *Musurgia Universalis* leads to what he calls the "musurgical ark," a music-making machine (figure 7). In essence, this "ark," one of a consid-

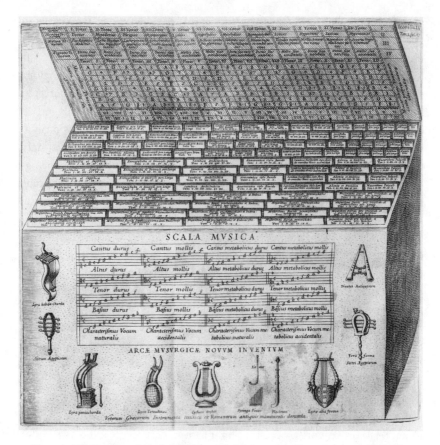

Figure 7. The music-making ark. Foldout, facing page 185, lib. 2, Athanasius Kircher, Musurgia Universalis, sive, Ars Magna Consoni et Dissoni . . . Rome: ex typographia hæredum Francisci Corbelletti, 1650. From the Archives at New England Conservatory of Music, Boston.

erable number of such devices invented by Kircher—and at least in some cases actually constructed and given to friends and patrons—allowed non-musicians to develop complete four-part polyphonic settings by drawing preconstructed fragments from a box. Each such element, inscribed on a wand, was classified by a number of syllables, with the wand giving both a simple note-against-note (species 1) counterpoint and a more complex (florid) version. Although this process certainly imposes an established "grid" on the given data (the melodic text to be set), the ark itself constitutes not only a classification but what one might almost call a generative gram-

The Occult Mind

mar, seeking to reduce musical composition to a mathematical basis and thus reveal once again the continuity (here numerical) between music and other forms of knowledge.[70]

In essence, Heninger reads such generations as metaphorical, as poetic play upon both cultural and natural structures. Vickers, by contrast, insists that whatever structures might be discerned by such a procedure are simply human impositions on the given realities of nature. But both views presume that the connections or links among disparate sorts of data are necessarily analogical—either poetic metaphor or pseudoscientific model. For Kircher, however, the links sought lie at a deeper level: he seeks *homology*, not analogy, rather like Eliade or Goethe.

To return briefly to paleontology, which presents a particularly concrete example, Kircher wants to know why one finds peculiar, anomalous traces embedded in ancient rock: images of the Virgin, apparent inscriptions, and the like. As Gould demonstrates, his purpose is by no means to undermine organic explanations for what have come to be called fossils; on the contrary, he hopes to find some *continuous* solution to the whole problem. If such traces appear, they must succumb to explanation. Just as Eliade sought a means to explain disparate phenomena as so many expressions of a single principle, so Kircher too works morphologically to discern the principles and systematics of all his vast data sets. By this reading, such machines as the musurgical ark, which produce morphologically legitimate results by purely mechanical means, should be understood as congruent with Goethe's Urpflanze: "With such a model . . . it will be possible to invent plants *ad infinitum*. They will be strictly logical plants—that is to say, even though they may not actually exist they could exist—they would not be mere picturesque shadows or dreams, but would possess an inner truth and necessity."[71]

Vickers demonstrates an important and subtle category mistake in scholarship on the occult. In comparing such systems to scientific ones, he takes for granted that the primary object is the passive interpretation of nature; indeed, he does not seem to see that there *could* be other purposes at work. Thus he draws two comparative (and negative) conclusions:

One concerns the applicability of models to science. Whatever one's estimate of the debt of experimental science to occult science—on this count I cannot see that any constructive borrowing took place. . . . In the experimental tradition analogies function as intermediaries between theory and observation, in a process that constantly evolves, and uses computational and verificational procedures. In the occult, by contrast, there seems to be no dialectical interplay between theory and observation, and no interest in computation and falsification. Observation is not an open-ended inquiry but a form of classification that is used to support theory in an unquestioning manner. . . . [The occult correspondence] is both the theory governing the processing of material and the material itself—a circular, self-justifying process.[72]

[Second,] the positive aspect of the occult's use of hierarchical and evaluative categories is that in grading and discriminating reality in animistic and socioreligious terms, they gave a comforting sense of the universe as having been constructed in man's image and likeness. In the course of the sixteenth century [however] men no longer needed to see the universe in such homocentric terms, and granted inanimate nature its own purely neutral categories of space, volume, density, and velocity. It is not the case that they abandoned the need to understand the universe as a system, but that they stopped constructing a system out of human social, sexual, and religious categories.[73]

Ultimately,

For all its attractiveness the occult's use of analogy in fact constituted a closed system, which constantly reduplicated its very limited understanding of the universe. The fusion of tenor and vehicle, while seemingly favorable to metaphor, actually destroyed the flexibility and creativity of metaphor, and its proper functioning in an open-ended system. In the occult, metaphor tends to become coagulated, rigidified. Instead of lamenting the breaking of the circle, one should celebrate that the seventeenth century finally dissolved the tyranny of the grid.[74]

In short, because Vickers does not recognize or accept the legitimacy of analytical systems outside the scientific modes, because he takes science as known and certain and thus an absolute touchstone with which to evaluate any epistemology or episteme, he ends up demonstrating only what we already knew: occult thought is not identical to science.

Despite its difficulties, Vickers's criticism moves us forward analytically. He rightly attacks the rhapsodic celebration of occult-thought-as-poetic-brio that Heninger and others present, and while the primary force of such discourse died within a few years of Vickers's work, in the mid-1980s, it still undergirds a good deal of ill-informed scholarship. He rightly connects such paeans to the specter of Yates: poor scholarship in this field can often be identified simply by examining whether Yates appears in it as a visionary or prophet.

The Occult Mind

What he fails to achieve, however, is a valid account of "The Function of Analogy in the Occult," as his title has it. Nevertheless, the logical and analytical flaws of his work allow him to serve as a Thrasymachian interlocutor, helping us antagonistically to identify categorical slippage. In particular, we can see Vickers tripping up because he does not see that early modern occult thinkers were aware of his concerns, and in fact went to some trouble to deal with them—with varying success. Thus the result of this extended examination of his discussion is the realization that Vickers is a *participant* in the occult discourse of the early modern period, or better, that occult thinkers already participated in our theoretical discourses. Vickers, like so many others working in these areas, implicitly denies that occult thinkers could understand his questions, *presumes* rather than proves an absolute disjuncture between scientific analysis (with which he identifies his own methods) and occult thought. In short, he has imposed a set of traditional categories on the objects of study and then claimed to find proof in them of those categories— precisely the fallacy he ascribes to the occultists.

⁞⁞⁞

We have seen Vickers assuming that all classification systems, at base, seek the same natural truths; any classification of natural things can be correlated to later and more successful scientific systems in order to evaluate their worth. But there is good reason to think that classification cannot be evaluated globally in this way. As Lévi-Strauss and later especially Marshall Sahlins demonstrate, there are other ways of knowing, other systems of categories, and the fundamental objects of these methods are not always commensurable.[75] We have yet to establish whether Kircher should be evaluated as a classifier against the backdrop of encyclopedism, Linnaean taxonomy, Goethean morphology, or of the *pensée sauvage*, an apparently radically different system that has its criteria of truth elsewhere. And if the latter is the case, then many criticisms—both recent and contemporary to Kircher— miss the mark.

Yet, this formulation is too simple. The abstract comparison Lévi-Strauss draws between *ingénieur* and bricoleur, like the historical one Sahlins famously examines in the death of Captain Cook, is intrinsically binary. This is not to raise the old canard that all structuralism imposes binary dichotomy on its objects, a criticism that rarely recognizes the many ways in which Lévi-Strauss in particular insists he is simply analyzing by means of the simplest possible logical system—a binary—and does not claim this is exactly adequate to the systems under analysis (note that Bourdieu's devastating cri-

tique of structuralism in the opening of *The Logic of Practice* explicitly sets
Lévi-Strauss to one side as far more careful and precise).[76] Rather, the *comparative stance* undertaken by Lévi-Strauss is intrinsically binary, and Sahlins
does to some degree annul his own distance from the Hawaiian situation in
order to express the problem in binary terms.[77] As we have already seen with
Bruno, however, and it is even more pointed in Kircher, matters become
more complex when the people studied already recognize the epistemic difficulty in question and work actively to overcome it. Even if, as Derrida elegantly points out, this overcoming is ultimately impossible (a point with
which Lévi-Strauss would I think agree), Derrida also recognizes that the attempt is itself not an overcoming of but a differance out of which emerges
the epistemic binarism.[78]

In other words, the difficulty of examining Bruno and Kircher—and Dee
for that matter—in terms of the epistemological stances of science and the
occult is that none of them falls entirely within one or the other camp, *and
they know this*. In part, their projects grapple with those two epistemes, attempting to resorb one into the other (Dee), or to reformulate knowledge
itself to alter the evaluation of truth (Bruno), or . . . what? We return to our
original question, the question not yet fully asked: What is Kircher doing?

Occult thought should indeed be distinguished sharply from science. As
Vickers argues, such thought is self-justifying and in a sense circular,
founded on the resorption of event into structure. But does science really
not operate this way?[79] Consider Lévi-Strauss's formulation:

> Hence we understand how an attentive, meticulous observation entirely
> turned toward the concrete finds in symbolism both its principle and its
> result. Savage thought does not distinguish the moment of observation
> and that of interpretation any more than one first registers, upon observ-
> ing them, the signs expressed by an interlocutor, in order thence to seek
> to understand them: he speaks, and the sensible expression carries with it
> the signification. Articulated language decomposes into elements, each of
> which is not a sign but the medium of a sign: a distinctive unit that could
> not be replaced by another without its changing the signification, and
> that perhaps itself lacks some attributes of this signification, which it ex-
> presses in being joined or opposed to other units.[80]

Derrida argues, with considerable force, that precisely this sort of distinction between observation and interpretation, or sign and understanding,
threatens the whole logocentric worldview—including science. To shatter

sign from meaning, however intellectually we may accept it, would in the end require us to admit the absence of the interlocutor's presence within his speech: he speaks, we encounter the meaning, and we presume that in doing so we stand in the presence of our interlocutor. Indeed, this is part of the threat of writing: by externalizing the sign in a stable medium, it forces us to recognize a distinction between sign and signification, and thus to accept that the elements of meaning we encounter are indeed "units" that lack some qualities of the signification. Derrida goes farther than Lévi-Strauss, of course, in his examination of the means by which the joining and opposing to other units only defers this lack, supplements for it, and ultimately persuades us of the presence that is always absent.[81]

In magical thought, Cassirer, Izutsu Toshihiko, C. K. Ogden and I. A. Richards, Frazer, and so on had always argued that the savage does not understand the arbitrariness of the sign; Lévi-Strauss, however, notes that in his use of concrete objects as signs the "savage" only commits the same error we always do: he thinks that his expression carries meaning in itself. Insofar as the parallel continues into a recognition of the constitution of meaning through joining and opposition—in fact through a relational syntagmatic chain that refers back to the paradigmatic system itself—Lévi-Strauss suggests that such systems are means of motivating the sign, in the same way as we motivate signs through the constant supplementation of speech-acts.

Tambiah, whom Vickers admires, takes up this point—and misses it. He argues that of course the natives know that words and signs are arbitrary; they merely work functionally, dealing with signification in terms of social effect. If a speech-act has a social effect, it achieves its end; that it is arbitrary (and motivated) is irrelevant. For the native to believe that his speech-acts have real power, he need not believe foolishly that words are not arbitrary signs.[82]

This is giving up too soon. *All* human signification systems presume, at some level, that signification is not arbitrary, that meaning and presence really are carried in the sign. This is in part why Derrida refers to such systems as logocentric: it is not language or logic at stake, but the sign itself. And *la pensée sauvage* is no less logocentric than Western metaphysics: it merely projects its supplementary certainty elsewhere.[83]

And yet, thought that turns resolutely toward the concrete requires qualities at odds with historical and scientific abstractions. In particular, by deferring to natural things, magical thought constructs a system whose anchors lie in nonhuman stabilities. Lévi-Strauss insists on this: so-called totemic identifications are means of expressing difference, not similarity:

The fur, feathers, beak, teeth, can be *mine* because they are that in which the eponymous animal and I differ from each other: this difference is assumed by man as an emblem [*à titre d'emblème*] and to assert his symbolic relation with the animal; conversely the parts which are edible, thus assimilable, are the index of a genuine consubstantiality, but in reverse of what one might suppose the dietary prohibition has for its real aim to deny this.[84]

If I say I am an elk, I may wear elk fur because this is a quality of the elk that I do not possess and that may thus serve as a sign of my elk-ness. But if I should eat elk, this would suggest that in some sense I really am an elk: I now not only *wear* elk but have *absorbed* elk's substance, collapsing the distinction that it was the whole purpose of the totemic prohibition to set up. My neighbors of the bear clan may eat elk, because there is no danger of their *being* elks: they are bears, and bears are not elks.

But if this system thus enforces, at its very core, that all certainty in signification rests outside of the human sphere, it is in this sense different from that "Western metaphysics of presence" to which Derrida refers, in which after all the putative certainty is always human and in some sense social: it is not *any* presence, but *someone's* presence. By that logic, a concrete system would require a dehumanized projection of meaning.

Furthermore, the "savage mind," by shifting the difficulties of absence onto the stability of nature, asserts that the system, because it *is* natural, is unchanging and has always been so. It subsumes event into structure. When change takes place—and of course it always does despite the conservatism of these supposedly "cold" cultures—the power of the system demonstrates itself: it can, by interpreting diachronic change in synchronic terms, assert that the change has not occurred, that the effects of the change were always already present in the system. Borrowing from Peirce's notion of abduction, we may say that precisely in such moments of seeming crisis the system most effectively structures its own supports. If the system could not absorb the event, could not formulate the change as an already present element of the previously structured system, then it would indeed be in crisis. But because it succeeds, as evidenced by its own continuation, the system proves precisely that no change has occurred because no change needed to occur: the system appears perfect because it seemingly already knew about this possibility, had already taken account of it. And thus the cyclical and apparently timeless quality of savage thought is affirmed precisely by the dynamic encounter with time.[85]

The Occult Mind

Taking these points quite literally, may we not say, with Derrida, that the science of the concrete is a system of writing?[86] Its great strengths are indeed those qualities that cause writing to haunt the Western metaphysics of presence. And in the same way as the Johnny-jump-up (*viola tricolor*, *la pensée sauvage*) pops up just where we least expect it, every year in its season, and could theoretically be wiped out but in human practice is pleasantly ineradicable, just so such systems (writing, *la pensée sauvage*) haunt not really by threatening but by being surprisingly present just where we had thought we had eliminated them.[87] If this be so, it helps to explain why, in Lévi-Strauss's famous "writing lesson," the Nambikwara chief, far from being threatened by writing, immediately absorbed its qualities and used them for devious political purposes.[88]

Thus the distinction between cultures with and without writing, to which Lévi-Strauss ultimately grants some credence, would be more properly the distinction between *written* and writing cultures.[89] And this would disturbingly parallel the tendency of writing cultures to use the written as slates on which to write further, at the same time transforming them into fledgling writing cultures whose written natures have already been shattered. By inscribing upon them, we haunt these peoples with ghosts not of their making.

On this basis, we see that Vickers's account of science and magic as epistemologically divided could be entirely reversed by a genuinely structural transformation. Vickers reads occult thought as tending to project the human onto the universe or vice versa; as failing in its classifications because of an inability to discern inherent boundaries of determinism between the human and the cultural; as unable in the end to achieve empirical ends because of an incapacity to see that signs relate to things only arbitrarily, not naturally.[90] Conversely, the bricoleur would presumably see scientific systems as failing to distinguish between human and natural; as on this basis remaining utterly ignorant of human questions because they assume natural answers to have human significance; as unable in the end to achieve valid human ends because of an incapacity to see that human models have neither stability nor truth. And the history of science affords ample opportunities to demonstrate that these propositions are not without validity.

Writing has a striking power to walk such fine lines, to act as a distorting but revealing mirror. Rey Chow has pointed out that the cover image for Derrida's *Of Grammatology* in the first edition of the English translation by Gayatri Spivak—a piece of Chinese writing and painting—is unidentified. And as she notes, the cover of the corrected edition released in 1996 bears an

Egyptian image of Thoth.[91] Even in the imagery, the Western *imaginaire* of the outside of writing is Egypt-China, or an Ægyptian China. And while he may have been preceded in suggesting the connection, it is surely Kircher who first made this important: in a sense, Kircher constructs precisely the *imaginaire* that Derrida deconstructs.

In his dissertation on Kircher, Daniel Stolzenberg informs us repeatedly that Kircher has often been read as continuing the Hermetic tradition.[92] What he does not do is demonstrate that this is incorrect: he notes that there is some truth in it, then expands greatly on the Orientalist context of the *Egyptian Oedipus*. He insists that the primary point, for Kircher, is to translate the hieroglyphics. Suppose it is? Why is this at odds with his other projects? That remains the question, and the Grafton-style text history Stolzenberg constructs does nothing to alter it.

Despite his erudition, Stolzenberg underestimates the degree to which hieroglyphics were the key to something else and at the same time the problem themselves. In an admirable summary of the *Oedipus Aegyptiacus* (Egyptian Oedipus), Stolzenberg shows Kircher examining in twelve headings the manners in which hieroglyphic signification had been extrapolated across history into various degenerate systems.[93] Such systems thus provide correlative evidence from which to backtrack into hieroglyphics. But we must never forget that deciphering hieroglyphics was simultaneously a way of reading Egyptian text and a way of reading Ægypt herself, since for Kircher the wisdom of Ægypt was bound up in her system of graphic language.

Stolzenberg shakes his head bemusedly at the early moderns' fascination with alphabets and writing systems, noting that they seemed to think that something other than linguistic meaning might be carried within: "From its beginnings, the European study of Oriental languages demonstrated a peculiar fascination with alphabets, over and above their utility for understanding the languages that they are used to record."[94] For Kircher, to understand Chinese writing was in itself to understand Chinese thought and culture; for us, of course, it is obvious that Chinese writing is simply a way of expressing Chinese language.

But this is not at all obvious. Indeed, as Derrida demonstrated throughout *Of Grammatology*, writing systems carry meaning intertwined with but not equivalent to the linguistic meanings they express. If early modern thinkers formulated this on other grounds, notably metaphysical and occult grounds, they nevertheless had a legitimate point, one that vanished with the collapse of such intensional signification systems in the later seventeenth and eighteenth centuries.

For example, note that many native Chinese thinkers conceived of their writing as founded on pictography and ideography. Although of course they knew perfectly well that Chinese graphs encapsulate several different forms of meaning-expression as well as phonetic cues, they nevertheless sought out the underlying pictographic realities that for them grounded the system in the miraculous visions of Sage Emperor Fu Xi and in the *Yijing* (Classic of Changes).[95] In a great many ways, this Chinese grammatology was akin to Kircher's approach: they sought traces of ancient historical wisdom embedded in a written system that, if it was more legible, still had to be read against the grain to reveal its history. It is hardly a criticism of Kircher that he used Intorcetta's manuscript, and through it Chinese originals, to explicate Chinese grammatological discourse.

As to Egyptian hieroglyphs, Jean-François Champollion's decipherment of the Rosetta Stone revealed that Egyptian writing is not unlike Chinese in its formal structure, composed of both ideographs and phonetic cues, the latter often constructed as a kind of punning in rebuslike style.[96] Clearly the system did not operate allegorically, as Kircher and many others had thought.

But where did Kircher get his information to this effect? Greek texts had reported the hieroglyphic system quite early, often in the context of broader discussions of Egyptian achievements. Plato indicates that Solon visited Egypt and had the system explained to him. Herodotus visited Egypt and apparently talked to literate priests. And we could continue the list of references; they are well known.[97] In every such text, as well as those more difficult to track down to precise origins (such as the *Hermetica* and Horapollo), there is general agreement that hieroglyphics operate on an ideographic and perhaps allegorical principle, and in some respects at least contain deep mysteries quite unlike the notionally transparent alphabetic systems of the Greeks and later Romans. Even within the depiction of cultural contact, then, Egyptian writing was already constructed as the absolute outside of the alphabetic.[98]

How did this happen? How is it that no text or fragment correctly reported the really very simple principles on which hieroglyphics actually operate? Must we disregard *every* reported contact and say they all simply invented or distorted?

Suppose the same conversations had occurred with the Chinese—as in fact they did. What did Intorcetta, Matteo Ricci, and the other Jesuit missionaries report? How was it interpreted in the West during the baroque era? Again, what came back was a report of a basically ideographic system, not unlike the Egyptian, leading to Kircher's excited claims about the origins of the former in the latter, via Ham and the lineage of Noah. Whatever we may think of his analyses, Kircher's reports from China are accurate enough *as* reports.[99]

It seems Chinese scholars told these Western visitors about what was really important in the system. To be sure, the Chinese writing system is used primarily to transcribe language, but the great pride in such texts as the ancient classics and the Ruist (Confucian) and Daoist canons in part resides in the fascination with language, a fascination embedded deeply in the nature of the script. Already in the Ruist texts we have critical examination of the disparity between name and thing, and the claim that *written* poems may have a somewhat different (not necessarily more problematic) relation to the truths of the poet than do spoken ones. In some sense, it has for millennia been claimed that the Chinese script embeds the person of the author into the text—as well as that of the scribe, whose calligraphy is significantly an index (in Peirce's sense) of the mind and heart (*xin*). Surely when confronted with these educated, advanced, sophisticated barbarians, Chinese scholars wished to explain the extraordinary superiority of their native system, as contrasted to the merely phonetic and pragmatic Western alphabets.

Might we not draw a similar inference about the Egyptian priests? Again, the system was of course primarily used to transcribe language, and was fully functional in this way. But that was also true of the demotic and other scripts, and if practicality alone were at stake hieroglyphics would have disappeared, especially as scribes became increasingly poor readers of the glyphs (as evidenced by copying mistakes in their artistic renderings).[100] Yet it seems that hieroglyphics meant rather more than they meant. The characters *themselves* meant something, because the *system* meant something. These characters were hardly mere practical instruments: the gods themselves instituted them. Might the Greeks have misreported because they reported accurately? Might they have correctly reported what the Egyptian priests considered most important about their superior because divine writing system?

In that case, Kircher in a sense had it more right than we give him credit for. And to be fair, he was right because his predecessors in various kinds of occult thought had it right as well: the Egyptian system *was* what they described—or at least, the Egyptians may have thought so. What they got wrong, these early modern polymaths, was the difference between what people *say* about their writing and what is linguistically correct about it. But the same could be said of our own discourses about language, in which we take for granted that "obviously" the whole point of a writing system is to

The Occult Mind

transcribe speech, because we have, since well before Plato and with relatively few exceptions since, taken it for granted that this is what writing quite obviously is—because we use alphabets.[101] And just so, we resist strenuously the idea that a writing system can carry meaning outside its linguistic sense, to such a degree that even someone as insistent on Orientalist philological context as Stolzenberg is bemused and amused by the early modern fascination with writing systems—which of course he calls "alphabets."

In meditating on Kircherian themes in this fashion, my concern is not exactly to convince others of the accuracy of his readings or thought. Rather, I wish to open up the field to other ways of examining the issues, other ways of conceptualizing and evaluating his work. In effect, I am trying to explicate in modern theoretical terms a project sufficiently analogous to that of Kircher that it may stand in as akin to translation. Perhaps one might say that this translates Kircher in the same way as he translated Egyptian hieroglyphs. But by this logic, is there any means by which to evaluate the validity of my readings? If by decentering the epistemological certainty of the discourse of translation we make it impossible to dismiss Kircher's translations, if we open the gap so wide that a linguistically correct reading of a hieroglyphic inscription has no superiority over Kircher's fanciful allegories, do we not fall into the very sort of paratruth that Vickers and others decry?

I can only answer, for the moment, by examining Kircher's analyses within the context of classification, as compared to the classificatory discourses that led to encyclopedism and taxonomy in the sciences. By returning to the purely historical, some possibility of understanding may arise.

As noted before, Findlen's wonderful book on early modern museums, *Possessing Nature*, suggests that in the sixteenth century museums and collections focused on totality, on collapsing the world into a small space. In the seventeenth, collecting bifurcated into natural history and science on the one hand and an elite dilettante's hobby on the other. Kircher's position is unclear here; in some respects, this ambivalence with respect to later sciences prompted his posthumous notoriety.

Findlen, like Rossi, situates such collecting primarily within the intellectual trajectory that eventually produced the great *Encyclopédie*, a move she rightly interprets as part of the development of science out of natural philosophy. The emphasis here is on classification, on placing things within a larger, comprehensible framework and thus making them knowable. This sort of work culminates in Linnaean taxonomy, with Goethe's morphology an important follow-up. As the article "Botanique" in the great Enlighten-ment encyclopedia puts it:

> Method gives us an idea of the essential properties of each object which is classified, and presents the relationships and oppositions which exist between the different productions of nature. . . . For the beginner in the study of natural history, method is like a thread which serves to guide them through a complicated labyrinth; for those who are already expert in the science it is a sketch which represents all the facts and helps them remember them if they know them already. . . . A single method is suffi-cient for nomenclature: one must construct a kind of artificial memory for oneself, in order to retain the idea and the name of every plant, be-cause the number of plants is too large to dispense with such an aid to memory; for this purpose any method will suffice.[102]

This Enlightenment connection of labyrinths, memory, and method echoes Kircher, though surely not deliberately. Kircher's museum too was a labyrinth and a memory palace, but the obvious classical precedent came from Herodotus's awed description of a wonder of Ægypt:

> The pyramids . . . are astonishing structures . . . but the labyrinth sur-passes them. It has twelve covered courts—six in a row facing north, six south—the gates of the one range exactly fronting the gates of the other, with a continuous wall round the outside of the whole. Inside, the build-ing is of two storeys and contains three thousand rooms, of which half are underground, and the other half directly above them. I was taken through the rooms in the upper storey. . . . [It] is hard to believe that they are the work of men; the baffling and intricate passages from room to room and from court to court were an endless wonder to me, as we passed from a courtyard into rooms, from rooms into galleries, from gal-leries into more rooms, and thence into yet more courtyards. . . . The walls are covered with carved figures, and each court is exquisitely built of white marble and surrounded by a colonnade. Near the corner where the labyrinth ends is a pyramid, two hundred and forty feet in height, with great carved figures of animals on it and an underground passage by which it can be entered.[103]

Unsurprisingly, Kircher could not resist the impulse to represent this Ægyptian architectural marvel in his *Turris Babel*, providing an elaborate fold-out plan (figure 8). If we consider for a moment the fanciful possibility

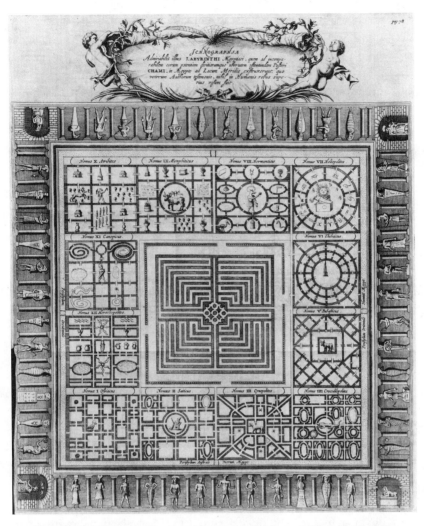

Figure 8. The Egyptian labyrinth. Foldout, page 78, Athanasii Kircheri e Soc. Jesu
Turris Babel, sive Archontologia . . . *Amsterdam: ex officina Janssonio–Waesbergiana,
1679. ƒ GC6 K6323 679t2. Houghton Library, Harvard University.*

that this rendering maps something akin to his method, we note immediately the rigid ordering, the connections between regions kept otherwise discrete, and that the labyrinth classifies and orders by a system of relations:
Heliopolites (VII) is just to the right of Hermonticus (VIII), and so on. But
we also note that the spiral labyrinthine paths in the center are all dead ends.
There is no way in. Once in the center, there is no way out.

By comparison to the *Encyclopédie*'s method, projects like Kircher's indeed appear incoherent. I should stress that Findlen does not read Kircher as entirely incoherent, but she does not see his work as part of the intellectual direction that would have scientific results.[104] But to read Kircher as a precursor to the *comparative* rather than the encyclopedic, and thus in a sense to the humanities rather than the sciences, we need an alternative perspective.

To expand briefly on the difficulty of encyclopedic classification: while particular things have clear positions, their interrelations are difficult to analyze. That an article on *finials* precedes one on *fish* tells us nothing; we should infer no claim from the juxtaposition of a 165–page article on "Anatomy" and the two-line one on "Anatoria" in the first edition of the *Encyclopedia Britannica*.[105] Linnaean taxonomy takes a further step in that the organization is not simply arbitrary as with alphabetization, but even there one must choose an arbitrary principle: Linnaeus chose reproductive organs, but he could just as easily have chosen something else. As noted in chapter 1, Goethe's morphology shifts the principle of organization into the plants and animals, leading to his selection of "leaf" as the ur-principle of plants. But all of this takes for granted that the *historical* status of the objects classified is essentially irrelevant; until Darwin, there simply was no way to discuss the differentiation of plants and animals on a historical basis.[106]

Unlike Goethe, however, Kircher arises from the context of a specifically Catholic humanism of the Republic of Letters, in which the process of situating things and ideas was a matter of rebuilding and restoring the past, of using the historical and the distant to understand the present. Thus Kircher's system, like the *pensées sauvages*, emphasizes differentiation as its core principle.

In effect, Kircher wants to compare different things, not classify similar ones. Although it is interesting and important that Chinese characters arose from Egyptian hieroglyphs, he prefers to discuss how the two systems differ. Thus his interest in wonders is not merely dilettantish fascination with the exotic—although certainly there is some of that!—but an analytic interest in what these exotica reveal about other things. For the pure encyclopedist, such wonders amount to poor data, outside the range of analysis, or at best interesting trivia; for the comparativist Kircher, wonders allow us to understand the mundane. What is most peculiar about this comparative project, however, is the emphasis on diachronic data—and perhaps history.

In a typically erudite article, Anthony Grafton argues that Kircher passes F. Scott Fitzgerald's "test of a first-rate intelligence": he had "the ability to hold two opposed ideas in the mind at the same time, and still retain the

The Occult Mind

ability to function."[107] Demonstrating the point in Kircher's chronological arguments, Grafton shows that:

> At times—as in his spectacularly detailed chapters on the cities of Nimrod and Semiramis in the *Turris Babel*—Kircher wrote as if he could think himself back into the past. A magnificently hyperbolic application of that primeval Jesuit discipline, composition of place, enabled him to rebuild the Tower of Babel and the Hanging Gardens, stone by stone and arch by arch, from the tiny references to them in his sources. The antiquary could raise not just individuals, but cities, from the dead. In these moods, Kircher probably thought—as many other Catholics did—that the longer chronology of the Septuagint could accommodate most of the new history he had discovered.
>
> In other moods, however, Kircher could deny that it was possible to restore the identity of much more recent monuments. . . . A splendid tirade—one directed as much against Kircher's Rome, the city of palaces, as against Nimrod's Babylon—shows the extent of the Jesuit's ability to entertain ideas about the past that were in sharp tension with one another—a skill to conjure with in the seventeenth-century heyday of the paradox. Kircher, who confidently called whole ancient cities back to life, could also feel and express the antiquary's characteristic nostalgia for an irrecoverable past. The master of historical time could evoke time's destructive tooth as eloquently as any epigrapher or numismatist. In these moods, Kircher—like Scaliger—may well have contemplated the mysteries and terrors of deep time.[108]

A more traditional reader than Grafton might have wished to see in this contradiction a development or progression: Kircher might, for example, have begun by accepting entirely the various devious means by which to insert Egyptian dynasties, Babylonian fragments, and so forth into the early years after the Flood, only late in life to find the evidence against this overwhelming. Conversely, one might attempt to read the other way, with a young, rebellious Kircher slowly ossifying into an old conservative. After all, Kircher's many works were often announced at one time, only to appear much later, and thus there is no great difficulty in manipulating Kircher's chronology—the chronology of his publications, that is.

Admirably, Grafton does nothing of the sort. Like Kircher himself, he willingly accepts contradiction. Rather than impose a narrative framework on Kircher, the sort of framework Kircher applied only irregularly to ancient history, Grafton reports the inconsistencies and explicates the debates and sources on which they (rather loosely at times) rest. And unlike many others who have studied Kircher, Grafton does not make a point of denigrating his various efforts, eccentric and unsuccessful though they often are.

Upon a solid scholarly base, what can we build? This is surely Kircher's question, but it also confronts those who read him. If we begin with Grafton, whose mastery of early modern chronological tradition is undisputable, we are left with a contradiction and no way to resolve it. Indeed, Grafton's fidelity to the texts leaves us without the possibility of resolution: the contradiction is there and cannot be annulled. What then?

What has not been asked, I think, is why *Kircher* accepts this situation. Even without recourse to secret histories and occult conspiracies, there can be no question that at times Kircher distorts or suppresses sources quite consciously, for eminently political ends.[109] Chronology—disputes over the Earth's history, today largely moribund outside of the creationism debates and perhaps the bickering about Velikovsky's catastrophe theory—was in Kircher's day a political and religious minefield. Given his eminence and position, he might have argued consistently either one of the positions he in fact argued inconsistently: the Septuagint chronology of some sixty-eight hundred years, or the "deep time" of Scaliger. We can see all sorts of reasons to pick one of these. We can see *that* Kircher thought chronology important, and *why* he thought so. But we simply do not yet understand why he remained so precariously perched on the fence.

I suggest that Kircher faced a similar difficulty to Bruno's. Bruno, as we know, saw that an infinite universe would require a new science, but he was unwilling to accept the latest mathematical tools to formulate it, preferring instead to restructure the art of memory. In a similar vein, Kircher saw that "deep time" would require a new history, or new historicism perhaps, but refused to accept the relentless philological precision of men like Scaliger and opted instead to revitalize the most traditional allegorical methods. How could this make sense as a project?

Eliade argued that Judaism broke the cyclical time of the "archaic ontology," that mode of time in which a New Year's festival could recreate the world ab initio, annulling the past. With such events as the Fall, the Tower of Babel, the Flood, and Moses's reception of the commandments, Judaism created a new type of illud tempus, one to which return was impossible. Christianity, with the Incarnation in historical time, furthered and completed this movement, such that time itself became a manifestation of a modality of the sacred. History became hierophany.[110]

Simplistic though it is, this argument helps us understand Kircher. For him, the chronology is a sacred structure, study of which may reveal the divine plan. And in the context of Kircher's vast collections of all sorts of data, history and time become structuring grids for classification. If Chinese writing has parallels to Egyptian hieroglyphs, this must both fit into the established chronology and also ensure its validity—thus Ham, as Zoroaster, becomes the Sage Emperor Fu Xi.

In an exceedingly complex and little-understood discussion, Lévi-Strauss analyzed this sort of thinking in *La pensée sauvage*. As we have seen continually throughout the present work, diachronic and synchronic data can be correlated, made to have a centered and certain truth value, only when approached from an episteme that prioritizes one over the other. In Lévi-Strauss's analysis, the modern Westerner prioritizes the diachronic and views data historically, while the "savage" prioritizes the synchronic to view data structurally.[111] But Kircher does not fit neatly in either category: he can, in fact, be read in either direction.

As a historian, Kircher emphasizes the chronology as a grid under which to classify his data: Egyptian hieroglyphs come before Chinese characters, the Flood comes before the nations, and so on. The interconnections among these data do not especially interest him, however: unlike most historians, he mentions influence mainly to classify, not for analysis. This differential, expansive history refuses the most basic reductions of data to systematicity and transformation. In fact, he proposes various causal links indifferently, as though unconcerned by the processes by which one item transforms over time into another. Here the historical operates as though prioritizing synchrony.

As a structuring thinker, a practitioner of *la pensée sauvage*, Kircher classifies differentially and uses the very ability to classify as a demonstration of the validity of structure, absorbing event and thus annulling history. Yet in doing so, he oddly fits Eliade's model: the structure in question is time, regained by the system as sacred chronology. This is structure prioritizing diachrony.

If Kircher had succeeded, he would have achieved a perspective on chronology that both respected historical development and change and, at the same time, validated the literal Biblical narrative by explicating disparate data as mutual transformations. The difficulty—apart from logical impossibility—was that either system must project an exterior center toward which truth may point. In "savage thought" that exteriority is nature (including time), against and from which cultural systems may be reconstructed endlessly. In the *ingénieur*'s historical or scientific approach, it is the intrinsic structures of nature's exteriority, its not-humanness, that attract attention: one attempts to achieve purely human, present ends by differential borrowing—a borrowing that never permits identification—from nature and time, while by precise inversion the other seeks clearer knowledge of nature or time without respect to present human ends. Where the scientist or historian enforces separation between observer and observed in order to use either one to structure the other, the "savage" bricoleur collapses the distinction to legitimate self-construction.

But where is the exterior of Kircher's chronology? It is the chronology itself—and therein lies the problem. The structures against which Kircher-bricoleur manipulates diachronic data are the very systems he wishes to legitimate: it is as if the shaman were to recite a cosmogonic origin of disease not to cure the sick but to prove that disease exists. Conversely, the historical and natural data that Kircher-*ingénieur* interrogates for higher principles and purposes are already the ends he seeks—as though the scientist performed endless expensive experiments in hopes of never finding the slightest imperfection in an established model.

I suggest that Kircher sought a purely differential system that would nevertheless satisfy his historical sensibilities. In essence, he hoped to find a way of resorbing history into structure, conceived as *ars magna sciendi*, such that time would become a classifying axis rather than a transformative one. What Lévi-Strauss sometimes (following Saussure) calls the "axis of successions" would then be compressed into the total system.[112] Kircher's difficulty, however, was that by projecting his anchors of certitude *in* time rather than *out* of it, he made impossible any intrinsic validation of what he had found. His system, unlike *la pensée sauvage*, rapidly became relative or even relativistic: depending on one's position within the axis of time, the total system necessarily altered. Deprived of an absolute grounding for his synchrony, he fell continually into diachrony without achieving history.

For the two must always be kept distinct. Diachrony is only time, another factor to be manipulated, classified, interpreted. But history is the formulation of meaning as occurring diachronically. And within a synchronic differential system, diachrony that cannot be absorbed manifests as crisis. The only way to overcome this crisis is then to deny it, to refer outside of time to a total system in which certain knowledge has always been achieved. This Ægypt, for Kircher, because it was already lost, provided infinite opportunity for reflection, but none for resolution.

Coming full circle, to Smith and Ginzburg, we face a considerable embarrassment. On the one hand, we have through Bruno and Kircher seen why the project of a methodology at once morphological and historical remains so refractory. On the other, we have also seen validation for the desire to formulate it. All these thinkers seek a kind of total knowledge, a way to think without center or play, a way to overcome the distance between ourselves and Ægypt without in that very gesture annulling all that makes her mystery compelling.

In my various examinations of the problem, I have relied ever more on Lévi-Strauss for guidance. But Smith's criticism quoted at the outset remains trenchant: "The morphological and the historical [should be seen] as two ways of interpreting the *same* data analogous to synchrony and diachrony in Saussure's formulation (unlike Lévi-Strauss, who all but mythologizes them as opposing forces)." The difficulty lies in the analogy: In what sense are morphology or structural analysis and history *analogous* to synchrony and diachrony? Indeed, the problem of occult analogy that has concerned us throughout this chapter, and implicitly in much of the present book, remains deeply entwined in the very heart of Lévi-Strauss's own work. To extricate ourselves from the magic circle he has drawn will require an act of magic.

Before interpretation of any fall could be considered, . . . they must decide
how the cards themselves must at this moment be construed. "You can think
of them as a story, and then you must find the beginning, middle, and end; or
a sentence, and you must parse it; or a piece of music, and you must find the
tonic and signature; or anything at all that has parts and makes sense."

John Crowley, *Little, Big*

Athanasius Kircher's Ægypt did not last. The discovery of the Rosetta
Stone in 1799 transformed perceptions of hieroglyphics, and with Champollion's decipherment in 1822 arose the new discipline of Egyptology. To judge
from the wealth of publications on the subject, the story of this decryption
continues to fascinate readers, who are instructed to see in it another triumph of science and reason over superstition and ignorance. Indeed, the advent of Egyptology expunged most occult speculation on Ægypt from re-
spectable discourse. Not coincidentally, the nineteenth century saw a deep
divide between scholarly and occult Egypts, a division we might properly
read as between Egypt and Ægypt. Despite the rise of Egyptology, this division liberated Ægypt: no longer required to justify their claims to skeptics,
occultists could indulge in Ægyptian fantasies that Kircher would have
found laughable. One of the most enduring such fantasies, second only to
speculations on the occult geometry of the Great Pyramid, is that tarot cards
are divinatory objects encapsulating high Ægyptian wisdom.

Tarot has extraordinary prominence as an occult symbol. The card images appear regularly on film and television, decks executed in a wide range
of artistic styles may be purchased in mainstream bookstores, and professional cartomancers abound. It will come as no surprise that Tarot cards do
not come from Egypt; rather less known is that the cards were not originally
used for divination at all but for a trick-taking card game akin to bridge. It is
an extraordinary situation: the scholarly skeptic "knows better" than to believe in the fabulous antiquity of these occult objects, but at the same time he
or she has come to accept them *as* occult objects. Even more strikingly, the
claim is recent, arising during a gathering of courtly hangers-on in late
eighteenth-century Paris.[1]

At this party, the hostess, "Madame la C. d'H. who came from Germany or Switzerland," brings out a deck of tarot cards, intending to play the game associated with them, which has become fashionable in the last year. Suddenly, one of the court's odder polymaths grabs the deck and recognizes in them a book of ancient Egyptian wisdom. He quickly publishes his results, and furthermore finds a like-minded nobleman who believes the cards were used for divination. Within the space of at most two years, a fairly ordinary deck of playing cards has been transformed into an occult object.

Just over fifty years later, Eliphas Lévi (1810–75) interprets the twenty-two trump cards as a series of hieroglyphs parallel to the twenty-two letters of the Hebrew alphabet, affording a means to restore Kabbalistic speculation to European occultism without having to consider its Jewish roots. For Lévi, as for perhaps the majority of occultists since the late nineteenth century, tarot is thus a magical analytical system without specific cultural baggage, without ordinary history; by referring the deck to Ægypt, occultists read whatever history or imagery they like into the cards. By the late twentieth century, only a few specialists know that tarot was not always used for occult purposes, though the ordinary skeptic likely scoffs at claims made about their efficacy and extreme antiquity.

To make sense of occult tarot, we must understand that its claims to antiquity, like its actual historical origins, are in a sense irrelevant. The process of visionary discovery by occult thinkers amounts to a reinvention, a re-creation of tarot as an object out of time, a self-enclosed, hermetic collection.[2] Insofar as the cards have origins, they must refer to a time outside history, to Ægypt. From this perspective, tarot reading represents an abstract mode of symbolic thinking, founded on an arbitrary cluster of signs. To read this mode of divination, then, we must compare tarot to an equally abstract and combinatorial semiotics.

In his landmark 1955 essay "The Structural Study of Myth," Lévi-Strauss briefly proposes cartomancy as a metaphor for myth, though he apparently discarded this parallel very quickly:

The other comparison is somewhat different. Let us take an observer ignorant of our playing cards, sitting for a long time with a fortune-teller. He would know something of the visitors: sex, age, physical appearance, social situation, etc. . . . He would also listen to the séances and record them so as to be able to go over them and make comparisons. . . . Mathematicians to whom I have put the problem agree that if the man is bright and if the material available to him is sufficient, he may be able to reconstruct the nature of the deck of cards being used, that is, fifty-two or thirty-two cards according to the case, made up of four homologous sets consisting of the same units (the individual cards) with only one varying feature, the suit.[3]

Lévi-Strauss's mythographic method developed over the course of his career, culminating in the four-volume masterpiece *Mythologiques*, and on numerous occasions Lévi-Strauss has suggested that all these works represent pieces of a single, continuous development.[4] In support of this, we not only find the methods constant but that even the metaphors—apart from cards—continue to grow through sixteen years of work. In particular, his methodological meditations harp on artistic productions, including painting and poetry, but most especially music, which haunts the entirety of *Mythologiques*, from "Overture" to "Finale," by way of "Bororo Song," "Well-Tempered Astronomy," and "The Harmony of the Spheres."

Oddly enough, there have to my knowledge been few serious attempts to make sense of the musical metaphor in Lévi-Strauss, and none readily accessible to scholars who are not musically trained. Perhaps the complexity and technical nature of music theory has daunted previous scholars; more likely, few readers have taken the metaphor very seriously, reading it simply as a literary structuring device. Some have analyzed his mathematical ideas more carefully, although he himself downplays the importance of mathematics to *Mythologiques*. Yet careful examination of Lévi-Strauss's musical thought reveals a good deal more about his methods than one might expect, and also clarifies some of their weaknesses.[5] As an alternate point of entry, then, let us continue exploring the magical theory of tarot cards through a comparison to Lévi-Strauss's musical composition.

We must first distinguish playing cards in general from tarot cards in particular.[6] The tarot deck is divided into two main groups: fifty-six suited cards and twenty-two trumps, commonly known to occultists as Minor and Major arcana, respectively. The suited cards are essentially equivalent to the Anglo-American deck of fifty-two, but have four face cards rather than three: Page, Knight, Queen, and King. There are four suits, with somewhat varying names: swords (Ital. *spade*, modern ♠); rods or wands (Ital. *bastoni*, modern ♣); cups (Ital. *coppe*, modern ♥); coins or pentacles (Ital. *denari*, modern ♦). The trumps are the distinctive mark of tarot packs: twenty-two unsuited cards, bearing unique images and names. They are first mentioned sometime between 1440 and 1457, the latter certainly a reference to tarot as such; it is now agreed that *tarocchi* were invented in connection with the court of Filippo Maria Visconti, duke of Milan.[7] The names of the first trumps were not written on the cards, but the order and imagery have remained relatively constant since the fifteenth century.[8]

The following chart shows the card names and numbers for three decks, spanning several centuries. The "archetypal" tarot is a standard or usual deck derived from the surviving fifteenth- and sixteenth-century decks, particularly Italian ones. The *Sermones* is an account of games that includes a brief description of the cards from the fifteenth century. In the last column I give A. E. Waite's version of the deck, which has become essentially standard in English and American neo-pagan tarot use. Waite switches Strength and Justice for occult structural reasons, and thus this reversal has become usual in modern occult decks; tarot decks deriving from Aleister Crowley's Thoth deck are the most common ones that retain the older order.[9]

"Archetypal" Tarot	*Sermones de Ludo Cum Aliis*	Rider-Waite Tarot
the Fool	22 El matto	0 the Fool
I the Mountebank	1 El bagatella	I the Magician
II the Popess	2 Imperatrix	II the High Priestess
III the Empress	3 Imperator	III the Empress
IV the Emperor	4 La Papessa	IV the Emperor
V the Pope	5 El papa	V the Hierophant
VI Love	6 La temperentia	VI the Lovers
VII the Chariot	7 L'amore	VII the Chariot
VIII Justice	8 Lo caro triumphale	VIII Strength/Justice
IX the Hermit	9 La forteza	IX the Hermit
X the Wheel of Fortune	10 La rotta	X the Wheel of Fortune
XI Fortitude or Strength	11 El gobbo	XI Justice/Strength
XII the Hanged Man	12 Lo impichato	XII the Hanged Man
XIII Death	13 La morte	XIII Death
XIV Temperance	14 El diavolo	XIV Temperance
XV the Devil	15 La sagitta	XV the Devil
XVI the Tower	16 La stella	XVI the Tower
XVII the Star	17 La luna	XVII the Star
XVIII the Moon	18 El sole	XVIII the Moon
XIX the Sun	19 Lo angelo	XIX the Sun
XX the Angel or Judgement	20 La iusticia	XX Judgement
XXI the World	21 El mondo	XXI the World

Figure 9. (left) The Hermit. Giuseppe Maria Mitelli. Bologna, c. 1690. Gioco di Carte di Tarocchini. *121 x 57 mm. Single figure. Engraving.* Back *turned over, standing figure:* All Aquila. *Square borders, square corners. ITA 16, Cary Collection of Playing Cards, Beinecke Rare Book and Manuscript Library, Yale University.*

Figure 10. (right) The Hermit. B. P. Grimaud, Chartier, Marteau and Boudin, 54 rue de Lancry, Paris, c. 1910. Tarot Italien. *119 x 62 mm. Single figure. Color lithography, surface polished.* Back *brown. Square borders, round corners, gilt edge. FRA 159, Cary Collection of Playing Cards, Beinecke Rare Book and Manuscript Library, Yale University.*

To demonstrate continuity and consistency across five centuries of tarot, we may note a few points with regard to symbolism. Choosing a card more or less at random, card IX (the Old Man, the Hermit, and so forth) shows a Diogenes-like figure carrying a lamp. In the earliest cards, the figure is an old man, often a hunchback (Ital. *gobbo*), carrying an hourglass and likely represents time (see figure 9). Quite early, with the Marseilles tarot especially, the

The Occult Mind

glass becomes a lamp, and the meaning shifts toward wisdom (see figure 10).[10] Such slight iconographic shifts are typical of the cards' history; examination of the many decks pictured in Kaplan's four-volume encyclopedia reveals considerable consistency, such that one can speak of a "standard" tarot deck, of which the Marseilles design is fairly representative. Significantly, the cards are single headed, as was usual for all playing cards until the late nineteenth century; in an occult context, the trumps have an *orientation*: they can be right side up or "reversed."

As noted before, the historical record reveals no occult associations to the tarot deck before the late eighteenth century. Not that *cartomancy* did not exist earlier, though it is unclear whether the practice extended back much before the late seventeenth century, but tarot as an occult device has an absolute origin, a moment of creative interpretation.[11]

Tarot as an occult system begins with Antoine Court de Gébelin (1725–84), a Protestant pastor and royal censor much involved with French "speculative" Freemasonry, which movement produced such notables as Cagliostro and the Comte de Saint-Germain.[12] In volume eight (1781) of his work *Le Monde Primitif*, Court de Gébelin suggests that the tarot trumps are actually a surviving work of ancient Egyptian provenance.

> If it were announced that there still existed in our times a Work of the ancient Egyptians, that one of their Books escaped from the flames which devoured their superb Libraries, which contained their purest doctrine on interesting subjects, everyone would, undoubtedly, be anxious to read a Book so precious, so extraordinary. If it were added that this Book were widespread in a great part of Europe, that for many centuries it had been in the hands of everyone, the surprise would certainly increase: would it not peak, if we were assured that no one had suspected it was Egyptian, that it was treated as though of no value, that no one had ever tried to decipher a page: that the fruit of an exquisite wisdom were regarded as a heap of extravagant figures which signified nothing in themselves? Would we not think that it was a joke, playing upon the credulity of the Listeners?[13]

Although this passage is quoted repeatedly in the few scholarly works on tarot (and a few less scholarly ones), the context rarely receives attention, probably because *Le Monde Primitif* is an unwieldy nine volumes of wild speculation on the ancient origins of mankind. Rather than range broadly in the forest of tarot literature, then, let us instead examine these earliest claims closely.

Le Monde Primitif is a fascinating, largely forgotten ancestor of the comparative history of religion, in which the author attempts to reconstruct the ancient golden age through comparative philology and mythology. Court de Gébelin's guiding principles are simple enough: everything is imitation, that is, interpretable "allegorically";[14] and every aspect of the primitive world lies hidden within our own and can be drawn out by comparative analysis: "One need only know well the things of today in order to know those of all the ages: the physical and moral constructions [*séries*] are necessary in themselves; they are before our eyes, under our hands."[15]

The majority of the nine volumes consists of speculations on the ancient language, spoken and written. The principles here are Cratylian, insisting upon the essential referentiality of language, in unusual and fascinating ways: "natural languages are merely dialects of one single language," and "the prevailing differences between natural languages do not prevent us from recognizing that they have the same origin."

> We have said, and it cannot be repeated enough: speech is nothing but a painting of our ideas, a painting of objects we know; therefore, a necessary relationship must exist between words and the ideas they present, as one exists between ideas and their objects. Indeed, the act of painting cannot possibly be arbitrary; it is always determined by the nature of the object to be painted. In order to designate an object or an idea, men were thus forced to choose the sound most analogous to that object, to that idea.[16]

Volume 8 considers "diverse *Objects* concerning History, Heraldry, Coinage, Games, the Voyages of the Phoenicians around the World, the *American Languages*, &c.," and here occult tarot has its inaugural moment: two essays, one by Court de Gébelin, the other by "M. le Comte de M***," that is, Louis-Raphaël-Lucrèce de Fayolle, count of Mellet (1727–1804).[17]

Court de Gébelin's essay begins with the famous passage quoted above, and goes on to analyze "this Egyptian Book" in some detail. His analytical principles are, as usual, allegorical:

> The 22 Trumps show in general the temporal and spiritual Leaders of Society, the Physical Leaders of Agriculture, the Cardinal Virtues, Marriage, Death, and resurrection or creation: the diverse plays of fortune, the Sage and the Fool, Time which consumes all, etc. One should thus understand in advance that all these Cards are Tableaux as much allegorically relevant to the entirety of life, and susceptible to an infinity of combinations. We

shall examine them one by one, and strive to decipher the particular allegory or the enigma which each of them encloses.[18]

Rather than list all the cards and his glosses on them, I give one example that shows how this first essay on the occult tarot works. Cards XI (Strength), XIII (Temperance), VIII (Justice), and XII (Hanged Man) are referred to the four cardinal virtues, the last of these as follows:

No. XII. *Prudence* is one of the four Cardinal Virtues: could the Egyptians have forgotten it in their painting of Human Life? Nevertheless one does not find it in this Game. One sees in its place under the number XII, between Strength and Temperance, a man suspended by his feet: but what is this hanged man doing? it is the work of a wretched presumptuous Card-maker who, not understanding the beauty of the allegory hidden under this tableau, took it upon himself to correct it, and by the same token entirely disfigured it.

Prudence could not be shown in a manner perceptible to the eyes except as a man upright, with one foot planted [on the ground], advancing the other, and holding it suspended while examining what place he can plant it securely. The title of this card was thus the man with a foot suspended, *pede suspenso*: the Card-maker, not knowing what that meant, made of it a man suspended by a foot.

Then one might ask, why a hanged man in this Game? and one would not lack a response, for it would be the just punishment for the Inventor of the Game, for having shown a Popess.[19]

But placed among Strength, Temperance and Justice, who does not see that it is Prudence which was wanted and which it must have represented originally?[20]

The four suits refer to the "four Estates into which the Egyptians were divided," with swords for the military rulership, cups the priesthood, rods (because of an association with Hercules) agriculture, and coins the merchants.[21] The structure of the deck depends on the "sacred number seven," as shown in the fourteen (2x7) cards per suit, the twenty-one (3x7) trumps (not including the Fool, number 0), the seventy-seven cards in the whole deck, and so forth. We learn further that the word *tarot* "is composed of the word *Tar*, which means way, road; and the word *Ro, Ros, Rog*, which means King [*roi*], Royal. Thus, word by word, the Royal road of life"; that the twenty-two trumps correspond to "the XXII Letters of the Egyptian Alphabet common to the Hebrews and the Orientals, and which served also as numbers"; that noble tourneys or quadrilles were based on tarot symbolism; and other interesting facts of this kind. The essay ends with a polite introduction to de Mellet's essay, "in which the author proves how the Egyptians applied this Game to the art of divination, and in what manner this same point of view was transmitted to our playing Cards made in imitation of them."[22] Note that Court de Gébelin himself does not discuss tarot in the context of divination.

De Mellet disagrees mildly with Court de Gébelin about a few points in the history and meaning of tarot, but not about essentials. He agrees, for example, that the deck is an ancient Egyptian work of moral and religious importance, but he explains the etymology as from T-A-Rosh: "*A*, Doctrine, Science; and *Rosch* [*sic*], Mercury, which, joined with the article *T*, signifies Tableau of the Doctrine of Mercury; but as Rosh also means *Beginning*, this word Ta-Rosh was particularly consecrated to his Cosmogony."[23] On the assumption that the Egyptians read right to left, he sets the first card of the trumps as XXI and counts downward, subdividing the deck into three groups of seven cards each referable to one of the ages of the world: thus XXI to XV is the Golden Age, XIV to VIII the Silver Age, and VII to I the Iron or Bronze age. The Fool, number 0, is "without a number and without force . . . ; it is the zero of magic calculations."[24]

The entire series is understood as a set of hieroglyphs, "which placed in their natural order retrace the History of the first times, but they are also so many letters which, combined differently, can make up so many sentences."[25] Such combination—the practice of divination with the tarot—consists of a random drawing of such "letters" to make up an oracular sentence, as follows:

Let us suppose that there are two men who want to consult the Fates, one having the twenty-two letters, the other the four suits, and that after having shuffled the characters, and given the packs to each other to cut, they begin to count together up to fourteen, taking out the tableaux and the cards face-up so as not to see the backs; when they arrive at a card in its proper rank, that is to say, which bears the number called, it must be put aside with the number of the letter [the Trump] drawn at the same time, which will be placed below it: the one who has the tableaux places there this same letter, because the book of Destiny must always be complete, and one cannot have, in any case, incomplete sentences; then he reshuffles and gives the pack again to cut. Then they continue three times through the cards with the same procedures; and then this operation is

The Occult Mind

complete; it only works by reading the numbers which express the letters drawn. The good or ill fortune which each presages, must be calculated from what each card means and what card it corresponds to, similarly their force in greater or lesser measure is determined by the number of this same card, multiplied by that which characterizes the letter. And here is why the Fool produces nothing, is without number: it is, as we have said, the zero of this calculation.[26]

De Mellet proposes that such divination was performed, among the Egyptians, by two special priests: a Jannes, or Explainer, and a Mambres, or Permutator, who kept careful records of "their interpretations, their discoveries, their miracles" such that "their Memoirs formed a body of Science and Doctrine, where the Priests could read physical and moral learning." These diviners also served as counselors to the pharaohs, and "one of the functions of the Magi was to explicate dreams."[27] As an example of interpretation by means of tarot cards, de Mellet imagines an Egyptian priest called to interpret the famous dream of Pharaoh in the Genesis story of Joseph, that is, the seven fat cows devoured by seven thin ones (Gen. 41:17–32). The cards drawn, on the two lines, are:

| Ace of Rods | King of Rods | Knight of Rods | :: | 2 of Rods | 5 of Rods |
| XIX Sun | X Fortune | 0 Fool | :: | XV Typhon | XIII Death |

In the first section, the suited cards add up to seven: ace (=1) plus king (=4) plus knight (=2). Thus "the Sign of Agriculture [i.e., rods] gives seven." "The Sun announces happiness"; "Fortune (preceded by a fortunate card) the same"; and "The Fool or zero puts the Sun into hundreds. . . . One thus reads, seven years of fortunate agriculture will give an abundance one hundred times greater than it has ever been. The second part of this sentence, closed by the two and the five of rods, also gives the number seven which, combined with Typhon and Death, announces seven years of drought, famine and the evils which follow."[28]

De Mellet further glosses each of the trumps in this reading with Hebrew letters, each of which has a meaning. We then learn that bibliomancy was "envisioned as a sort of antidote to the Egyptian Divination by the Book of Destiny," i.e. the tarot, and the essay concludes with a discussion of the meanings that modern fortune-tellers assign to the cards of a piquet pack.[29]

Interpretation of tarot here rests on the same allegorical principle as *Le Monde Primitif* in general. A fixed number of elements are understood as both allegorical tableaux and pieces of a larger allegory. These elements can be recombined in various ways according to rules, albeit not very clearly stated ones. Tarot divination is an interpretive and creative endeavor, requiring the diviner to construct a new allegory out of the various elements and their intersections, which allegory serves as an explanation of some stated problem, dream, or myth.

⣿

Structural analysis of myth rests on the simultaneous distinction and correlation of two axes, synchronic and diachronic. In his original formulation, "The Structural Study of Myth," Lévi-Strauss suggested that a single myth be laid out in a chart of several lines, such that each vertical column represents a single repeating element synchronically, while the horizontal rows represent the plot of the myth as a series of elements in chronological (diachronic) order.[30] In "Structure and Dialectics," he proposed that several myths might serve as the horizontal rows, even if those myths should be geographically disparate. This all comes to fruition in *The Raw and the Cooked*, volume 1 of *Mythologiques*, which in effect aligns hundreds of myths in a vast table of transformations and correspondences.

In the "Overture" to *The Raw and the Cooked*, the relation between synchrony and diachrony is described as a "discontinuity" between the "natural" relational meanings of elements and their meanings within the diachronic context of any given myth.[31] Here the musical metaphor becomes particularly powerful. Where in "The Structural Study" Lévi-Strauss had compared the vertical, synchronic dimension to the relationships among multiple instrumental parts in an orchestral score, he now suggests that this dimension is akin to a musical scale.

This shift means more and less than it seems to. At least in *Mythologiques*, Lévi-Strauss intends both analogies simultaneously. For him, every note in a score has a natural significance in at least two senses. First, in a scale, each note has a significance with respect to the harmonics of that scale. If the work is written in C major, a G has the specific meaning of being a fifth above the C; since a fifth is a strongly consonant interval, as can be demonstrated mathematically or with an oscilloscope, it is exceptionally easy to shift keys temporarily from C major to G major, and for this reason the fifth above the *tonic* (here C) is known as the *dominant* in music theory. By way of contrast, F♯, a half-step lower than G, is strongly dissonant with C, related by an interval called a *tritone*. To give a well-known example, in the song "Maria" from *West Side Story*, the repeated notes sung on the syllables "Ma-ri-a" and "I've just met" are a tonic, tritone, and dominant, equivalent to C,

F♯, G. In this melody, the first interval seems incomplete, because of its strong dissonance, but it is completed or *resolved* by the move to the strong consonance of the third note. With regard to structuralism, the point is that it does not really matter whether the notes in question are C, F♯, G or D, G♯, A: in both cases the intervals are the same, and it is the *intervals*, the *relative* meanings of the notes that carry harmonic meaning.

The second "natural" significance refers to notes as played by particular instruments. While an A on a piano and a violin may be tuned to the same number of cycles (now commonly 440 Hz), one could hardly mistake one for the other—they have distinctive timbres arising from the instruments' physical constructions. From a structuralist perspective, it is also essential that the "meanings" of these particular instrumental sounds again arise from relations. That is, the sound of a violin has in itself no particular meaning, but the relationship between violin and cello (both strings) is quite different from that between violin and trumpet (string and brass). Furthermore, particular instrumental sounds have historical associations of genre; for example, we associate saxophones with jazz, electric guitars with rock, and violas with so-called classical music.

A similar relationship among meaning-types occurs in tarot as described in *Le Monde Primitif*. To begin with, de Mellet provides a structure of the deck that may serve as the key myth, the starting point for constructing a brief structural breakdown of tarot divination:

Each of the lines refers to an age, such that we can understand them as shorter variant myths: M_2, the Golden Age, XXI–XV; M_3, the Silver Age, XIV–VIII; and M_4, the Bronze/Iron Age, VII–I.

In order to clarify the synchronic structuring here, note that within each of these three variants, at least one fixed grouping cannot be separated. In M_2, the three specific creations (XIX–XVII) are a set; in M_3, the initial instruction (XIV–XIII) is a kind of two-part phrase, as is the final pairing IX–VIII; and in M_4, the two rulers IV–III are not distinguished, and the final two consequences of the Iron Age fall (II–I) appear to form some sort of set, although it is not clear how strongly. By examining these three myths in parallel, we know that the synchronic, vertical dimension remains constant throughout the variants. Thus each of M_{2-4} has a tripartite clustering:

A-B: Preconditions of the Age; C-D-E: Ruling aspects of the Age; F-G: Consequences

Comparing this construction to an alternate mythology of tarot, that of Court de Gébelin himself, de Mellet's series runs from XXI to I while Court

M₁: The History of the World

M₂

XXI: Universe	XX: Creation	XIX: Sun	XVIII: Moon	XVII: Star	XVI: Tower	XV: Devil
Isis in an egg; four seasons	Osiris speaks world into being	Creation of the Sun and man and woman	Creation of the Moon and the animals	Creation of the stars and the fishes	Fall of/from paradise, the house of God	Descent into the rule of evil

M₃

XIV: Temperance	XIII: Death	XII: Prudence	XI: Strength	X: Wheel	IX: Hermit	VIII: Justice
Comes to instruct man how to avoid →	To which man is newly subject	Required to avoid mishaps	Required to overcome savagery	Injustice of fortune; virtue alone succeeds	Wanders the earth seeking →	Justice

M₄

VII: Chariot	VI: Love	V: Jupiter	IV: King	III: Queen	II: Juno	I: Mountebank
War, combat, strife, crime	Wavering between vice and virtue; lust	Creates kings in his anger	Insatiable desire to rule	Same as IV?	Arrogance of the mighty; invention of idolatry	Trickery and deception of the credulous

de Gébelin moves in the opposite direction: "One has thus the two methods: ours [Court de Gébelin's] is easier when one wishes to consider the Cards only in themselves: and the other, useful for conceiving better the totality and the relations [between cards]."[32] The interrelations discovered in de Mellet are thus primarily diachronic, those in Court de Gébelin synchronic.

In Court de Gébelin's allegory, cards o (Fool) and I (Magician/Mountebank) are a pair, establishing the defining dialectic of folly: o is the fool, I he who fools. The foursome II–V divide in two ways: "they are the temporal and spiritual Heads of Society," male and female, temporal and spiritual; "numbers II and III show two women: numbers IV and V, their husbands," at the same time as the pair II–V is priestly and III–IV is temporal. For reasons not immediately clear, cards VI and VII are presented in reverse order: VII is Osiris Triumphant, VI is Marriage; Court de Gébelin posits no direct connection between them, but says that VII suggests a divine eternal return and VI the "constant fidelity" of true love. Next come the four cardinal virtues: XI (Strength), XIV (Temperance), VIII (Justice), XII (Prudence). IX (Hermit or Sage), XIX (Sun), XVIII (Moon), and XVII (Dog-Star/Isis/Star) form another foursome, this time "all the tableaux relevant to light: thus after the dark-lantern of the Hermit, we will review the Sun, the Moon and the brilliant Sirius or flashing Dog-Star." The next four are XIII (Death), XV (Typhon), XVI (House of God), and X (Wheel of Fortune), all related to misfortune or destruction. Finally comes a pair, XX (Creation) and XXI (Time/Universe).[33] Thus, we have a second synchronic classification of cards.

	0–I	II–III/IV–V *or* II–V/III–IV	VII–VI	XI–XIV–VIII–XII	IX–XIX–XVIII–XVII	XIII–XV–XVI–X	XX–XXI
M_5	folly	Temporal/spiritual; male/female	Return/constancy	Virtues	Lights	Destruction	Creation

One could continue such analysis for some time. We have barely begun a *Mythologiques* of tarot, since we have as yet only used two extremely closely related sources, neither bringing in the now-standard issue of orientation, that is, whether a card is right side up or reversed. The structuralist flights this would engender are perhaps all too obvious—reversal, inversion, and so forth. Similarly, we have not considered the issue of the *gematria* values of Hebrew letters as calqued on tarot cards, such that I–IX are ones, X–XVIII tens, and XIX–XXI hundreds. And where does the Fool (o) come in? Court de Gébelin more or less leaves it to one side, while de Mellet considers it "the zero of magical calculations." With Eliphas Lévi, however, the Fool becomes central, largely because he places it between XX and XXI, as ש (*šin*), the twenty-first letter of the Hebrew alphabet and one of the three mother letters of the *Sefer Yetsirah*.[34]

Even without fuller analysis, however, it should already be clear that a structuralist analysis of tarot is, in a sense, pointless. Such analysis merely reveals tarot as itself an analytical mode, a kind of simplistic and overdetermined structuralism, and the attempt to analyze it through what amounts to a variant of itself leads into a methodological hall of mirrors.

At the same time, the continual reflections that this analysis prompts have value for further understanding of Lévi-Strauss. In the next section, then, I shall examine the musical metaphor so central to his work—interestingly an analogy present in other volumes of *Le Monde Primitif*. In other words, using music as a conceptual bridge, I shall attempt a tarot reading of Lévi-Strauss.

⁙

I have already briefly discussed the phenomenon of tonal intervals and scales in the context of Lévi-Strauss's reference to the "natural" or "objective" foundation to the synchronic relations within myth and music. This issue lies at the heart of his musical metaphor and serves as the basis of an important critique of Arnold Schoenberg and serialist music. Although a full understanding of the music-myth relation in Lévi-Strauss's work must await a much longer article drawing on musical semiology, I shall make use of this critique to explicate some central principles.

In the preceding discussion, I remarked that the perfect fifth interval, as between C–G or D–A, exists regardless of the notes involved, since it is a pure relation; as Lévi-Strauss is well aware, however, this is not strictly speaking true.[35] Imagine a string vibrating at 440 Hz (A). If I now pinch the string exactly in the center, the two halves will each vibrate at 880 Hz and sound a note exactly one octave above the previous note (A'); the relationship of the perfect octave is thus produced by a 2:1 ratio of string lengths. A perfect fifth (A–E, C–G, and so on) is precisely the same, except that the ratio of string length is now 3:2, and for a perfect fourth (A–D, C–F) it is 4:3. Returning to the fifth for simplicity's sake, and supposing we hear a chord of a C and a G tuned exactly as described here, they will be perfectly in tune; if the ratio is just a hair off, however, the listener will hear "beats" in the sound—slight, regular pulses in sound intensity caused by the overlap of sound waves. By listening for these beats and tuning carefully, we can eliminate the beats and thus produce an acoustically perfect fifth.

Now suppose we create a scale based on this perfect interval: this is the Pythagorean scale, described in Plato's *Timaeus*. Begin at C, go up one fifth to G, up one fifth to D and so forth. Going down from C, we reach F, then B♭, and so on. At the far ends, we reach A♭ on the low end and G♯ on the high, and—as everyone with any musical experience knows—these two notes are the same.

Unfortunately, they are *not* the same: they differ by 23.5 cents, about one-quarter of a semitone (the distance between, say, C and C♯); this interval is known as the Pythagorean comma. Put simply, in a scale constructed this way, the resulting A♭ and G♯ are badly out of tune.

One way of resolving this problem is to divide the comma across all twelve notes to compress (diminish) all the intervals between notes by about 2 cents, just enough that the resulting endpoints will be equivalent. This system, known as *equal temperament*, has a serious disadvantage for close harmony, however, in that *every* interval will produce the "beat" effect already mentioned. In addition, prior to the advent of accurate pocket tuning devices, it was exceedingly difficult to tune every note just that requisite hair off, equally. Certainly the most famous solution to the problem is the *well-tempered* scale, one of a number of systems that distribute the Pythagorean comma unequally, such that less obvious intervals are less acoustically pure and the most essential intervals can be perfect. As is well known, J. S. Bach wrote a series of short works for this scale, under the title *The Well-Tempered Clavier*.[36]

All this may seem remote from Lévi-Strauss, but it is central to his comments on serialism:

> Contemporary musical thought . . . rejects the hypothesis of the existence of some natural foundation that would objectively justify the stipulated system of relations among the notes of the scale. According to Schönberg's significant formula, these notes are to be defined solely by "the total system of relations of the sounds with one another." However, the lessons of structural linguistics should make it possible to overcome [this claim].[37]

He continues:

> The serial approach, by taking to its logical conclusion that whittling down of the individual particularities of tones, which begins with the adoption of the tempered scale, seems to tolerate only a very slight degree

of organization of the tones. It is as if one were trying . . . to destroy a simple organization, partly imposed from without . . . to leave the field open for a much more supple and complex, yet declared code. . . . In serial music, according to [Pierre Boulez], "there is no longer any preconceived scale or preconceived forms—that is, general structures into which a particular variety of musical thought can be inserted." . . . [In effect the serialists] are trying to construct a system of signs on a single level of articulation.[38]

Let us be clear. Lévi-Strauss objects mildly to a tempered scale, by which he likely means equal temperament, because it eliminates the "individual particularities" of tones. By making the relations among notes identical, this form of temperament permits a "supple and complex" harmony, but at the same time it substitutes a formal element for a natural one. When the trajectory that begins with scale tempering reaches its conclusion in Schoenberg and serialism, the entirety of natural relations has been replaced by formal constructions, and there is thus no natural meaning or character to any interval or note. In Lévi-Strauss's view, this attacks the synchronic dimension of music. Before, music modulated the relation between harmony and rhythm, between synchrony and diachrony; in serialism, harmony itself is undermined, leaving only temporal relations:

> [The serialists] maintain [that] they still have two levels. We have had in the past the ages of monody and polyphony; serial music is to be understood as the beginning of a "polyphony of polyphonies"; through it the previous horizontal [diachronic] and vertical [synchronic] readings are integrated in an "oblique" reading. But in spite of its logical coherence, this argument misses the essential point: the fact is that, in the case of any language, the first articulation is immovable, except within very narrow limits. And it is certainly not interchangeable. The respective functions of the two forms of articulation cannot be defined in the abstract and in relation to each other.[39]

Put this way, it might seem as though Lévi-Strauss has betrayed structuralism: he seems to demand a kind of extreme nonarbitrariness of the sign, a natural and intrinsic—almost Cratylian—signification. But in focusing on the synchronic dimension, we have thus far ignored the diachronic; if we are to deal with the problem and critique posed here, we must deal with polyphony, in which diachronic relations dominate. Fortunately, the problem of polyphony receives extended treatment in *The Naked Man*, and by

The Occult Mind

combining the discussion there with our outstanding questions about the "natural" and "objective" foundation of scales, we will at last begin to see what Lévi-Strauss has in mind. At the same time, although the musical analysis here is indeed coherent, consistent, and an essential window onto the workings of structural myth analysis, comparison to tarot by way of the critique of serialism reveals the musical metaphor as both a defense against and an attack on the latent possibility of deconstruction.

The discussion of polyphony revolves around the fugue:

> It would seem that the point at which music and mythology began to appear as reversed images of each other coincided with the invention of the fugue, that is, a form of composition which, as I have shown on several occasions, . . . exists in a fully developed form in the myths, from which music might at any time have borrowed it. If we ask what was peculiar about the period when music discovered the fugue, the answer is that it corresponded to the beginning of the modern age, when the forms of mythic thought were losing ground in the face of the new scientific knowledge, and were giving way to fresh modes of literary expression.[40]

Fugue is like mythology, in that it depends on concurrent melodies (diachronic expressions) that have their own internal rhythmic and harmonic logic yet simultaneously refer to each other synchronically through the scale. This analogy plays out in a detailed analysis of Ravel's *Boléro*, seen as "a sort of fugue 'unpicked and laid out flat [*mise à plat*],' so that the different parts are set end to end in linear sequence, instead of chasing each other and overlapping."[41] The oddity is that *Boléro* is very much unlike the musical form of fugue.

The fugue, like the canon from which it derives, was never a particularly rigid structure in the history of Western music, but it has a few distinctive characteristics.[42] First, it rests on imitation, in that the subject (the initial theme) undergoes formal imitation, transposition, inversion, and so on, which then become answer, countersubject, and so forth. Second, it is polyphonic, which means that several voices, entering successively, play parallel parts; importantly, these parts are *internally* driven, rather than depending mainly on the other lines as in pure harmony.

The use of *Boléro* strongly suggests problems in Lévi-Strauss's analogy. Fugue declined sharply in the late eighteenth and nineteenth centuries, concomitant with the decline of purely polyphonic forms in general. Having reached its height with Bach's *Art of the Fugue*, the form never regained its pride of place. At least one reason for this was that the ever-increasing complexity of harmonic structure and size of ensembles made nearly impossible the performance of fugue in its most typical aspect, the *improvisational fugue*. This aspect of the form, so standard in Bach's time, required tremendous mastery of particular instrumental techniques, often to the detriment of others. Specifically, it is difficult enough to maintain the logic of an improvised line and at the same time keep track of what other performers are doing with their own lines, without having simultaneously to emphasize acoustic purity in the tuning of intervals and harmonies. (Note that the reintroduction of improvisation with jazz avoids these difficulties by having only one performer solo at a time, downplaying the aesthetic valuation of extremely pure harmony, and, often, playing in very small performing groups such as trios or quartets.)[43] Even setting aside the originally improvisatory character of fugue, however, Lévi-Strauss has chosen highly aberrant examples of the form: Ravel's *Boléro* and (obliquely) Wagner's operas. Surely Bach would have been a more obvious example, be it specifically his fugues or perhaps an enigma canon or two, for example, the fascinating "Quaerendo inveniete." Indeed, an enigma canon, in which only the subject is given and the remainder improvised by following an obscurely written or even implied rule, seems to offer a convenient analogy for myths as Lévi-Strauss describes them.[44]

Specifically, enigma canons have three explicit dimensions: synchronic harmony, diachronic elaboration and development, and a *rule*, a definite subject matter or focus driving diachronic exploration of the synchronic material. To use more of Lévi-Strauss's terminology, the diachronic consistencies are *armature*, "a combination of properties that remain invariant in two or several myths"; the particular scale and its tonalities are *code*, "the pattern of functions ascribed by each myth to these properties"; and the rule that "modif[ies] the discontinuity without challenging its principle"[45] is *message*, "the subject matter of an individual myth."[46]

Let us combine our questions about *Boléro* and fugue with our earlier ones about Lévi-Strauss's apparent abrogation of the sign's arbitrary nature. On the one hand, we have in *Boléro* a diachrony that appears utterly divorced from synchrony, a series of variations strung end to end rather than stacked up vertically. On the other, we have in the critique of serialism an unwillingness to set aside "preconceived" or "natural" synchrony among notes in favor of extreme diachrony. Thus far, Lévi-Strauss's musical metaphor seems incoherent.

I suggest, however, that these two problems amount to the same, and that by considering their "discontinuity" we can see a latent debate. In addi-

The Occult Mind

tion, absent from the dialogue between synchronic and diachronic elements is the *message*, particularly as it arises in the *performance* of music.

In his reading of *Boléro*, Lévi-Strauss wants to demonstrate that structural analysis of myths never has active polyphony to work with, only implicit polyphony, and that his analytical method thus treats mythology as a fugue *mise à plat* or a spread of tarot cards. When a number of related myths are aligned and stacked up vertically, as in *Mythologiques*, the parallelism of armatures becomes apparent, and we hear the polyphony of voices in strict counterpoint. Sometimes this parallelism is very close, and something akin to canon or stretto occurs; sometimes it is less clear, analogous to free counterpoint and fugue per se.

With the critique of serialism, Lévi-Strauss defends his method against the charge of infidelity to the cultures that constructed the myths. Unlike serialism, he claims, structuralism presumes that the code elements are embedded in webs of meaning irrespective of their deployment in mythological diachrony; far from a natural or Cratylian signification, then, Lévi-Strauss is suggesting a human and cultural motivation of the sign that always already stands behind the myth, that is, the paradigmatic system of *langue*. If the serialist's thought "creates the objects it needs and the form necessary for their organization,"[47] as Boulez says, then the composer is like an engineer who "presuppose[s]" that there are, "at least in theory, as many sets of tools and materials or 'instrumental sets' as there are different kinds of projects." By contrast, with the mythological thinker or bricoleur:

> His universe of instruments is closed and the rules of his game are always to make do with "whatever is at hand," that is to say with a set of tools and materials which is always finite and is also heterogeneous because what it contains bears no relation to the current project . . . but is the contingent result of all the occasions there have been to renew or enrich the stock or to maintain it with the remains of previous constructions or destructions. The set of the bricoleur's means cannot therefore be defined in terms of a project.[48]

Thus serialism, by freeing itself of the bonds of "previous constructions" of notes, risks cutting music loose to such a degree that it no longer has any means to refer to anything but itself, becoming not unlike the unlimited semiosis that Umberto Eco ascribes to "irresponsible deconstructionists" who, by taking arbitrariness to an extreme conclusion in the elimination or nonrecognition of motivation, authorize themselves to make any text say anything about anything.[49]

There are two important problems here. First, Lévi-Strauss has misunderstood the serialists' liberation of scales and rhythms from preconceived structures. At least in Schoenberg, such a move permits music to serve as a critique of prior conceptions. Theodor Adorno analyzes this approach in considerable detail, labeling such prior structures "musical material." As Max Paddison describes it,

> "Material" . . . is what the composer controls and shapes, ranging from sounds (as pitches, timbres, durations, dynamics), through connections of any kind made between them (as melody, harmony, counterpoint, rhythm, texture), up to the most advanced means available for integrating them at the level of form (. . . he considers form, genres, and also styles to be part of the material . . .). For Adorno, the material "is all that the artist is confronted by, all that he must make a decision about, and that includes forms as well, for forms too can become materials." . . . Adorno insists that the composer's choice of material is always constrained by the stage reached by the development of expressive needs and technical means at any particular historical period.[50]

Thus,

> Each individual composition should be in effect an indicator of the stage reached by the musical material at any particular historical period. . . . [However, it] at the same time also acts as a *critique* of it, in [that] . . . it negates and reconceives the pre-formed, handed-down material, as a historically "necessary" response to the problems posed by the material at its previous stage.[51]

In short, Lévi-Strauss misses the fact that Schoenberg, and after him the serialists, wishes to replace synchronic note-relations only in the sense that he wants to see them as *historical* structures:

> In the last hundred years [since the mid-nineteenth century], the concept of harmony has changed tremendously through the development of chromaticism. The idea that one basic tone, the root, dominated the construction of chords and regulated their successions—the concept of *tonality*—had to develop first into the concept of *extended tonality*. Very soon it became doubtful whether such a root still remained the centre to which every harmony and harmonic succession must be referred. Furthermore, it became doubtful whether a tonic appearing at the beginning, at the end, or at any other point really had a constructive meaning. . . . [Fur-

The Occult Mind

thermore] the ear had gradually become acquainted with a great number of dissonances, and so had lost the fear of their "sense-interrupting" effect. . . . This state of affairs led to a freer use of dissonances . . . as if there were no dissonance at all.[52]

As a result, Schoenberg argued, the whole notion of tonality itself collapsed: with no root or center, and no way to distinguish consonance from dissonance, the structure of harmony as a series of logical relations becomes meaningless. To restore order and coherence to harmony, it is necessary to recognize that the *historical* system can be challenged and overcome by a *logical* one. The construction of a "polyphony of polyphonies" is thus the *critical* activity of recognizing that the apparently synchronic note-relations are actually the products of diachronic historical and political relations.

The second, related problem appears when we consider the scholar-analyst's position with respect to the myth or music analyzed. If myths are like *Boléro*, then only the analyst bridges the "discontinuity" of diachrony and sees the underlying synchrony; that is, the polyphony of *Boléro* only appears in the course of structural analysis. If myths are polyphonic, they require something resembling structural analysis in order to achieve a full performance.

By this reasoning, we have come full circle to a central argument of this book. As with Goethe's or Eliade's morphology, we see in Lévi-Strauss's structural myth analysis the construction of a historylike structure in the absence of history itself. More important, perhaps, we again encounter the possibility that the "native" might act exactly like the scholar, the occultist like the scientist. After all, if the myth tellers are entirely unaware of the structural underpinning of their constructions, how do they continue to hear polyphony? If Lévi-Strauss has revealed that myth has a fugal character, he has simultaneously demonstrated that the natives know this is the case.

This point is clearer if we return to tarot. Tarot does indeed have the double structure Lévi-Strauss demands. On the one hand, each card has its own meaning, in several senses: the trumps relate hierarchically (and indeed are numbered), have their own independent meanings outside of the deck (as images, concepts, and so forth), and relate at the level of a cosmogonic cycle. At the same time, they appear in a new, random order within a given spread, and this new order is essentially linear. By aligning the various levels and seeking to formulate the spread as a "score" made up of these elements, we have a musical activity, a mythological procedure.

This interpretation, let us note, differs considerably from Lévi-Strauss's claims about what the structuralist observer could identify in an ethnography of card reading. For him, the only important points to discern are the natural relations, the structure of the cards within the deck, their number, and so forth; in his metaphor he ignores the process by which they are interpreted from the spread. Given the brevity of that statement, however, we must certainly not assume that this is all Lévi-Strauss would really have to say, faced with such an ethnography in actual fact.

On the contrary, it seems certain that he would and could analyze the spreads and their procedures, and would be interested to know exactly how the diviner (and quite possibly the querent) aligned the various elements of the spread to construct meaning. But we are starting to shift ground: the analyst now seeks to discern the *analytical* procedures of the informants; in other words, to interpret tarot reading as we have done requires viewing the diviner as a kind of structuralist.

Of course, this is to some degree tautological: I set up the comparison in this fashion and can hardly claim to have discovered it in the process. But it is nevertheless revealing that Lévi-Strauss does not seem to want to see mythical thinkers in quite this way. He wants to see them as thinking mythologically at an *unconscious* level, as part of his project to discern the underlying structures of the human mind. If, however, we can see all this at work in tarot readings, as I have suggested, then the possibility arises that the structure of human mental processes, interpreted by Lévi-Strauss, will turn out to be founded on structuralism itself.

There are several readings of this. On the one hand, as has been suggested many times, it may be simply that Lévi-Strauss overreads to the point that he sees only himself in the material he analyzes. And yet, wholly to accept this interpretation entails that the natives do *not* think analytically. If Lévi-Strauss's analysis has logical flaws, it is at least generous about the natives' considerable intellectual powers. From our reading of tarot, I suggest pushing the analysis in the opposite direction: rather than presume that native mythological thinking arises from the structure of the mind, let us grant the possibility that it is not only modern scholars who can think in terms of structural rigor.

One upshot of this for *Mythologiques* is that we can set aside the concern with binarism and its "actual" presence or absence in native thought. We can see Lévi-Strauss's work as a *translation* of the mythical material into binary structures, making overt the logical relations, binary or otherwise, with which the native bricoleur works. Native thought is thus every bit as complex as Lévi-Strauss makes it, but this is not simply an artifact of the human

The Occult Mind

mind: rather, the natives are every bit as intellectually sophisticated as we are. Those who find *Mythologiques* heavy going at least have the justification that native thought really is that difficult.

I cannot complete a musical analysis of *Mythologiques* here. I hope only to have demonstrated the importance of the musical metaphor and to have gone some way toward clarifying the stakes involved in understanding it. In constructing his vast opus, Lévi-Strauss has necessarily modulated the native mythological musical material into an entirely new form. If with Adorno and Schoenberg we respect the possibility of composition as a critique, we must grant Lévi-Strauss his success as a composer. Ironically, he does not give himself that credit, nor accept the validity of the peculiar musical form he has invented. Still, in the "Finale" to *The Naked Man*, the anthropologist reveals his creative purposes:

> To me, at any rate, it appears certain—since I embarked on this *Introduction to the Science of Mythology* in full consciousness of the fact that I was trying, in a different form and in an area accessible to me, to make up for my congenital inability to compose a musical work—that I have tried to construct with meanings a composition comparable to those that music creates with sounds: it is the negative of a symphony of which, some day, some composer could well try to produce the positive image; I leave it to others to decide whether the demands that music has already made on my work can be said to prefigure such an image.[53]

As a coda, let us examine de Mellet's discussion of Pharaoh's dream. The analysis begins with a specific question: What is the meaning of the dream?

M_6: Pharaoh's Dream

Then Pharaoh said to Joseph, "Behold, in my dream I was standing on the banks of the Nile; and seven cows, fat and sleek, came up out of the Nile and fed in the reed grass; and seven other cows came up after them, poor and very gaunt and thin, such as I had never seen in all the land of Egypt. And the thin and gaunt cows ate up the first seven fat cows, but when they had eaten them no one would have known that they had eaten them, for they were still as gaunt as at the beginning. Then I awoke. I also saw in my dream seven ears growing on the stalk, full and good, and seven ears, withered, thin, and blighted by the east wind, sprouted after them, and the thin ears swallowed up the seven good ears. And I told it to the magicians, but there was no one who could explain it to me."

To interpret this dream, two lines of cards are drawn, one each by the Explainer (Jannes) and the Permutator (Mambres). The Permutator finds a series of hieroglyphic trumps in two groups: Sun, Fortune, Fool, Typhon, and Death. The Explainer's line is of necessity parallel, because of the technique: Ace, King, and Knight of Rods, then 2 and 5 of Rods. These two lines may be considered as separate myths M_{jannes} and $M_{mambres}$, but de Mellet gives the impression that they more properly constitute two stages of movement between M_6 (the dream) and M_{1-5} (the various structures of the deck)—that is, they allow us to situate Pharaoh's dream within the context of tarot in general.

The spread of cards is the basis of a question. If M_6 is equivalent to M_{1-5} transformed by a function of M_{jannes} and $M_{mambres}$, then what is that function? To put it like an enigma canon, what rule allows us to continue the line M_6 if we know the key and signature (M_{1-5}) and that the rule may be derived from M_{jannes} and $M_{mambres}$?

Suppose we lay out the dream (M_6) as the subject of the fugue and M_{jannes} and $M_{mambres}$ as answering lines. To continue within the key, we cannot move harmonically outside the confines of tarot. First, then, the answers M_{jannes} and $M_{mambres}$ must link structurally with M_6; de Mellet accomplishes this by paralleling two groups of sevens in the subject and the answers: fat cows : thin cows :: 1+4+2 rods : 2+5 rods. Since the two answers must also be structurally parallel, fat cows : thin cows :: Sun + Fortune + Fool : Typhon + Death.

Rods	$7 =$	1	+	4	+	2	::	2	+	5	$= 7$
Trumps		Sun		Fortune		Fool		Typhon		Death	
Cows	$7 =$	Fat cows / good agriculture					::	Thin cows / bad agriculture			$= 7$

Next, we must place the answers at some interval from the subject and perform any necessary minor alterations (accidentals) to have each note remain within the key. Since the key of the dream (M_6) seems to be agricultural (cows, ears of corn), rods must also be agricultural; as this is their usual interpretation, we have thus far confirmed our analysis. Furthermore, the two clusters of trumps must be glossed in similar terms. Thus Sun (creation, generation) = agricultural production, Fortune (luck) = good agricultural luck, Fool (multiplier) = increase of abundance; Typhon (evil, descent) = collapse of agriculture, Death (destruction) = death of agricultural products, that is, blight or drought.

The Occult Mind

Having laid out the fugue's structure, we begin to improvise a performance on these themes, strictly maintaining their internal logic and also reacting to the general logic and harmony of the entire key of tarot. This is the critical lesson of the fugue analogy in the context of interpretation, divinatory or mythological: simply laying out the themes and variant structures does not in itself constitute interpretation, much less art. Just as Lévi-Strauss dismisses the mathematical formulae as unimportant and draws our attention to the myths themselves, so a musical score or spread of cards is a precondition, a prerequisite, but it requires a creative moment of performance in order to be heard as music.

For the myth analyst, where does this creative performance enter? Lévi-Strauss, at least, has a neat answer to this: as a structuralist, the meaningful act of interpretation can only happen *in between* myths, in their interrelations. Thus for him, the music of Pharaoh's dream will only be heard when we find a second myth standing in a strict counterpoint to it.

M_7: Joseph, Structural Anthropologist

Then Joseph said to Pharaoh, "The dream of Pharaoh is one; God has revealed to Pharaoh what he is about to do. The seven good cows are seven years, and the seven good ears are seven years; the dream is one. The seven lean and gaunt cows that came up after them are seven years, and the seven empty ears blighted by the east wind are also seven years of famine. It is as I told Pharaoh, God has shown to Pharaoh what he is about to do. There will come seven years of great plenty throughout all the land of Egypt, but after them there will arise seven years of famine, and all the plenty will be forgotten in the land of Egypt; the famine will consume the land, and the plenty will be unknown in the land by reason of that famine which will follow, for it will be very grievous. And the doubling of Pharaoh's dream means that the thing is fixed by God, and God will shortly bring it to pass."

Certainly the Art of Writing is the most miraculous of all things man has devised. . . . No magic Rune is stranger than a Book. All that Mankind has done, thought, gained or been: it is lying as in magic preservation in the pages of Books.

Thomas Carlyle, *On Heroes, Hero-Worship, and the Heroic in History*

I. Definition.
MAGICK is the Science and Art of causing Change to occur in conformity with Will. (Illustration: It is my Will to inform the World of certain facts within my knowledge. I therefore take "magical weapons," pen, ink, and paper; I write "incantations"—these sentences—in the "magical language" i.e. that which is understood by the people I wish to instruct; I call forth "spirits," such as printers, publishers, booksellers, and so forth, and constrain them to convey my message to those people. The composition and distribution of this book is thus an act of MAGICK by which I cause Changes to take place in conformity with my Will.)

Aleister Crowley, *Magick in Theory and Practice*

There remains to be written a history of this metaphor, a metaphor that systematically contrasts divine or natural writing and the human and laborious, finite and artificial inscription.

Jacques Derrida, *Of Grammatology*

It has long been fashionable to cite old-fashioned claims about savage absurdity to justify disuse of "magic" as an analytical term.[1] But in the first place, one would need on this basis to impose an arbitrary and illegitimate division between "their" magic and "ours," since as we have seen the European occult traditions hardly fall into such incoherence as Frazer attributed to "savages." Indeed, if Giordano Bruno was exceptionally perspicuous in recognizing an epistemological problem that endures in mathematical modeling of natural phenomena, there is nevertheless no reason to presume that his ideas did not arise from magic.

Whether one calls it magical or otherwise, moreover, any intellectual system of sufficient complexity affords ample resources for abstract thought. And the impossibility of discarding "magic" becomes all the more apparent when we note that differential usages of all kinds are also mustered as justification. When Durkheim and Marcel Mauss assigned to magic an antisocial character and E. E. Evans-Pritchard read it as a means by which a society manifests tensions and cleavage, they offered strongly differing views founded on structurally equivalent grounds.[2] In the former case, the scholar uses "magic" as a class term for practices grouped by a set of exterior criteria; in the latter, it is the natives themselves who classify behavior on parallel bases. But to postulate that the native distinction and the scholarly one are therefore interchangeable amounts to mistaking analogy for identity. Rejecting such an equivalence, many have gone on to emphasize the validity of the native categories at the expense of the scholarly, as though they did not by translating native terms propose in linguistic form the very metaphor whose legitimacy they wish to deny. And the value of the comparison has repeatedly manifested in studies of both witchcraft and alchemy.

In fact, the structure of classification varies so widely from culture to culture, and from discourse to discourse, that it often seems the most appropriate analogy to native definitions is not merely scholarly but rather disciplinary conceptualizations. European historians distinguish among a range of magical modes, all in continual use throughout the occult renaissance. At the same time, we must not be blinded by the naive claim that such distinctions arise simply from the material. As we have repeatedly seen, these divisions were often matters of contestation, whether in the service of further precision in classification or of synthetic overcoming. If historians hold to native disciplinary divisions, it is for reasons of methodological utility rather than accuracy as such—and the magicians themselves might rightly lay claim to interdisciplinarity.

The proliferation of definitions of magic, positive as well as negative, among scholars as well as those whom they study, certainly attests to the confusion or diffusion of the term, but it also indicates in magic an unusual power to manifest distinction and division. This differential character of magic, both in addition to and in place of *definitions* of magic, has been much neglected. Precisely when magic is defined negatively, in opposition to science and religion for example, the formulation obscures the positive possibility of a differential magic. Like the misdefinition of theory as that which is not practice, such approaches ignore the equal (il)legitimacy of the reverse proposal. In any case, an abstract differentiation opens the door to substantive definition.

Every discipline tends to overestimate the objective fidelity of its terminology. When we make the mistake of thinking that the purely differential, nonsubstantive quality of magic arises solely from native usage, we forget that magicians make the same claim in reverse. In the introduction chapter of his *Magick in Theory and Practice*, Aleister Crowley argues that the tendency of ordinary people to disdain or hate magic arises from their failure to recognize that magic is not at base different from supposedly mundane activities; properly speaking, "MAGICK is for ALL":

> My former work has been misunderstood, and its scope limited, by my use of technical terms. It has attracted only too many dilettanti and eccentrics, weaklings seeking in "Magic" an escape from reality. I myself was first consciously drawn to the subject in this way. And it has repelled only too many scientific and practical minds, such as I most designed to influence.[3]

Ignorant discrimination is hardly to be confused with proper scholarly distinction. But in ignoring the latter and overextending the former, Crowley simply repeats and turns to his own advantage a mistake of the same kind that A. R. Radcliffe-Brown made when he claimed that magic's inconsistency of classification showed that it did not exist.[4]

⁞⁞⁞

Mauss, in his 1902 *General Theory of Magic* written in collaboration with Henri Hubert, proposed that magic is first and foremost *different*: magicians are powerful because they are different, and those who are different have magical powers. Mauss referred this projection of power to the notion of mana—a theory famously borrowed by Durkheim in *The Elementary Forms of Religious Life*. And it could be said with some accuracy that the history of substantive definitions of magic since that time has amounted to a progressive repudiation of this thesis.[5]

It turns out that mana does not mean, in its original Polynesian context, what Mauss and Durkheim thought it did.[6] In addition, one should not generalize a local native theory as an explanation of a general principle or category, a point made well by Radcliffe-Brown: "The reasons given by the members of a community for any custom they observe are important data for the anthropologist. But it is to fall into grievous error to suppose that they give a valid explanation of their custom."[7] Thus not only native explanations but also native *classifications* should be accepted into scholarly discourse with suspicion, if at all.

The Occult Mind

At the same time, it has to a considerable degree been accepted that "magic," insofar as one can use it substantively at all, is indeed primarily differential in character. Yet if local differentiation systems (which is to say classification systems) do not rest on strongly generalizable principles—if, that is, we are dealing with differentiation itself as a principle and not something else like mana—then there is little reason to suppose a generalizable magic. Magic becomes simply a rough and problematic way of collapsing the differences among native differentiations, in a sense of making native differences similar. And as we know, such familiarization tends to blur difference. Of all things *not* to blur, the difference of difference tops the list: it makes a difference!

Nevertheless, a grave logical slippage manifests here. We can presumably agree that difference *itself* is generalizable, that the natives (including ourselves) do in fact make distinctions and have principles on which they found them. And as Mauss quite rightly pointed out, radical differentiations, the extremes of difference in whatever sense, do often get ascribed some sort of supernatural (broadly speaking) power. Victor Turner and others have looked to the dramatic social power of marginal positionality and so on, which goes a long way toward classifying and specifying what Mauss already intuited, but a serious problem remains: Why *magical* power? In fact, we have come full circle. Having come to understand far more clearly than our predecessors ever did why marginality and differentiation have the potential for a range of powers and their limitations—explaining, for example, why women especially have been persecuted as "witches" in a strikingly large number of societies—we still do not understand clearly why this potential should manifest in such a particular and peculiar fashion.

No reader who has followed me to this point in the present book will be surprised to hear that Claude Lévi-Strauss made a very striking suggestion about this. I hope readers will also be unsurprised that I find his proposal fascinating and usefully incorrect.

In his *Introduction to the Work of Marcel Mauss*, a lengthy introductory essay to the 1950 edition of Mauss's works, Lévi-Strauss makes a typically elegant inverting remark. He grants that "despite all the local differences, it seems quite certain that *mana, wakan, orenda* do represent explanations of the same type; so it is legitimate to construct the type, seek to classify it, and analyse it."[8] Indeed, "Conceptions of the *mana* type are so frequent and so widespread that it is appropriate to wonder whether we are not dealing with a universal and permanent form of thought."[9] After a brief examination, he comes to his proposal:

Always and everywhere, those types of notions, somewhat like algebraic symbols, occur to represent an indeterminate value of signification, in itself devoid of meaning and thus susceptible of receiving any meaning at all; their sole function is to fill a gap between the signifier and the signified, or, more exactly, to signal the fact that in such a circumstance, on such an occasion, or in such a one of their manifestations, a relationship of non-equivalence [*inadéquation*] becomes established between signifier and signified, to the detriment of the prior complementary relationship.[10]

To unpack this proposal, we must recognize where Lévi-Strauss takes it. Having remarked that language must have arisen all at once, he suggests that "at the moment when the entire universe all at once became *significant*, it was none the better *known* for being so."[11] That is:

The universe signified long before people began to know what it signified. . . . [But] man has from the start had at his disposition a signifier-totality which he is at a loss to know how to allocate to a signified, given as such, but no less unknown for being given. There is always a non-equivalence or "inadequation" between the two, a non-fit and overspill which divine understanding alone can soak up; this generates a signifier-surfeit relative to the signifieds to which it can be fitted. . . . I believe that notions of the *mana* type . . . represent nothing more or less than that *floating signifier* which is the disability of all finite thought (but also the surety of all art, all poetry, every mythic and aesthetic invention). . . . In other words . . . I see in *mana*, *wakan*, *orenda*, and all other notions of the same type, the conscious expression of a *semantic function*, whose role is to enable symbolic thinking to operate despite the contradiction inherent in it.[12]

As Jonathan Z. Smith puts it with typical wit and clarity, "Rather than the popular, 'hot' analogy of electricity to mana, Lévi-Strauss has provided one of temporary cold storage."[13]

This idea of a "signifier-totality" has received criticism, as has the interpretation of mana in its local Polynesian sense,[14] but I am not convinced that the argument has been thought through fully on appropriately abstract grounds. Clearly this interpretation laid a foundation for *La pensée sauvage* and serves as something of a manifesto for structural anthropology, as has often been remarked, but there remains a considerable disjuncture here. Lévi-Strauss has provided us with something of a floating signifier of his own. It is not only in Mauss and Durkheim that "*mana* really is *mana*."[15]

The Occult Mind

In effect, *mana*—but here I must specify. The precise local interpretation of mana or its various cognates in Polynesian societies is emphatically not my bailiwick. When I refer to mana here, I refer *solely* to its use in Lévi-Strauss— and in Mauss and Durkheim. It is certainly possible that, as Smith claims, Lévi-Strauss has "proposed a proper explanation; one that can be challenged only on theoretical grounds,"[16] but I will not even go so far. What interests me is the theory *as* a theory, as an explanatory *categorical* formulation.

In effect, mana is a signifier with no signified, which functions to defer signification and hold it in abeyance. That which has mana is *significant* but not *meaningful*. But we have as yet failed to answer the question: Mauss did not get from nowhere the idea that mana in some sense indicated magical power, and indeed it does appear that such terms as *mana*, *wakan*, and *orenda* do carry supernatural (loosely speaking) overtones in many contexts. But *why?* To say that mana delays or defers the signification process does not by itself explain the ascription of power. Lévi-Strauss has deferred the question: Mauss did not seek to explain *mana* but rather *magic*, and he thought mana a good example of a general type—a belief Lévi-Strauss shares. Yet Lévi-Strauss ducks the issue of why mana should be *magical*.

From a broader reading of Lévi-Strauss, it seems possible to answer the question. First of all, mana has a dangerous tendency to expose the limitations of a signification system that depends on its own cohesion, on the denial of anomie. Thus mana is dangerous and furthermore *outside system*— hence outside what is classifiable (nature and society), hence *unnatural* and the like. Furthermore, and here again Lévi-Strauss follows Mauss rather than most of his detractors, that same examination of limits entails that magical thinking can serve to extend the known, to extend the system itself, by means of bricolage: by familiarizing the unfamiliar, that which had been mana becomes part of the system. Thus magical thinking can serve to stabilize a system by grappling with the unknown—a notion that meshes smoothly with a wide range of notions about great magicians, historical and otherwise.

Yet there is a problem here. Bricolage works with the shattered remnants of past systems, the odds and ends, the *bribes et morceaux*. It is not, at base, creative, except insofar as it makes new things out of old ones. And every example presented us of bricolage appears as the endpoint of a process, not as process itself. Magical *thinking* would thus have to be different from its result, because the result—bricolage as we know it—would necessarily already have incorporated itself into the system. The *process* then would be strictly unknowable, because it could not be expressed or acted on within the symbolic system outside whose limits it works.

We thus return to one of Lévi-Strauss's favorite problems: abstract and concrete thought. Insofar as magical thought is concrete, it is constrained by the symbolic system of which the objects are a part. Insofar as that thought is truly abstract, it cannot be observed or expressed: Lévi-Strauss's analyses of bricolage thus amount to back calculations of a process never observable in its own terms. Concretizing thought makes it nonmagical.

If we can have any confidence whatever thus far, we know only that notions of the (Lévi-Straussian) mana-type amount to a gross contradiction. They label, without defining, precisely that which cannot be defined, precisely that which stands most outside classification itself. They operate—and it is *process* we must consider here—in the interstices of signification as a way of setting aside while simultaneously exploring the nature of reality itself, reality as it is understood and interpreted. In short, magic appears to be a way of labeling for future consideration that which has no reality to label, that which potentially violates reality. Magic then is not different because of its nature or its power; magic is considered powerful because first of all it *differentiates*.

::: :::

It may be objected that a category of pure differentiation can hardly have a practical manifestation or analytical value. To this I reply that in being formulated and deployed *as* a category, it naturally becomes substantive and thence practical. Nevertheless, it meets intellectual requirements at least as much as it satisfies practical ends.

The real question is not whether a given magical class does in fact differ from such putative opposites as science or religion. It is rather whether there is an analytical position from which religion or science require differentiation for their own definition, and whether some preliminary clarity can be introduced by the formulation of an antithesis. Any positive definition requires an implicit negative one, and the starker the contrast the more positive the whole often appears. The classifications designated by "magic" depend on such demands for opposition and difference. This is necessarily the case of all analysis, yet the more rigorous drawing of such analogies affords the best means of interpreting seemingly alien thinking.

Lévi-Strauss makes the insightful comment that "magic postulates a complete and all-embracing determinism."[17] It could even be said that this striving for deterministic totality is what makes a system magical, for if the causal relations among elements were broken or limited, the entire structure would move into arbitrariness of a scientific kind. Magical ideas thus contribute to

The Occult Mind

theoretical formulation of certainty by seeking out and attempting to overcome the limits of epistemological structures. Examined superficially and externally, the gradations of magical classification can appear empty and unnecessary. They can however be explained by a demand for what one might call "differential adjustment"—the necessity to delimit every conceptual class and thus linguistic term against its exterior. Stanley Tambiah's application of Austinian "performative utterance" to magical words is particularly illuminating in this respect, although only because it draws on so many previous attempts. In postulating, against Cassirer, Toshihiko Izutsu, C. K. Ogden, and I. A. Richards, that the natives cannot be so foolish as to imagine a causal link between arbitrary linguistic signs and their putative referential effects, Tambiah unwittingly reintroduces a sharp distinction between magic and its other—the other now of a linguistic and theoretical nature rather than a scientific one. Returning to a remark from Lévi-Strauss quoted in a previous chapter:

> Hence, we understand how an attentive, meticulous observation entirely turned toward the concrete finds in symbolism both its principle and its result. Savage thought does not distinguish the moment of observation and that of interpretation any more than one first registers, upon observing them, the signs expressed by an interlocutor, in order thence to seek to understand them: he speaks, and the sensible expression carries with it the signification. Articulated language decomposes into elements, each of which is not a sign but the medium of a sign: a distinctive unit that could not be replaced by another without its changing the signification, and that perhaps itself lacks some attributes of this signification, which it expresses in being joined or opposed to other units.[18]

This exhaustive differentiation embedded dynamically in classifications called magical entails that, as Smith notes, the positive formulations sometimes manifest as weak identities or privative definitions, in which magic is religion or is science *but for the lack of* some desirable quality.

> In the history of its imagination, ["magic"] has been doubly dual, being counter-distinguished from *both* elements in another persistent and strong duality—from both "science" *and* "religion." . . . In the "prelogical" modes of thought that so often characterize anthropological and religious studies discourse within the human sciences (and so rarely characterize the thought of those peoples they claim to study), the law of the excluded middle has long since been repealed, most commonly by means

of a shift from a logical to a chronological rhetoric. Employing an evolutionary hierarchy, the one ("magic") is encompassed by either one of its opposites ("religion" or "science"), with "magic" invariably labeled "older" and "religion" or "science" labeled "newer."[19]

These identities should not be isolated from their close cousins, those definitions that make magic a degraded or defective would-be science or religion. "It may rather be the case that magical thought, that 'gigantic variation on the theme of the principle of Causality' as Hubert and Mauss called it, can be distinguished from science not so much by any ignorance or contempt of" any particular concept, principle, or quality, but rather by an uncompromising necessity for difference itself that expresses an uncertainty and instability that science would prefer not to acknowledge.[20]

From this point of view, the first difference between magic and other types of intellectual systems is that magic takes irreducible difference, as between sign and referent or signifier and signified, as a principal object of thought. Science, on the other hand, requires a distinction among spheres, only some of them marked by the radical difference that makes modeling endlessly preliminary, while for others (e.g., mathematics) is asserted a transparency of sign and phenomenon. In this way, magic may be seen as a kind of prophecy of a structural thought yet unborn.

The fact of such an anticipation ensures that on occasion the parallel may be very close. Indeed, in a previous work explicating the semiotic theories of the sixteenth-century magician Cornelius Agrippa, I have shown that his approach to what Saussure calls the motivation of the sign prompts difficult questions for modern linguistic philosophy.[21] Moreover, magical classifications may imply or entail not only structural differentiation but even its analytical methods, as we have seen in reference to tarot. Arguably, magical systems of thought begin with the most extensive and encompassing formulation of the problem of knowledge, in which the first issue is the overcoming of the distinction of man and nature, subject and object, from which science in its very instauration prescinded. And the later history of philosophy demonstrates numerous occasions on which these magical anticipations have encouraged subsequent developments, as with Giordano Bruno and the infinite universe.

⁖

I am not however suggesting a return to the notion of magic as protoscience, nor proposing the inclusion or substitution of theory (structural,

The Occult Mind

semiotic, poststructural) in the old magic-science-religion triad. Whatever value such a move might have would already be undermined by the necessary analogy, rather than identity, of the formulation. Analysis of an abstract, dynamic motion of thought cannot be limited by the fact that, at some historical moments, magic has served as or been differentiated from any particular or definite conception. Magic as a substantive must (be made to) form a coherent, articulated specificity; it is the *kind* and not the *nature* of this specificity that requires determination. It is therefore best, when comparing magic with any of its various shadowy parallels, to understand the latter on the basis of the former, and not the reverse, as is usual. At the same time, no form or type of data may be excluded on a priori grounds, for those grounds could only come from outside a conceptuality which, preliminarily at least, has only differential and literally indefinite epistemological criteria.

The methodological difficulties entailed by differential handling of what it seems is already a differential term should not be underestimated. In recent moves to avoid substantive formulations, scholars try thereby to control the manner of their own participation in discourses of difference. Yet in so doing, they often become entangled in circularities of paradox.

Wouter Hanegraaff's neoempirical approach, for example, attempts to remove the scholar from what we might call the transaction of signification. Like Frances Yates in a different way, Hanegraaff tries only to *report*, and then in an entirely separated gesture he moves to interpret on other grounds:

> The principal theoretical tool to safeguard scientific legitimacy . . . is the distinction between *emic* and *etic*. Emic denotes the "intersubjective patterns of thought and symbolic associations of the believers" or, expressed more simply, the "believer's point of view." An accurate presentation of the religion under study as expressed by the believers themselves must be the basis of research. On the part of the researcher, the reconstruction of this emic perspective requires an attitude of empathy which excludes personal biases as far as possible. Scholarly discourse about religion, on the other hand, is not emic but etic. This means that it may involve types of language, distinctions, theories, and interpretive models which are considered appropriate by scholars on their own terms. . . . The final results of scholarly research should be expressed in etic language, and formulated in such a way as to permit criticism and falsification both by reference to the emic material and as regards their coherence and consistency in the context of the general etic discourse.[22]

"Magic"—although like many historians in their workaday positivism he prefers seemingly more concrete terms such as "esotericism"—would then be irreducibly *theirs*, an emic signifier having no signified in our etic language. But this once again amounts to pure alterity: there is not even a structural parallel to their sign that would permit a rendering into our language, entailing that the term remains utterly alien and that interpretation can only rest on sand.[23]

The most sophisticated meditation on these issues is Smith's article "Trading Places." The first portion levels a traditional, if unusually comprehensive, challenge to definitions of magic as a substantive, at the same time hinting that matters are not so simple. Having noted that "the largest single family of theoretical, substantive definitions of 'magic'" is that in which "'magic' is 'religion' or 'science' . . . but for the lack of this or that—or, less commonly, but for an excess of this or that," Smith notes that such definitions "break the conventional definitory rules (especially those against the use of a negative definiens)" but worries more that "many phenomena that we unhesitatingly label 'religious' or understand to be 'religion' . . . differ among themselves, on some scale of absent or excessive characteristics, at least as much [as], if not more than 'magic' does from 'religion' in many theories." The logical problem entailed is one of essence: "If the heart of [a model's] explanatory power . . . is that it does *not* accord exactly with any cluster of phenomena ('map is not territory'), by what measurement is the incongruency associated with those phenomena labeled 'magical' . . . so great as to require the design and employment of another model?" To put that somewhat differently, what makes the difference between "religion" (or "science") and "magic" not only *significant* enough but also *specific* enough to warrant a parallel distinction in theory? As to the countervailing trend, what Smith calls "the second family of theoretical, substantive definitions," this amounts to the subsumption of magic into religion (or less commonly science), and this fails for the same reason in reverse: "Synonymy is theoretically useful precisely in that two . . . terms are thought to be so close that their microdistinctions take on enormous clarificatory power. . . . But if one cannot specify the distinctions with precision, . . . the difference makes no difference at all." In short, attempts to formulate substantive definitions of magic founder on *difference itself*: "These flaws have been brought about by the fact that in academic discourse 'magic' has almost always been treated as a *contrast* term, a shadow reality known only by looking at the reflection of its opposite ('religion,' 'science') in a distorting fun-house mirror." In sum, Smith sees "little merit in continuing the use of the substantive term 'magic' in second-order, theoretical, academic discourse."[24]

But having drawn this conclusion, the *data* force a reversal:

The matter, however, will not be so simply disposed of. As with a large class of religious studies vocabulary (e.g., "myth"), the name will not be easily rectified. Abstention, "just say 'no'," will not settle "magic." For, unlike a word such as "religion," "magic" is not only a second-order term, located in academic discourse. It is as well, cross-culturally, a native, first-order category, occurring in ordinary usage which has deeply influenced the evaluative language of the scholar. Every sort of society appears to have a term (or, terms) designating some modes of ritual activities, some beliefs, and some ritual practitioners as dangerous, and/or illegal, and/or deviant. (Even some texts, conventionally labeled "magical" by scholars, themselves contain charms and spells against what the text labels "magic".)[25]

The difficulties of a purely othering magic, for example the post–Evans-Pritchard understanding of magic as a third-person ascription, are equally great. Smith notes five, which for present purposes I reduce to three: (1) the data rarely suffice to interpret the ascription fully, and never when dealing with societies at a historical remove; (2) the emphasis on accusation rather than action entails an inability to analyze magic: only the *magician* exists; (3) peculiarly, this in turn makes of the magician precisely someone who does *not* perform magic.[26]

Nevertheless, three remarks buried in the rubble Smith leaves where definitions once stood suggest a quite different approach to the problem, an approach founded on difference. First, Smith recognizes, and in fact stresses, that "the notion of 'magic' as 'other' is far more deeply engrained [than an ordinary matter of scholarly ideologies]. It is already present, to be used rather than created by these ideologies."[27] In other words, differing, alterity of some kind, does indeed bind first-order and second-order usage in a manner that at least potentially ought to afford appropriate means for modeling. Second, it is not the case that "magic" is simply "othering" itself but, rather, somehow *different from difference*: "Any form of *ressentiment*, for real or imagined reasons . . . , *may* trigger a language of alienating displacement of which the accusation of magic is *just one possibility* in any given culture's rich vocabulary of alterity."[28] It makes a difference which difference is ascribed. Finally, in his concluding discussion of the Greek Magical Papyri, Smith notes that the miniaturization of rituals in that corpus parallels and extends the "microadjustment" normally found in ritual, such that the magical act "becomes a sort of *ritual of ritual*, existing, among other loci, in a space best described as discursive or intellectual."[29] This language should remind us of Aristotle's "representation of representation"—a connection confirmed by the fact that "the chief ritual activity within the Greek Magical Papyri appears to be *the act of writing itself*."[30] It seems that the modes of differing and differentiating proliferate and yet somehow combine in magic, and that the necessary correlation-without-identity between first-order and second-order terminology manifests precisely in difference.

Ultimately, to eliminate "magic" from second-order scholarly discourse would require that the native, first-order term refer to nothing at all—nothing anyway that cannot be designated otherwise. Their "magic" is *really* something else. But this entails that magic *really is* something—or that it is a sign of a vast chain of deferral whose ultimate end *we* (alone) can identify as nonexistent. That in turn requires us to know the difference between terms or concepts that ultimately end in fixed meaning and those, like magic, that merely walk in circles. Yet one cannot have it both ways: either *all* signification depends on endless circularity and deferral whose end one only determines pragmatically, or one must have recourse to a transcendental signified (God, Being, and so forth). From no position can one legitimately pick out a term from another discourse as *uniquely meaningless*, such that the word itself need not even exist, because the selection and delineation itself reifies the object, or better identifies it as an already meaningful sign—albeit an endlessly receding one, like Lévi-Strauss's mana. Thus the very ease with which it seems "magic" can be discarded demonstrates that there is an "it" to *be* discarded.

I stress Smith's examination not only because of its clarity, depth, and precision. Too, his insistence on rigorous, logical formulation serves, in my estimation, to show exactly what he hopes to prove: that "magic" *cannot* legitimately be defined such that it (1) operates appropriately in second-order, academic discourse; (2) functions as an explanatory basis for interpretive analysis of first-order, "native" discourse; and (3) rests on a logical foundation in which it might be comparable (in the broadest sense) to such second-order terms as "religion," "science," or the like. Yet one could nevertheless imagine that magic somehow stands outside logic and reason, something not uncommonly ascribed to it pejoratively, and thus a proper definition might achieve the first two while failing the third. Such a definition would "break the conventional definitory rules," not in this case because of a failure but because the structure of difference so defined would be such that non-differential qualities could not be predicated of it; one could only pinpoint it by its absence or in opposition. Properly speaking, then, we would not be

The Occult Mind

talking of magic as such; magic would be a sign of such difference, an indicator of a differential dynamic that one could not unmask. We would need to define magic as an opposite that is not an opposite-of, a difference not different-from.

⁞⁞⁞

There exists in recent Continental philosophy a concept (though this is the wrong term) that on the purely abstract plane gives a good analogical means of understanding what I have begun to formulate for magic. This is that most famous neographism of Jacques Derrida, "différance." The orthography draws on a kind of double pun. First, the active, participial sense indicated by the *a* makes indistinguishable the root meanings indicated in English as *to differ* and *to defer*. And at the same time, the French pronunciation makes equally indistinguishable *différence* and *différance* when spoken aloud, thus gesturing to the differance underlying writing and speaking. The characteristic qualities of magic too are a simultaneously active and passive differentiation and being-different-from. Magic therefore can be seen as a sort of relative of differance, which helps explain also the peculiarly consistent haunting presence of magic within discourses on writing.[31]

Reading Derrida for thinking magic is a fascinating, endlessly frustrating task. Magic haunts Derridean discourse, from the necromancy of making specters speak to the "occult" movements of logocentrism, from Saussure's "exorcism" of writing to meditations on Hermes and the Ægyptian dream of hieroglyphs. And yet in the only extensive consideration of these themes *as* themes known to me, the ground shifts: in *Specters of Marx* Derrida ruminates on the logic of the specter, of invocation, necromancy, summoning. But while a magical reading of the text demands consideration, it depends on an engagement with Hegel (especially in the wildly experimental *Glas*) *after the fact* of Derrida's reformulation of the problem of language vis-à-vis writing, *after* "writing before the letter."

The analogy is worth pursuing, because it provides a respected and relatively accessible model for thinking differentiation in itself and in isolation. Furthermore, the tendency already mentioned for Derrida's discussions to become haunted by magic, and conversely for magic to become entwined with writing, as we have seen throughout this work, suggests that the analogy may have a deeper basis that requires investigation.

Consider the relatively simple case of signification as formulated in the structural model of Saussure. The signifier (*signifiant*) links to the signified (*signifié*) through differentiation: it is not that the signifier *is* connected to the signified, but rather that it is *not* connected to the other possible signi-fieds. In speech, a sound strikes the ear, forming a percept that the mind im-mediately transmutes into a potential signifier and then distinguishes as a specific sign (a signifier-signified relation) by differentiating it from other signs in their perceptual (signifying) natures; for example, "walk" is distin-guished as "walk" by differentiating it from "talk" and "chalk" and "wall." Once the percept is recognized (or formulated) as a sign, the conceptual end (signified) arises from the structure of language (*langue*). But Derrida points out that this entails a *trinary* rather than *binary* relation: signifier (percept/image), signified (concept), and a kind of "not-ness" or "non-ness"—a kind of active differentiation that defers or puts off signification by deflecting it through the entirety of *langue*. Thus this "autonomous nega-tion," to use a term from Hegel criticism, stands as the only consistent and real ground of signification, for without it nothing could legitimate (or claim to do so) the postulated connection of signifier and signified.[32] Thus signs stand on the ground of a differing and deferring negativity. And this negativity is not itself a thing, because it cannot exist within the relations of truth or theoretical legitimation for which it is the grounds; and it is not a concept, because concepts are within the closed circle of *langue*; and it is not properly designated with a word, because words (like all signs) are again within this closed circle to which such an autonomous negativity would al-ways stand in a prior relation, always already *there* without ever having been or having been able to be *present*. And this negativity or negation Derrida calls *différance*.

If we consider subjectivity, that is, the constitution of the subject as it stands in subject-object relations of reflection, we find the same haunting triplicity. If *I* (subject) look into a mirroring *object*, presumably what I see is myself in reflection. But how do I know that this is what I am looking at? If I have no prior conception of myself, because such a conception could only be an *effect* of reflection, then how is it that I recognize this image in the mir-ror *as* myself? There must once again be some sort of negative, some *not*-ness that preconditions and in a sense validates this reflective relation such that I can see myself in the mirror and know that it *is* myself rather than something else. And thus differance stands outside the subject, yet as we know it is not an objectifiable thing. In this analysis, the transcendental sub-ject collapses into an effect of differance.[33]

Magic too has this endlessly haunting, never quite definite or signifiable quality. We have seen this with definitions of magic, but the same can be predicated of its manifestations. In Kircher's differential classifications in history we noted his strange inability to decide among contradictory choices. Bruno's brilliant use of the *ars memorativa* as a solution to the failure of finitude in the face of the infinite capitalizes on endless deferral to constitute a para-infinite seemingly graspable because it always already exists (but without limit) within the mind. And Dee's deflection of his monad outside himself—and thus outside the human and the political—in order to constitute it as the very grounds of the human and the political, again uses what we might perhaps call the "differantial" quality of magic to think the literally unthinkable.

With Derrida's most famous and perhaps most important examination of these issues, in the context of writing, the magical can be specified—and *differentiated*, for the parallel I am here constructing is not an identity, even if such a thing might heuristically be thought in reference to something (though it is not a thing) so literally without identity and thus without the possibility of a predication of identity as differance. In *Of Grammatology*, Derrida summarizes the traditional view of writing within what he calls (following Heidegger) the "Western metaphysics of presence":

> Writing is that forgetting of the self, that exteriorization, the contrary of the interiorizing memory, of the *Erinnerung* that opens the history of the spirit. It is this that the *Phaedrus* said: writing is at once mnemotechnique and the power of forgetting.[34]

To this Derrida responds,

> Deconstructing this tradition will . . . not consist of reversing it, of making writing innocent. Rather of showing why the violence of writing does not *befall* an innocent language. There is an originary violence of writing because language is first, in a sense I shall gradually reveal, writing. "Usurpation" has always already begun. The sense of the right side appears in a mythological effect of the return.[35]

The point is clear if we recall what we have seen about differance in reference to signification. We saw in chapter 1, with Hermes' prophecy of linguistic collapse, the nostalgia for a language in which words are self-identical; in the *Phaedrus* we saw the further distinction made between spoken language, in which there is still some identity and presence, however attenuated, and written language, which is merely a shadowy tomb of and for presence. Derrida's emphasis on the "mythological effect of the return" points to just this gesture, this attempt magically to restore a lost presence to a language that never had it—or only before the fall of Ægypt.

Speech readily deceives us into thinking that language immediately represents thought, that even if language does not carry truth and meaning, at least I am present to myself in my speech—thus the *Cogito*. Writing, however, reveals that this is not the case: the written character is obviously not simply identical to my thoughts as they formed themselves in my inner self—thus Aristotle's formulation of writing as a "representation of a representation." At its simplest, Derrida's point is no more (and no less) than this: because signification is always already different and deferred, speech as traditionally conceived, that is, speech as a bodying forth of interiority, never existed. *All signification is writing*.

> Writing is the name of these two absences {of the signatory and of the referent}. Besides, is it not contradictory to what is elsewhere affirmed {by Saussure} about language having "a definite and [far more] stable oral tradition that is independent of writing" to explain the usurpation by means of writing's power of *duration*, by means of the *durability* of the substance of writing? If these two "stabilities" were of the same nature, and if the stability of the spoken language were superior and independent, the origin of writing, its "prestige" and its supposed harmfulness, would remain an inexplicable mystery.[36]
>
> . . . . If "writing" signifies inscription and especially the durable institution of a sign (and that is the only irreducible kernel of the concept of writing), writing in general covers the entire field of linguistic signs. . . . The very idea of institution—hence of the arbitrariness of the sign—is unthinkable before the possibility of writing and outside of its horizon.[37]

As a demonstration of this universality, Derrida examines Lévi-Strauss's ethnocentrism as it manifests when discussing writing. The claim is not so much that Lévi-Strauss falls into ethnocentrism (and logocentrism is the "original" ethnocentrism), but more interestingly that this ethnocentrism *always* manifests when we speak—or rather, write—of *writing* and of *violence*.

The parable in *Tristes Tropiques* is famous: Lévi-Strauss introduces writing, shorn of its linguistic content, to the innocent Nambikwara; their clever chief spots the political implications of the technique, manipulates it (and Lévi-Strauss) to gain further ascendancy; Lévi-Strauss muses, alone in the pampa, on the violence inflicted on these most innocent, childlike people by this most destructive *tekhnē*. Derrida makes several points in an analytical tour de force. The Nambikwara were *not* in fact innocent and childlike, strangers to violence, but constructed so by Lévi-Strauss for parabolic purposes. Further, the supposed innocence is the same as that ascribed to speech prior to the violence of writing; Lévi-Strauss projects the presentist (logo-centric) view of language onto the Nambikwara because he cannot imagine that writing does not arrive as a new violence by contrast to innocent spoken language.

Derrida argues that the instant appropriation of writing as political technique gives sociological evidence that the Nambikwara already knew writing. Lévi-Strauss's logocentrism manifests as the assumption that writing is equivalent to its medium and its (practical) method. Under the assumption that writing is, at base, inscription on paper (wood, bark, metal) of language as voice, Lévi-Strauss sees that the Nambikwara do not have writing until he reveals it; but if writing be described formally and philosophically, not pragmatically—and language is not normally described pragmatically—the Nambikwara already had writing, and the chief's appropriation is recognition of a type. No small achievement, but not one permitting the anthropologist his agonistic self-recriminations, nor his formulation of the "extraordinary incident" as high tragedy.[38]

To be sure, magic cannot be defined as differance, but it often plays the part of its sign or, to be more precise, coexists with the thinking of or toward differance, and inasmuch as such purely negative formulations are rarely present, it can hold a place open for differance and make its contours apparent differentially. Magic is in any given manifestation a fixed sign, even if not linked to any particular signified or referent. Unlike differance, magic lends itself to a kind of permutation and manipulation, allowing the possibility of thinking differance within the order of signs, things, and actions. In this way, the extension and intension of magic collapse into a unity: what "magic" signifies is always a system of differential relations that at once depends on magic for its foundation and also encloses magic within itself as a structure. Magic works by analogies and comparisons, yet at the same time it attempts to think *itself* and in such a way that it might escape its own formulations. Lévi-Strauss remarks that "the practico-theoretical logics governing the life and thought of so-called primitive societies are shaped by the insistence on differentiation";[39] but penetrating though this is, he fails to take into account that such total differentiation is the very principle on which *all* signification rests, and thus the magic of "so-called primitive societies" is equivalent to the writing of so-called advanced societies.

This formulation, which could serve as a first gesture toward Derrida's grammatology, does not however sufficiently consider the totalization that Lévi-Strauss rightly ascribes to the differential principle. Differance is precisely *not* total or insistent, because it stands properly outside (because before) the system itself. And this distinction allows us to formulate magic differentially once more, as different from differance:

> Now if differance i̶s̶ (and I also cross out the "i̶s̶") what makes possible the presentation of the being-present, it is never presented as such. It is never offered to the present. Or to anyone. Reserving itself, not exposing itself, in regular fashion it exceeds the order of truth at a certain precise point, *but without dissimulating itself as something, as a mysterious being, in the occult of a nonknowledge.*[40]

Thus Derrida defines magic through exclusion: magic would be that expression or manifestation, effect or progression of the movement of differance that *does* dissimulate itself as something, as a mysterious being, professing a knowledge exterior and superior to knowledge and by that token an occult nonknowledge. Better, it would be a sign of this dynamic. It would, within Derridean thought, be a failure to think differance coexisting with a claim to have done so. It would (now) be a cheap deconstructionism, an ill-informed Derrideanism, a false show of deconstructive elegance and insight that blinds itself to its impotence. It would be a thinking-the-trace become distracted, deferred, by its cleverness. Too clever by half—a *prestige*. But it may nevertheless act as a liberator by its protest against the deceptive demand for presence and truth with which magic's various opposites (science, religion) mystify their operations.

⁝⁝⁝

I have by now stepped fully out of the analytical and discursive stream provided by the first chapter of Lévi-Strauss's text, which I have imitated somewhat slavishly. In borrowing much of the structure and some of the language of "The Science of the Concrete," I am in part motivated by a wish to gesture toward that extension of *La pensée sauvage* into Western magic to which my title refers. But more important I have hoped to demonstrate, through the very rigidity of the parallel, just what sort of an extension this would be. And by substituting differance for bricolage, Derrida's emblematic term for Lévi-Strauss's (though neither thinker would wish to be signified in this fashion), I have tried to wrench the structural stream of thought into the deconstructive. The first question to be resolved, then, is methodological: I must examine and evaluate the analytical yield of the strange definition proposed.

In the course of this book, I have periodically leveled strong criticisms at scholars who have worked on magic. At times, I have even suggested a kind of blindness, an inability to read magical texts in their relatively obvious senses. Furthermore, I have tried to reveal a peculiar tendency to fall into quite straightforward logical and analytical problems. Readers outside the field might wonder whether I have not simply exaggerated, or whether on the other hand those who study magic are afflicted by a sort of madness.

The definition of magic on the basis of differance offers something of an explanation. Because magic is at once fully outside of and entirely caught within reason, magic exercises a disturbing antilogical influence on those who study it. This is not to say that magic is irrational in the sense usually meant; rather, magic is properly speaking *non-* and *anti-*rational. The analogy of differance helps us to see this, for it is a fundamental point in Derrida's work that differance, because it is a precondition of logic, cannot be thought within logic, and similarly because it is not identifiable as a unity it cannot stand at the center of an episteme—in fact, it makes the center of any such episteme decentered.

Lest there be any confusion, I emphasize both that magic *is not* differance nor a sign thereof and also that I do not see Derrida as the ultimate *telos* of magical (or any) thinking. On the latter point, I am furthermore entirely persuaded by the argument that Derrida's criticism of the "Western metaphysics of presence," however insightful and important, slightly misses its target in part because of an unfortunate overreliance on Heidegger's account of this "metaphysics."[41] Nevertheless, such conceptions as Hegel's "autonomous negation," even in Schelling's restructuring, are less useful for the analysis of magic, which after all is the point here. I suggest, in fact, that Derrida offers us the best analytical tools for thinking (about) magic. It is by standing upon Derrida's perhaps unwilling shoulders that we can learn to evade through recognition the destructive effects of magic as an object of thought.

As an example, I argued in chapter 4 that historical and morphological (or structural) knowledge are not commensurable, and referred in passing to Derrida as a limited justification for the claim. In light of this differance-based formulation of the problem of magic, we can see more clearly why overcoming the distinction would, as I have said, require a spell.

With both Dee and Bruno, we saw clearly magical attempts to overcome such distinctions. In Bruno's case, the logical discontinuity of infinite, finite, and infinitesimal prompts the formulation of the *ars memorativa* as a rigorous analogy through which to think the divine. In Dee's case, the disjuncture between an individual, mystical ritual and a sociopolitical activity requires projecting the hieroglyphic monad outside the human sphere and into a distanced divine mind. To understand these efforts philosophically and theoretically, I suggest reading them as attempts to think differance as an occult object, a concept arising from the dynamic movements of thought, society, and nature that is nevertheless not captured within the closure of the episteme which thinks it. Derrida would certainly argue that such attempts were foredoomed to failure, and not only because of conceptual contradictions: objectivity, conceptualization, *thing*ness itself could only be thought within an episteme founded on a centered certainty, and thus such reifying formulations necessarily fail to constitute the object they seek, achieving only another supposedly self-present metaphysical construction that in the end deconstructs itself.

At the same time, this very criticism reveals a continuity with the various manifestations of "the Western metaphysics of presence" that generally concern Derrida and his followers. We might say that Bruno's and Dee's work here finds a satisfactory conceptual common ground with the mainstream trajectories of Western philosophy. The sole absolute difference, and it is an important one, between magical and nonmagical philosophical metaphysics would, in this account, be the insistence of the former on thinking the center differentially, as opposed to the latter's search for a center within the unity of some form of transcendental subject. And whatever might be the ultimate conclusion of the ongoing debates with Derrida's arguments, such a reading affords both analytical grounds for interpreting magical thought within the history of philosophy and reasons to suspect that such thought might have developed valuable resources for the continuing project of thinking difference philosophically.

A comparative approach to European magic would therefore always begin with a *choice*. Having made it, one would no longer be able to rethink.

The preliminary grounding gesture I have just made is morphological, formulating similarity and difference, progression and development, on the basis of synchrony. Like Goethe's "leaf," difference serves as a formal ground for the unfolding of a vast range of possible ways of thinking, and differance in turn serves as an external means of deconstructing, of analyzing backward the total construction of, such philosophical movements.

Conversely, one could begin with a historical choice, seeking means of linking disparate expressions of a common problematic diachronically so as to understand the links as themselves revealing developments of thought over time. Here the work would be genealogical or (to use Foucault's terms) archaeological; one would approach the same deconstructive project by revealing a progressive sedimentation of ideas and seek further horizontal con-

The Occult Mind

nections to other ideas and trajectories of the same discursive era. Foucault's *The Order of Things*, however dubious factually, was an important move in this direction, and many others have worked on such projects with varying degrees of success.

As we know, Smith rightly argues that morphological and historical methods are different approaches to the same objects; each offers legitimate means of seeking to know a given object of study, and by this logic we may reasonably see them as complementary. But to *overcome* this distinction, to synthesize the results of such complementary researches, requires ultimately that the logical grounds of each method culminate in the same objective center, which in the case of magic would have to be differance. Yet differance simply cannot function this way; to forestall precisely this deployment Derrida insists that differance is not a concept, not an object, not an idea—indeed, not a word. To constitute it as such, one would have to think differance as a hidden (occult) concept whose real and logical contours might be revealed through sufficiently extensive study. And this is just how I have characterized the magical, with "magic" or its various cousins commonly operating as a sign of such a concept, as a sign of the thinking of such a thing, as a sign of theoretical thinking about others grappling with such a notion. It is in this sense that to overcome the historical and the morphological in a synthetic and synoptic methodology would require a spell. In part for this reason as well, magic, like this methodological overcoming, "remains an urgent *desideratum*"—or rather, the same desire for a *solution* to a fundamental problem of thought drives both Smith's search for a methodological overcoming and Dee's search for the truth of the monad.

At the same time, I do not consider this logical impossibility to constitute an insuperable obstacle to scholarly analysis. We have seen that the difficulty lies in the fact that morphology and history cannot refer ultimately to the same epistemological center, that morphological and historical knowledge are expressions of incommensurable epistemes. In order to overcome this, one would have to postulate a transcendental center—a problematic metaphysical gesture. But it remains the case that the materials studied, be they magical or otherwise, do postulate such centers, explicitly or implicitly; indeed, the revealing of such metaphysical postulation amounts to the simplest formulation of the deconstructive project. Thus a dialectical movement between morphology and history could ground itself in the metaphysics of the epistemologies studied.

Such a method would be relentlessly comparative, as Smith insists. Even were it focused only on one apparent object, it would necessarily put into play the corresponding metaphysical formations within our own theoretical and analytical thought. Thus at the least, the comparison would be between the explicit object of study and ourselves, in this motion distanced and estranged. In short, the overcoming of history and morphology in one synthetic method would amount to a *historically founded deconstruction*.

In the present work, I have tried to realize a preliminary formulation of this method. I have worked progressively toward comparing modern theoretical epistemologies to magical ones, as with Yates and Bruno, and also tried to destabilize our sense of which thinkers or conceptions are modern, as with Dee and Nō. As we saw with Kircher, such comparison leads unavoidably into a reflection on and of magical epistemes as they surface in theory, be it Vickers or Smith or Ginzburg, and toward magical rereadings of analytical theory, as with Lévi-Strauss via tarot. If the common gesture of recent historians is to do history by means of theory, I have tried to open the possibilities of doing theory by means of history. Future study of magical thought, I suggest, must recognize itself as an intrinsically theoretical and comparative endeavor. In this sense, more Derridean than Lévi-Straussian, bricolage is inevitable.

Lévi-Strauss's use of bricolage is a matter of metaphor, an analogy gracefully borrowing from the homely and concrete world of French hobbyists to clarify the eminently worldly yet aesthetically and intellectually satisfying processes of mythological thought. With few exceptions, uses of bricolage that do not recognize this purely provisional, heuristic character go astray insofar as they seek thence to comment on Lévi-Strauss's work.[42] Yet Derrida's elegant evaluation reverses this precisely by taking the analogy literally (in all senses) and showing what its formulation and employment reveals about Lévi-Strauss and about structuralism.[43] In displacing bricolage with differance, then, I cannot claim that analogical intent can annul further implications.

Reading magic by means of both differance and its outside opens possibilities beyond the confines of analytical study (historical, morphological, comparative) of magic. Indeed, I have hoped throughout this book to have opened the question of "magic" to and for those who have not previously considered it germane. In arguing that magic haunts and inhabits the interior of many fundamental methodological and theoretical issues I have tried to suggest not only means by which to study magic but also, and more important, reasons to do so.

The Occult Mind

Taking up the question or gesturing toward its formulation in light of Derrida's differance necessitates some evaluation of Derrida's thought. This was, after all, part of Derrida's own point about Lévi-Strauss and bricolage: the legitimacy or value of the metaphor cannot reside solely in what it illuminates in the metaphorically described object, for the same reason as Lévi-Strauss cannot step outside the circle of mythmaking through a self-refusal of the *historical* formations he reveals. And even on the basis of the present studies of magical thought, taking seriously uses of words and metaphors as Derrida teaches us to do, we can already begin to see questions announcing themselves.

Could it be said that, by defining (or rather formulating) differance so as to exclude magical self-identification and self-legitimation, yet permitting magic to work metaphorically in his texts, Derrida asserts a kind of truth-value to his discussions as against the nonlegitimacy of magic? Such a transgressive, deconstructive reading of Derrida is worth pursuing. But such a reading must not forget that this exclusion is properly an *in*clusion: it is differance that is (or was always already) excluded from logic and reason; Derridean rhetoric would by this account seem (correctly) to place magic within the sphere of traditional philosophical discourses. That said, I have nevertheless not entirely addressed the haunting presence of haunting itself.[44]

Within the sphere of criticism of the subject, an issue Derrida takes up in numerous early works, especially those concerning Hegel, magic again comes to haunt a discourse from which it had seemingly been excluded. The Tübingen philosopher Manfred Frank, in a number of scintillating lectures, argues persuasively that Derrida's analysis of the subject as an effect of differance collapses because it rests on a Hegelian reflective theory of subjectivity that Schelling already attacked and overcame. Frank suggests that in some sense Derrida completes Schelling's *critical* assault on the Hegelian subject, but at the same time he fails to destroy the subject *itself* and in fact goes some way toward justifying Schelling's formulations on what amount to post-Saussurean structural grounds.[45] Frank does not mention, however, that Schelling found resources for this criticism and reformulation in Isaac Luria's Kabbalah, particularly the notion of *tzimtzum* — inhalation by an infinite God to generate a negative space, a space without God, as a prerequisite to the emanation by exhalation of Creation.[46]

Ultimately, Frank suggests that the philosophical projects of hermeneutics and what he calls "neostructuralism" must come into conversation.[47] Although, as a hermeneutical thinker, he thinks conversation is necessarily productive, one can hardly disparage the scope of the project he proposes: a rethinking of signification and subjectivity on the basis of Charles Sanders Peirce, Saussure, and Friedrich Schleiermacher, by way of Schelling and Derrida. Given the historical orientation of philosophy, is it unreasonable to suggest a wider cast of the net upon the deep waters of magic?

I have tried to show that magic continually manifests similar impulses and constructions to those we associate with mainstream philosophical intellectual trajectories, particularly those loosely called "theoretical." By encountering magical thought *as* theory, rather than as an object to be analyzed through theory, we come to new understanding of a thought that looks back at us from a fun-house mirror. By way of conclusion, of *ceasing* rather than *closing* a work that hopes to serve as a preliminary, let me note the problem with mirrors: barring an external certainty not to be found in differentiation, one cannot know which is the original and which the distorted reflection. To exclude from philosophy the vast range of endeavors to which the sign "magic" has pointed requires that we already know how to distinguish. But has it not been said that objects in mirrors are closer than they appear?

The Occult Mind

1. ÆGYPT

1. For critical assessments of Yates, see chapters 2 and 3 in this book, as well as the excellent discussion in H. Floris Cohen, *The Scientific Revolution: A Historiographical Inquiry* (Chicago: University of Chicago Press, 1994), 169–83, 285–96. On the more charged question of Eliade's work and fascism, see especially Steven Wasserstrom, *Religion after Religion: Gershom Scholem, Mircea Eliade, and Henry Corbin* (Princeton: Princeton University Press, 1999); Bryan Rennie summarizes the debate fairly well, although his defense of Eliade is unconvincing: *Reconstructing Eliade: Making Sense of Religion* (Albany: State University of New York Press, 1996). On Dumézil, the literatures of both criticism and support are very large and varied; for a masterly summation and critical analysis, see Bruce Lincoln, "Dumézil's German War God," *Theorizing Myth* (Chicago: University of Chicago Press, 2000), 121–37. Endnotes 13 and 14 on page 270 of Lincoln's book also provide useful bibliographies of the debates on both Eliade and Dumézil.

2. As an example of this influence: when a Greek manuscript copy of the *Corpus Hermeticum* was brought to Florence, Cosimo de' Medici turned it over to Marsilio Ficino in 1463 for immediate translation. "Though the Plato manuscripts were already assembled, awaiting translation, Cosimo ordered Ficino to put these aside and to translate the work of Hermes Trismegistus at once, before embarking on the Greek philosophers. . . . It is an extraordinary situation. There are the complete works of Plato, waiting, and they must wait whilst Ficino quickly translates Hermes, probably because Cosimo wants to read him before he dies" (Frances A. Yates, *Giordano Bruno and the Hermetic Tradition* [1964; Chicago: University of Chicago Press, 1979], 13), which is also essential for an understanding of the Renaissance *prisca magia* and *prisca theologia*. See also D. P. Walker, "The *Prisca Theologia* in France," *Journal of the Warburg and Courtauld Institutes* (1954): 209, and esp. Walker, *Spiritual and Demonic Magic from Ficino to Campanella* (1958; Notre Dame: University of Notre Dame Press, 1975).

3. Born Alphonse Louis Constant, Lévi was made abbé and professor of Hebrew at the Petit Séminaire St. Sulpice. In 1848 he left his position in the Church and married Noëmie Cadiot, a novelist, sculptor, and journalist working under the name Claude Vignon, but the marriage was brief. Renaming himself Eliphas Lévi Zaed (the Zaed is rarely used), he became active in the nascent *décadent* occultism, and pro-

ceeded to publish numerous highly influential works on the subject. Perhaps most important for later occult thought, Lévi discovered in tarot a preeminent divinatory system, and restored the centrality of Kabbalah to (more or less) Christian occult praxis. Despite his almost incredible importance for the whole of later occultism and its connections to modernist artistic movements, Lévi is sadly ignored by academic scholarship. The most important work is Christopher McIntosh's *Eliphas Lévi and the French Occult Revival* (London: Rider, 1972), long out of print. Considering the importance of the occult revival for such artists as William Butler Yeats, J. K. Huysmans, Gustave Moreau, and, more problematically, T. S. Eliot and Somerset Maugham, one wonders at the willful blindness of the scholarly community toward this movement. Other references include Paul Chacornac, *Eliphas Lévi, renovateur de l'occultisme en France, 1810–1875* (Paris: Chacornac frères, 1926); Thomas A. Williams, *Eliphas Lévi: Master of Occultism* (Tuscaloosa: University of Alabama Press, 1975); Christiane Buisset, *Eliphas Lévi: Sa vie, son oeuvre, ses pensées* (Paris: G. Trâedaniel, Editions de La Maisnie, 1984).

4. On the occult tarot, see "Tarocco and Fugue," chapter 5 of this book. On occult Freemasonry, see Ronald Hutton, *The Triumph of the Moon* (Oxford: Oxford University Press, 1999), 52–65. On Atlantis, Lemuria, and Mu, see H[elena] P[etrovna] Blavatsky, *Isis Unveiled*, 2 vols., new ed. (Wheaton, Ill.: Theosophical Publishing House, 1972; 1st ed. 1877), and *The Secret Doctrine*, 2 vols. (London: Theosophical Publishing Company, 1888), esp. vol. 2; for less directly Theosophical interpretations see, inter alia, James Churchward, *The Lost Continent of Mu: The Motherland of Man* (New York: William Edwin Rudge, 1926), which invented the Mu myth, and Ignatius Donnelly, *Atlantis, the Antediluvian World* (New York: Harper, 1882). On Druidic telluric magic, see (indirectly) Alfred Watkins, *The Old Straight Track: Its Mounds, Beacons, Moats, Sites and Mark Stones* (1923; London: Abacus/Little, Brown, 1974), and the extended discussion in "The Ley of the Land," chapter 2 of this book. On Murray's theory of witchcraft, see Margaret A. Murray, *The Witch-Cult in Western Europe* (Oxford: Oxford University Press, 1921), *The God of the Witches* (London: Faber, 1934), and Murray's entry on "Witchcraft" in *Encyclopedia Britannica*, 23.687, 1965 ed.; scholarly attacks on Murray are too numerous to list, but for an idiosyncratic appraisal see Mircea Eliade, "Some Observations on European Witchcraft," *Occultism, Witchcraft, and Cultural Fashions: Essays in Comparative Religions* (Chicago: University of Chicago Press, 1986), 69–92, whose annotated references provide a more usual bibliography.

5. There is extensive scholarship on the historical context and situation of the *Hermetica*. See, most importantly, Garth Fowden, *The Egyptian Hermes: A Historical Approach to the Late Pagan Mind*, new ed. (Princeton: Princeton University Press, 1993); Fowden's bibliography and notes provide detailed and sophisticated apparatus for such study.

6. Several editions and translations of the *Hermetica* are readily available. I have used primarily Brian P. Copenhaver, *Hermetica: The Greek "Corpus Hermeticum" and*

the Latin *"Asclepius"* in a New English Translation with Notes and Introduction (Cambridge: Cambridge University Press, 1992); other editions of particular importance are Walter Scott, ed. and trans., *Hermetica: The Ancient Greek and Latin Writings Which Contain Religious or Philosophical Teachings Ascribed to Hermes Trismegistus*, 4 vols. (of which vol. 4 was completed by A. S. Ferguson) (London: Dawsons, 1968; first ed. 1924–36); A.-J. Festugière, *La révelation d'Hermès Trismégiste*, 4 vols. (Paris: J. Gabalda, 1950–54). Copenhaver's introduction and bibliography (xiii–lxxxiii) provide an excellent starting point for historiography of the *Hermetica*.

7. *Asclepius* 24–26, pp. 81–82. References are to Copenhaver's edition. Text in angled braces is inserted by Copenhaver; ellipses are mine. These long quotations are reprinted with permission of Cambridge University Press.

8. *Asclepius* 24, p. 81.

9. *Phaedrus*, 274c–275b. On the philosophical implications of this text, see esp. Jacques Derrida, "Plato's Pharmacy," *Dissemination*, trans. Barbara Johnson (Chicago: University of Chicago Press, 1981), 61–171. I shall return to this story, and to Derrida's interpretation, periodically.

10. *Asclepius* 37, p. 90.

11. *Asclepius* 24, p. 81.

12. *Hermetica* 16.1–2, p. 58.

13. Mircea Eliade, *Patterns in Comparative Religion: A Study of the Element of the Sacred in the History of Religious Phenomena*, trans. Rosemary Sheed (Cleveland: Meridian, 1963). This translation is problematic and should be corrected against the revised original: *Traité d'histoire des religions*, 2nd ed., preface by Georges Dumézil (Paris: Payot, 1970).

14. See Jonathan Z. Smith, "Acknowledgments: Morphology and History in Mircea Eliade's *Patterns in Comparative Religion* (1949–1999)," *History of Religions* 39, no. 4 (May 2000): 315–31, 332–51; reprinted in *Relating Religion* (Chicago: University of Chicago Press, 2004), 61–100. See also Smith's discussion of Goethe and morphology in "Adde parvum parvo magnus acervus erit," *Map Is Not Territory* (Leiden: E. J. Brill, 1978; repr. University of Chicago Press, 1993), 240–64, esp. 253–59. The significance of Rudolf Steiner's work as a link between Eliade and Goethe has yet to be explored. Although Smith makes use of Steiner's *Goethes Weltanschauung* (Weimar: E. Felber, 1897) (trans. as *Goethe's Conception of the World*, ed. H. Collison [London: Anthroposophical Publishing, 1928] and as *Goethe's World View*, trans. William Lindeman [Spring Valley, N.Y.: Mercury Press, 1985]), and the introductory materials of Steiner's five-volume edition of *Goethes Naturwissenschaftliche Schriften* (Dornach: Rudolf-Steiner-Verlag, 1973) (now available as *Nature's Open Secret: Introductions to Goethe's Scientific Writings*, trans. John Barnes and Mado Spiegler [New York: Anthroposophic Press, 2000]), he does not attempt a systematic comparison or correlation of Eliade and Steiner. Other important Steiner works on Goethe include *A Theory of Knowledge Based on Goethe's World Conception*, trans. Olin D. Wannamaker (New York: Anthroposophic Press, 1968), and *The Spiritual–Scientific Basis of*

Goethe's Work (London: Rudolf Steiner Press, 1982); see also Steiner's lectures on *The Origins of Natural Science* (Spring Valley, N.Y.: Anthroposophic Press, 1985), which characterize non-Goethean science as antispiritual. Even a quick reading of these works strongly suggests the possibility of a radical reinterpretation of Eliade, without which a much-needed reappraisal of morphology's potential value in comparative study cannot be satisfactorily completed. Of major value here are Goethe's own *Scientific Studies*, ed. and trans. Douglas Miller, vol. 12 of *Goethe: The Collected Works* (Princeton: Princeton University Press, 1988), on which I have drawn for the present analysis.

15. Mircea Eliade, *Shamanism: Archaic Techniques of Ecstasy*, trans. Willard R. Trask (Princeton: Princeton University Press, Bollingen, 1964), xiv. Most of the foreword to *Shamanism*, esp. xiii–xx, is an extended discussion of the value (or lack thereof) of history for Eliade's studies, and much clarifies what Eliade takes "history" to be. See also his *Cosmos and History: The Myth of the Eternal Return*, trans. Willard R. Trask (New York: Harper Torchbooks, 1959) and pt. 2 of Smith, "Acknowledgments."

This foreword is interestingly parallel to that of Goethe's *On Morphology*, where we see Goethe differentiating his approach from the traditional reductionist or classifying approach:

> In observing objects of nature, especially those that are alive, we often think the best way of gaining insight into the relationship between their inner nature and the effects they produce is to divide them into their constituent parts. Such an approach may, in fact, bring us a long way toward our goal. In a word, those familiar with science can recall what chemistry and anatomy have contributed toward an understanding and overview of nature.
>
> But these attempts at division also produce many adverse effects when carried to an extreme. To be sure, what is alive can be dissected into its component parts, but from these parts it will be impossible to restore it and bring it back to life. ("The Purpose Set Forth," in *Scientific Studies*, 63)

Here we see an important source for Eliade's conception of the irreducibility of the sacred. It would be interesting to compare Eliade's various introductions closely against Goethe's.

16. Goethe remarks: "The *Urpflanze* is to be the strangest creature in the world—Nature herself shall be jealous of it. With such a model . . . it will be possible to invent plants *ad infinitum*. They will be strictly logical plants—that is to say, even though they may not actually exist they could exist—they would not be mere picturesque shadows or dreams, but would possess an inner truth and necessity." Goethe, letter to Herder, May 17, 1787; trans. in Erich Heller, *The Disinherited Mind: Essays in German Literature and Thought* (New York: Harcourt, Brace, Jovanovich, 1959), 10; quoted in Smith, "Acknowledgments," 327 (*History of Religions*), 71 (*Relating Religion*).

17. A number of nineteenth-century thinkers made the mistake of assuming that Darwin had simply found a historical explanation and foundation for morphology, or alternatively that Goethe was "Darwinian before Darwin." Ernst Cassirer refuted this interpretation and attempted to place Goethe more accurately within the trajectory of scientific epistemology; see *The Problem of Knowledge: Philosophy, Science, and History since Hegel*, trans. William H. Woglom and Charles Hendel (New Haven: Yale University Press, 1950), 137–50.

18. This is to some degree what Jonathan Z. Smith proposes in "Fences and Neighbors" and related articles: *Imagining Religion*, 1–18. I return to the problem of morphology and history in chapter 4.

19. Goethe, "Observation on Morphology in General," in *Scientific Studies*, 57.

20. For Eliade's most sustained meditation on the problem of time, see his *Cosmos and History*.

21. Yates, *Giordano Bruno*, 1–2.

22. Ibid., 398.

23. Ibid., 455.

24. See his discussions of early modern magical and occult thought, particularly alchemy, in *The Forge and the Crucible*, trans. Stephen Corrin (Chicago: University of Chicago Press, 1962). Less valuable but interesting are "Religion, Magic, and Hermetic Traditions before and after the Reformation," chapter 38 of *A History of Religious Ideas*, vol. 3, trans. Alf Hiltebeitel and Diane Apostolos-Cappadona (Chicago: University of Chicago Press, 1985), 221–61; and "The Occult and the Modern World," *Occultism, Witchcraft, and Cultural Fashions*, 47–68, esp. 56–7.

25. Properly speaking, morphological and structural analysis provide context through the achronic or synchronic frame formulated by the method. I return to this point in chapters 2 and 4; for the moment, I limit the question of context to its more usual historical usage.

26. "In Comparison a Magic Dwells," *Imagining Religion*, 20–22.

2. THE LEY OF THE LAND

1. Paul Devereux, "Leys/'Ley-lines'," abridgment of paper given at the "Wege Des Geistes—Wege Der Kraft" (Ways of Spirit—Ways of Power) conference, October 1996, in Germany (city not given); the abridged paper is available at Devereux's website, http://www.pauldevereux.co.uk/. See also Danny Sullivan, "Ley Lines: Dead and Buried: A Reappraisal of the Straight Line Enigma," *3rd Stone* 27 (Autumn 1997): 44–49.

2. Alfred Watkins, *The Old Straight Track*; also *Early British Trackways* (London: Simpkin Marshall, 1922) and *Archaic Tracks around Cambridge* (London: Simpkin Marshall, 1932). The son of Alfred Watkins wrote a biography, which I have not seen: Allen Watkins, *Alfred Watkins of Hereford* (London: Garnstone, 1972).

3. Roger Sandell, "Notes towards a Social History of Ley–Hunting," *Magonia* 29

(April 1988). The article is based on a talk given, largely extempore, at the Anglo–French UFO meeting held at Hove in March 1988.

4. Ibid.

5. According to his website, "Devereux delights at crossing subject boundaries with his research, and dealing with audiences and readerships that range from the popular level to the academic. Devereux is a highly informed and original thinker in his fields of interest, and is concerned to remove the fantasy and misinformation that plagues many of them. He feels that the real mysteries are wonder enough."

6. Devereux, "Leys/'Ley-lines'." Amusingly, Devereux refers to Buck Nelson as "Rogers," presumably reminded of Buck Rogers; I have corrected this in square brackets. See Aimé Michel, *Mystérieux objets celestes* (Paris: Editions Arthaud, 1958); Buck Nelson, *My Trip to Mars, the Moon, and Venus* (Grand Rapids: UFOrum, Grand Rapids Flying Saucer Club, 1956); J. A. D. Wedd, *Skyways and Landmarks* (Chiddingstone, Kent: privately printed 1961; repr. Hull: P. Heselton, 1972). There appears to be considerable variation in the length of the Nelson text, from twenty-eight to forty-four pages, with the original at thirty-three; I have not been able to track copies of these for comparison. The prolific Aimé Michel was the subject of Michel Picard's *Aimé Michel, ou la quête du surhumain* (Paris: JMG, Collection Science-Conscience, 2000).

7. John Michell, *The View over Atlantis* (London: Garnstone Press for Sago Press, 1969); the revision, *The New View over Atlantis* (London: Garnstone, 1972; London: Thames and Hudson, 1983), reveals some changes in Michell's thinking, notably a moderation of his views on UFOs as alien spacecraft, while retaining the main argumentative thrust.

8. Simon Broadbent, "Simulating the Ley Hunter," *Journal of the Royal Statistical Society*, ser. A (General) 143, no. 2 (1980): 111. Michell's response to this paper at the meeting in question appears on pages 133–34 of the same journal; unsurprisingly, he finds Broadbent "partisan" and dismisses his statistical work as "quibbles."

9. Broadbent's practical suggestions may be found in pt. 6 of his paper, 122–23.

10. E. W. MacKie, "Archaeological Tests on Supposed Prehistoric Astronomical Sites in Scotland," *Philosophical Transactions of the Royal Society of London*, ser. A (Mathematical and Physical Sciences) 276.1257, "The Place of Astronomy in the Ancient World" (May 2, 1974), 170–71. Most of the second half of this volume of *Philosophical Transactions* is devoted to the problem of the megalithic yard and the Alexander Thom and Gerald Hawkins views.

11. To the best of my knowledge, there has been no serious assessment of the question by modern archaeologists. This seems rather a pity. Although Broadbent proved that it would be difficult indeed to discern a genuine ley within the evidence, a refusal to consider the possibility does no good at all. Unfortunately, the field seems understandably to consider this question tainted, and thus to ask the question is to lend credence to mania. But this is not a scholarly or scientific perspective—it is a defensive one. Furthermore, should any such leys actually exist, the longer they are left

entirely to occult thinkers for speculation, the more difficult it will be for serious scholarship to examine them.

12. Erich von Däniken, *Chariots of the Gods? Unsolved Mysteries of the Past*, trans. Michael Heron (New York: Souvenir Press, 1969; original ed., Econ-Verlag, 1968). Oddly enough, the 1999 reprint (New York: Putnam Berkeley) asserts that "this is a work of fiction. Names, characters, places, and incidents are either the product of the author's imagination or are used fictitiously, and any resemblance to actual persons, living or dead, business establishments, events, or locales is entirely coincidental." This despite von Däniken's discussion in the book of several well-known persons and theories about such apparently fictional places as the Great Pyramid and Easter Island!

13. The omission of Stonehenge is not accidental. Von Däniken's theory clearly has a racist dimension, such that ancient *white* people presumably could build fabulous monuments; it is only others who required alien assistance. In an interesting debunking article, the stage magician and skeptic James Randi notes several examples of von Däniken's more glaring errors of fact. For example, the claim that the Easter Island statues could not have been set up with primitive technology had long been contradicted by Thor Heyerdahl, who organized a demonstration of the procedure. Heyerdahl remarks of von Däniken, "Together with my colleagues I am to blame for not promptly having used the modern mass media for telling the public not to take his references to Easter Island seriously." Randi's article is "The Paper Chariots in Flames," in *Flim-Flam!* (Buffalo, N.Y.: Prometheus, 1982), 109–30; the quote from Heyerdahl, which Randi gives without citation, appears on 113. For Heyerdahl's demonstration, see *Aku-Aku: The Secret of Easter Island* (Chicago: Rand McNally, 1958).

14. Properly speaking, Michell does not claim that the ancients were Atlanteans in a simple, literal sense; rather, he refers to an "archaic world-order" whose memory "was preserved into historical times by certain groups or castes of priestly initiates, such as the keepers of the Egyptian temples from whom indirectly Plato received it. His name for the lost world, Atlantis, is respected in the title of [Michell's] book": *The New View over Atlantis*, 8. For catastrophic geological history, see Immanuel Velikovsky, *Worlds in Collision* (London: Gollancz, 1950).

15. The assertion that the Great Pyramid predates the other structures on the Pyramid Plain is traditional in this sort of speculation and is argued in great depth in Piazzi Smyth's *Our Inheritance in the Great Pyramid* (London: A. Straham, 1864), as well as in Michell.

16. Eliade is thinking of Rudolf Otto's idea of divinity as *ganz andere*; see Otto, *The Idea of the Holy*, trans. John W. Harvey (London: Oxford University Press, 1923).

17. Eliade, *Traité d'histoire des religions*, 330. The distinctly Eastern Orthodox (or Catholic, for that matter) theological perspective is important in Eliade, who at times seems to perceive the Reformation as destroying true Christianity and precipitating the "terror of history" as an inescapable condition.

18. *Cosmos and History*; orig. ed., *Le Mythe de l'éternel retour: Archétypes et répétition* (Paris: Gallimard, 1949). Note that Eliade, in his preface to the 1959 Harper Torchbook edition, remarked that he should not have used the term "archetype" because of its specifically Jungian connotations, which he did not intend: "I use the term 'archetype,' just as Eugenio d'Ors does, as a synonym for 'exemplary model' or 'paradigm,' that is, in the last analysis, in the Augustinian sense" (viii–ix).

19. *Cosmos and History*, 104.

20. Frances Yates, *Ideas and Ideals in the North European Renaissance: Collected Essays*, vol. 3 (London: Routledge and Kegan Paul, 1984), contains a complete bibliography.

21. For biographical information, Yates's *Ideas and Ideals* includes an autobiographical sketch of her early years, unfortunately never completed. See also *Dictionary of National Biography* 1981–85: 433–34.

22. H. Floris Cohen, *The Scientific Revolution: A Historiographical Inquiry* (Chicago: University of Chicago Press, 1994), 295–96; the quote is Yates, "The Hermetic Tradition in Renaissance Science," in *Ideas and Ideals*, 227–46 (London: Routledge and Kegan Paul, 1984), 228, which originally appeared in C. S. Singleton, ed., *Art, Science, and History in the Renaissance* (Baltimore: Johns Hopkins University Press, 1967).

23. In the Modern Library's 1998–99 list of the one hundred best nonfiction books of the twentieth century, *The Art of Memory* comes in at number sixty-five in the board's list and number twenty-nine in the readers' list. For the complete list, see the Modern Library's website: http://www.randomhouse.com/modernlibrary/100 bestnonfiction.html.

24. Brian Vickers, "Frances Yates and the Writing of History," *Journal of Modern History* 51, no. 2 (June 1979): 287–316. Analysis of Yates, *The Rosicrucian Enlightenment* (London: Routledge and Kegan Paul, 1972).

25. Vickers, 302, quoting Yates, *Rosicrucian Enlightenment*, 202; italics are Vickers's.

26. Vickers, 304–5, quoting Yates, *Rosicrucian Enlightenment*, 198 and 223, with Vickers's italics.

27. Yates, *Giordano Bruno*.

28. Yates sometimes made a distinction between Hermetism, the teachings of Hermes Trismegistus in particular, and Hermeticism, a mode of essentially Neoplatonic thought inspired by the Ægyptian sage. This distinction was not, however, maintained rigorously by Yates's admirers and critics, nor by Yates herself. See Ingrid Merkel and Allen G. Debus, eds., *Hermeticism and the Renaissance: Intellectual History and the Occult in Early Modern Europe*, papers presented at the "Hermeticism and the Renaissance" conference held in March 1982 (Washington, D.C.: Folger Shakespeare Library, 1988), 8.

29. Yates, *Giordano Bruno*, 447.

30. Yates, "The Hermetic Tradition in Renaissance Science"; this text is cited at length in Vickers, "Introduction," 4–5.

31. Major contributors include Brian Copenhaver, Allen Debus, B. J. T. Dobbs, Eugenio Garin, A. Rupert Hall, Mary Hesse, Hugh Kearney, J. E. McGuire, Frederick Purnell Jr., Edward Rosen, Paolo Rossi, Charles Schmitt, Charles Trinkaus, Cesare Vasoli, Brian Vickers, Richard Westfall, and Robert Westman. For surveys of the debates, see esp. Brian Copenhaver, "Natural Magic, Hermeticism, and Occultism," in *Reappraisals of the Scientific Revolution*, ed. David C. Lindberg and Robert S. Westman (Cambridge: Cambridge University Press, 1990), 261–302, and several other articles in the volume. Other useful volumes of essays are Vickers, ed., *Occult and Scientific Mentalities in the Renaissance* (Cambridge: Cambridge University Press, 1984), and Merkel and Debus, eds., *Hermeticism and the Renaissance*. See also H. Floris Cohen's discussions in *The Scientific Revolution*, esp. 285–96.

32. I return to this point next chapter.

33. Yates, *Giordano Bruno*, 447.

34. Ibid., 448, 449, 450, 455.

35. Ibid., 449–50. In this passage Yates is referring also to A.-J. Festugière's *La révélation d'Hermès Trismégiste*, vol. 1 (Paris: J. Gabalda, 1950–54), 61–64.

36. Yates, *Giordano Bruno*, 449.

37. Ibid., 452; the footnotes here refer specifically to Bruno's atomism.

38. Ibid., 454.

39. Ibid., 1.

40. For bricolage, see "La science du concret," chap. 1 of *La pensée sauvage* (Paris: Plon, 1962; ed. cit., Paris: Brodard et Taupin, 1990). The unascribed translation as *The Savage Mind* is not satisfactory. Setting aside ungrammatical sentences and the like, the translators render technical terms drawn from Saussurean linguistics indifferently, undermining Lévi-Strauss's precise formulations. Although a book whose very title is "spectacularly untranslatable," as Clifford Geertz puts it (*The Interpretation of Cultures* [New York: Basic Books, 1973], 357; see also 351n2), meaning both "savage thought" and *viola tricolor* (Johnny-jump-up), can hardly be translated perfectly, even a workmanlike version is an urgent desideratum.

41. For Lévi-Strauss's "neolithic intelligence," see *Tristes Tropiques*, trans. John and Doreen Weightman (1974; London: Penguin, 1992), 53: "Today I sometimes wonder if anthropology did not attract me, without my realizing this, because of a structural affinity between the civilizations it studies and my particular way of thinking. I have no aptitude for prudently cultivating a given field and gathering in the harvest year after year: I have a neolithic kind of intelligence." In his article "The Cerebral Savage: On the Work of Claude Lévi-Strauss," in *The Interpretation of Cultures*, Clifford Geertz, working from the earlier John Russell translation, omits "I have no aptitude . . . after year," greatly distorting the sense.

42. See, for example, *Cosmos and History*.

43. Yates, *Giordano Bruno*, 324; see also Hilary Gatti, *Giordano Bruno and Renaissance Science* (Ithaca: Cornell University Press, 1999), 9n16.

44. Robert S. Westman, "Magical Reform and Astronomical Reform: The Yates Thesis Reconsidered," in *Hermeticism and the Scientific Revolution*, ed. Robert S. Westman and J. E. McGuire (Los Angeles: William Andrews Clark Memorial Library, 1977), 5–91.

45. Gatti, *Giordano Bruno*. Note that Westman recognized at least some of the scientific implications of Bruno's infinitism, though he did not carry this analysis into a thorough reading of Bruno's cosmology.

46. Westman, "Magical Reform," 72.

47. Edward A. Gosselin, "Bruno's 'French Connection': A Historiographical Debate," in Merkel and Debus, eds., *Hermeticism and the Renaissance*, 166–81.

48. Gatti, *Giordano Bruno*, 203.

49. "L'explication scientifique ne consiste pas dans le passage de la complexité à la simplicité, mais dans la substitution d'une complexité mieux intelligible à une autre qui l'était moins": *La pensée sauvage*, 295. *The Savage Mind* translates this as: "Scientific explanation consists not in moving from the complex to the simple but in the replacement of a less intelligible complexity by one which is more so" (248); Jonathan Z. Smith, in *Relating Religion*, proposes: "Scientific explanation consists not in a movement from the complex to the simple but in the substitution of a more intelligible complexity for one which is less" (106).

50. Gatti, *Giordano Bruno*, 1–9, provides an elegant overview of this problem, making clear her preference for the scientific Bruno without significantly distorting or dismissing the magical. For Bruno's images as logical tools, see Gatti, *Giordano Bruno*, 171–203, and especially Rita Sturlese, "Il *De imaginum, signorum et idearum compositione* di Giordano Bruno ed il significato dell'arte della memoria," *Giornale critico della filosofia italiana* (May–August 1990), and Sturlese, "Per un'interpretazione del *De umbris idearum* di Giordano Bruno," *Annali della Scuola Normale Superiore di Pisa*, 3rd ser., 22, no. 3 (1992). Also useful (indirectly) is Brian Vickers, "On the Function of Analogy in the Occult," in Merkel and Debus, eds., *Hermeticism and the Renaissance*, 265–92.

51. Note that at the opposite end of the scale, Bruno's atomism emphasizes the indivisible unity of the geometric point, with multiple atoms linked by equally indivisible distances. As Gatti shows convincingly, Bruno's infinite space and atomism amount to the same epistemological—and for him, nonmathematical—problem.

52. Gatti, *Giordano Bruno*, 83.

53. Yates, *Giordano Bruno*, 241.

54. Ibid., ix–x; see Westman, "Magical Reform," 6–8, for a different interpretation of the passage.

55. Yates, *Giordano Bruno*, 449.

56. The lost works have prompted various speculations, but little can be said with certainty; indeed, we must wonder whether all of these works ever existed. I find

Gatti's correlation of *Arca di Noè* with Kircher's 1675 memory book *Arca Noe* convincing; I am less sanguine about the actual completion of *Clavis Magna*.

57. These works have been translated: Giordano Bruno, *Cause, Principle and Unity: Essays on Magic*, ed. and trans. Robert de Lucca and Richard J. Blackwell (Cambridge: Cambridge University Press, 1998); *De Vinculis in Genere* is there translated as *A General Account of Bonding*.

58. Bruno, *De Vinculis* and *De Magia*. On Ficinian magic, see D. P. Walker, *Spiritual and Demonic Magic*. On Agrippa, see Christopher I. Lehrich, *The Language of Demons and Angels* (Leiden: Brill, 2003), esp. chap. 3; note that Yates's reading of Agrippa misunderstands him in a way Bruno does not, as indicated by Bruno's comments in *De magia*.

59. Emblems and devices (*imprese*) have received extensive treatment over the last few decades. Apart from Ashworth's helpful overview, "Natural History and the Emblematic World View," in Westman and Lindberg, eds., *Reappraisals of the Scientific Revolution*, 303–32, I would draw particular attention to Armando Maggi, *Identità e impresa rinascimentale* (Ravenna: Longo, 1998).

60. Ashworth, 312. For a less romantic view, see Umberto Eco, "Unlimited Semiosis and Drift: Pragmaticism vs. 'Pragmatism,'" in *The Limits of Interpretation* (Bloomington: Indiana University Press, 1990), 24–32.

61. Gatti, *Giordano Bruno*, 147.

62. Ibid., 147–48.

63. Giordano Bruno, *The Ash-Wednesday Supper*, trans. Edward A. Gosselin and Lawrence S. Lerner (Hamden, Conn.: Archon/Shoestring, 1977), prefatory epistle, 73. See also Gatti, *Giordano Bruno*, 192 and 202 n58.

64. E. E. Evans-Pritchard, *Theories of Primitive Religion* (Oxford: Clarendon, 1965), 120.

65. For a spirited defense of comparison on logical grounds, see Robert A. Segal, "In Defense of the Comparative Method," *Numen* 48, no. 3 (2001): 339–73.

66. Derrida, "Structure, Sign, and Play in the Discourse of the Human Sciences," *Writing and Difference*, trans. Alan Bass (Chicago: University of Chicago Press, 1978), 293.

3. THE THEATER OF HIEROGLYPHS

1. Dee states that his "mind had been pregnant" with the monad in *Monas Hieroglyphica* (Antwerp: G. Silvius, 1564), 10r.

2. Four translations are known to me: [Émile-Jules] Grillot de Givry, *Jean Dee de Londres, "Le Monade Hiéroglyphique"* (Paris: Bibliothèque Chacornac, 1925); J. W. Hamilton-Jones, *The Hieroglyphic Monad* (London: J. M. Watkins, 1947); C[onrad] H[ermann] Josten, "A Translation of John Dee's 'Monas Hieroglyphica' (Antwerp, 1564), With an Introduction and Annotations," *Ambix* 12 (1964): 112–221; *Die Monas-Hieroglyphe*, ed. Agnes Klein (Interlaken: Ansata-Verlag, 1982) [not seen]. The more

recent English texts I have seen, published in Edmonton, Washington, and York Beach, Maine, are more or less credited reprints of Hamilton-Jones. As Josten notes (148–53), Grillot de Givry omits Dee's letter to Silvius, his printer. Hamilton-Jones appears to be working from Grillot de Givry, at least in part, and further omits the whole dedicatory epistle to Maximilian II. Josten's translation is by far the best, and I have used it throughout; note that he also reprints the entire Latin text in xerographic facsimile, making his *Ambix* article the single most useful source for the *Monas*.

3. Dee, *Monas Hieroglyphica*, 3v; Josten 121.

4. Dee, *Monas Hieroglyphica*, 12r, 13r, 27v–28r; Josten 155, 159, 217–19.

5. The full title of this famous edition is almost never given:

A True & faithful RELATION OF What passed for many Yeers Between Dr. JOHN DEE (A Mathematician of Great Fame in Q. Eliz. And King James their Reignes) and some spirits: tending (had it Succeeded) *To a General Alteration of most STATES and KINGDOMES in the World*. His *Private Conferences* with Rodolphe Emperor of *Germany*, Stephen K. of *Poland*, and divers other Princes about it. The Particulars of his Cause, as it was agitated in the *Emperors* Court; By the Popes intervention: His Banishment, and Restoration in part. As Also The Letters of Sundry Great Men and Princes (some whereof were present at some of the these Conferences and Apparitions of Spirits:) to the said D. Dee Out Of The Original Copy, written with Dr. Dees own hand: Kept in the Library of Sir tho. Cotton, Kt. Baronet. WITH A PREFACE Confirming the Reality (as to the Point of Spirits) of This Relation: and shewing the several good Uses that a Sober Christian may make of All. By Meric. Casaubon, D. D. *LONDON*, Printed by *D. Maxwell*, for t. Garthwait, and sold at the Little North door of S. *Pauls*, and by other Stationers. 1659.

I have used the facsimile edition from Magickal Childe Publishing (New York, 1992).

6. A complete edition of Dee is in the works but not as yet announced for publication.

7. Nicholas H. Clulee, *John Dee's Natural Philosophy: Between Science and Religion* (London: Routledge, 1989); William H. Sherman, *John Dee: The Politics of Reading and Writing in the English Renaissance* (Amherst: University of Massachusetts Press, 1997); Deborah E. Harkness, *John Dee's Conversations with Angels: Cabala, Alchemy, and the End of Nature* (Cambridge: Cambridge University Press, 1999); Håkan Håkansson, *Seeing the Word: John Dee and Renaissance Occultism*, Ugglan Minervaserien 2 (Lund: Lunds Universitat, 2001); György Endre Szőnyi, *John Dee's Occultism: Magical Exaltation through Powerful Signs* (Albany: State University of New York Press, 2005); Benjamin Woolley, *The Queen's Conjurer* (New York: Henry Holt, 2001).

8. That Dee changed his mind about a number of matters, and that his thought developed over time, is not in question, certainly since Clulee's work. But if Sherman's

analyses are fully accepted in their rather overstated terms, we are left with Dee the magical thinker and Dee the political reader/writer—and ne'er the twain shall meet.

9. See Richard Popkin, *The History of Scepticism: From Savonarola to Bayle* (Oxford: Oxford University Press, 2003), a much-expanded version of his 1979 *The History of Scepticism: From Erasmus to Spinoza*, itself an expansion of the 1960 edition, which covered Erasmus to Descartes.

10. See, inter alia, Allen G. Debus, *Man and Nature in the Renaissance* (Cambridge: Cambridge University Press, 1978).

11. On Agrippa, see Christopher I. Lehrich, *The Language of Demons and Angels: Cornelius Agrippa's Occult Philosophy* (Leiden: Brill, 2003); on Trithemius, see Noel L. Brann, *Trithemius and Magical Theology: A Chapter in the Controversy over Occult Studies in Early Modern Europe* (Albany: State University of New York Press, 1998).

12. James Bono, *The Word of God and the Languages of Man: Interpreting Nature in Early Modern Science and Medicine; Ficino to Descartes* (Madison: University of Wisconsin Press, 1995), 200–207.

13. Szőnyi, *Dee's Occultism*, 181–91, surveys contemporary and modern sources for the move to angelic theurgy.

14. This is clearly presented in Woolley's *Queen's Conjurer*.

15. See Harkness, *Dee's Conversations*; also Szőnyi, *Dee's Occultism*, 204–27, esp. 220–21.

16. Dee, *Monas Hieroglyphica*, 3r; Josten, 119.

17. Catherine M. Bell, *Ritual Theory, Ritual Practice* (Oxford: Oxford University Press, 1992).

18. See Popkin, *History of Scepticism*.

19. On Artaud's stolen words, see Jacques Derrida, "La parole soufflée," *Writing and Difference*, trans. Alan Bass (Chicago: University of Chicago Press, 1978), 169–95, esp. 178–81.

20. See Lehrich, *Language of Demons and Angels*.

21. Ibid., chap. 3.

22. Pierre Bourdieu, *The Logic of Practice* (Stanford: Stanford University Press, 1992); Sherry Ortner, "Theory in Anthropology since the Sixties," *Comparative Studies in Society and History* 126, no. 1 (1984): 126–66; Bell, *Ritual Theory, Ritual Practice*.

23. Dee, *Monas Hieroglyphica*; Josten, 119.

24. Based on this passage, Håkansson (290–93) interprets this word as being derived by Dee from the Greek *gamos*, "marriage." He is clearly correct, as Dee calls this "matrimonii terram, sive influentialis coniugii, terrestre signum." But it is also a play on words, a reference to the Hebrew *kamea*, a (protective) amulet, from which *cameo* may derive:

> Heb. *Kamea*, a magical charm to protect from harm the one who possesses it or wears it. Despite the strong biblical opposition to magic and divination, white magic in the form of the amulet was tolerated by the Talmudic Rabbis, who al-

lowed a tried amulet (one written by an expert in the art, which had worked suc-
cessfully on three different occasions) to be carried even on the Sabbath when
carrying objects in the public domain is normally forbidden. Even the rationalist
thinker Maimonides records this rule in his Code. . . . The belief in amulets per-
sisted widely among Jews, along with similar superstitious practices, it was attacked by the Haskahal and Reform movements in the eighteenth century. To
this day the belief is still held in some circles, where amulets are worn as a protection against the evil eye and are hung around the room of a woman in child-
birth to protect her against the machinations of Lilith. The inscriptions on
amulets in ancient times would appear to have been various scriptural passages
that spoke of healing or protection. In the practical Kabbalah, various combinations of divine names are used for the writing of amulets on parchment. (Louis
Jacobs, *The Jewish Religion* [Oxford: Oxford University Press, 1995], 25)

See also Joshua Trachtenberg, *Jewish Magic and Superstition* (1939; repr. Philadelphia:
University of Pennsylvania Press, 2004). Maimonides, *Guide to the Perplexed* 1:62,
"Beware of sharing the error of those who write amulets [*kameot*]. Whatever you hear
from them or read in their works, especially with regard to the names which they
form by combinations—all of this is utterly senseless; [the amulet makers] call these
combinations *shemot* [names] and believe that their pronunciation demands sanctifi-
cation and purification and that by using them, they will be able to work miracles. An
intelligent person should not listen to these tales, let alone believe in them." Thus
Dee's hieroglyphs are simultaneously *marriages* of the spheres and *talismans*.

    25. Dee, *Monas Hieroglyphica*, 7r–v; Josten 135–37. Bracketed interpolations are by
Josten.

    26. Dee, letter to the Spanish ambassador: "Don Wilhelmo de St. Clemente,"
quoted in *True and Faithful Relation*, 230–31, also in Josten, 94.

    27. See Jonathan Z. Smith, "God Save This Honourable Court," *Relating Reli-
gion*, 379.

    28. I. R. F. Calder, "John Dee Studied as an English Neoplatonist," 2 vols., PhD
diss., Warburg Institute, 1952.

    29. Szőnyi, *Dee's Occultism*, 248–70, gives fascinating new information on Dee's
reception in eastern Europe, where it appears that "his apocalyptic and highly idiosyncratic message was frightening. . . . While he communicated the angelic messages
to king and emperor, he bluntly threatened them in the name of the celestial powers
unless they followed his directions" (250–51).

    30. Sherman, *Politics of Reading*; the quotation from Grafton appears on the back
cover.

    31. Ibid., 12.

    32. Ibid., 13.

    33. Ibid., 19–20.

    34. Ibid., 79–100.

35. Cf. Walter Benjamin, "Unpacking My Library," *Illuminations*, trans. Harry Zohn, ed. Hannah Arendt (1968; New York: Schocken, 1969), 59–67.

36. The literature on Nō is enormous. For a historical overview in relation to other Japanese theatrical forms, I have found most useful Benito Ortolani's *The Japanese Theatre: From Shamanistic Ritual to Contemporary Pluralism*, rev. ed. (Princeton: Princeton University Press, 1995). On the technical details of modern Nō performance and aesthetic theory, Komparu Kunio's *The Noh Theater: Principles and Perspectives*, rev. ed., trans. Jane Corddry (New York and Tokyo: Weatherhill/Tankosha, 1983), is extremely thorough and clearly presented. Richard A. Gardner's *The Art in Nō: A Reconsideration of the Relation of Religion and Art* (PhD diss., University of Chicago, 1988) covers the vast literature in Japanese and Western languages and situates Nō in the context of scholarship on religion.

37. These secret treatises, themselves the subject of a large scholarly literature, are available in English translation: *On the Art of the Nō Drama: The Major Treatises of Zeami*, trans. Thomas J. Rimer and Masakazu Yamazaki (Princeton: Princeton University Press, 1984).

38. Exact sectarian identification of Zeami's Buddhism is hotly contested. D. T. Suzuki (*Zen and Japanese Culture* [Princeton: Bollingen, 1959] argued for Zen; Arthur Waley and George Sansom claimed Amidist (Pure Land) leanings (Waley, *The Nō Plays of Japan* [New York: Grove, 1957]; Sansom, *Japan: A Short Cultural History*, rev. ed. [New York: Appleton-Century-Crofts, 1962]); Gaston Renondeau focuses on Tendai (*Le bouddhisme dans le nō* [Tokyo: Maison franco-japonaise, 1950]); and so on. Gardner surveys this material briefly, and smoothly dismisses such identification as irrelevant to understanding Zeami, although he does note that the undeniable influence of Zen on Nō clearly postdates Zeami, and further stresses that Shinto too must be added to the long list of religious influences: *The Art in Nō*, 93–116, esp. 104–12. On Shinto in Nō, see also Carmen Blacker, *The Catalpa Bow: A Study of Shamanistic Practices in Japan* (London: Allen and Unwin, 1975). William R. LaFleur argued that Nō drama in Zeami is consistent with "the *general* Mahayana viewpoint," and that sectarian identification, while interesting as a historical issue, is irrelevant to interpretation of the plays themselves, which "present the 'common, average Buddhism' of Japan . . . informed by a mode of thought often associated with Zen": *The Karma of Words: Buddhism and the Literary Arts in Medieval Japan* (Berkeley: University of California Press, 1983), 117.

39. Komparu Kunio, *Noh Theater*, xiii–xiv.

40. *Kokugaku* literally means "national learning," but since the exceptionally important work of H. D. Harootunian it has more often been rendered "nativism." Harootunian's *Things Seen and Unseen: Discourse and Ideology in Tokugawa Nativism* (Chicago: University of Chicago Press, 1988), while hardly light reading or uncontroversial, remains the seminal work in English on kokugaku. In addition, the very nature of Harootunian's argument and method entails a rewriting of the whole of kokugaku scholarship, in Japan and elsewhere. It is worth noting that the term "na-

tivism" is also used to render *nihonjinron*, a somewhat later discourse about Japanese identity, although I use the term here strictly in reference to kokugaku except as otherwise noted.

41. The term *shite* has no exact equivalent in English, significantly because Nō does not conform to European models of "character." LaFleur (*Karma of Words*) uses "protagonist" with quotation marks to indicate the term's problematic nature. After this point, however, I shall leave this word—and its complement, *waki*—untranslated.

42. This category is technically a miscellany and includes various historical dramas and others not readily categorized, but the Madness plays predominate and are usually taken as typical.

43. This now-standard division is not found in Zeami. See note 47.

44. Komparu Kunio, *Noh Theater*, xxii–xxiii.

45. "Drama is something that happens; Nō is someone that happens": Claudel, *Mes idées sur le théatre* (Paris: Gallimard, 1966), quoted in Komparu Kunio, *Noh Theater*, 8.

46. On *Okina*, see Ortolani, *Japanese Theatre*, 67–69. The earliest reference to the play seems to date from 1280, but it seems the mask and general form had already been in use for some centuries. It is variously interpreted; some identify Okina, and the two other characters Senzai and Samba, as kami who bestow longevity, fertility, and prosperity on the land, fields, and villages. Others read Senzai as the Buddha, Okina as Monju (Manjusri), and Samba as Miroku (Maitreya), and interpret the play as the invention of Buddhist monks of the Kōfukuji temple in Nara. Ortolani affirms that *shushi* magicians were certainly involved in *Okina* from an early period, but he also notes that there is little agreement on their place in its formation. He also remarks that some of the chanted words are apparently meaningless syllables, interpreted by some as spells and by others as distorted ritual formulae, possibly of Tibetan origin. On the issue of meaningless vocalizations and magical efficacy, the recent work of Robert A. Yelle on mantras should provide a foundation for future scholarship: *Explaining Mantras: Magic, Rhetoric, and the Dream of a Natural Language* (London: Routledge, 2003).

47. Komparu Kunio, for example, notes that "today, considerations of time often result in abbreviated programs of only two or three Noh plays, one or two Kyōgen pieces, and some short dances, but the five-play cycle *is the original and correct one*, and a full program begins with *Okina* and then continues through the day with a play from each category. This method was even made into law in the days of the regulation-obsessed Tokugawa shogunate" (*Noh Theater*, 32). And yet, the phrase I have italicized should certainly be read with suspicion, especially given the Tokugawa legislation mentioned. The now-standard division into five types of play is not found in Zeami, already suggesting that claims about Nō as simply continuing Zeami's and Zenchiku's theory and practice are, at the least, overstated; further, Zeami's notion of a full day of Nō involves as many as sixteen plays. It seems probable that the Toku-

gawa definition of a full program as a cycle of five plays running through the categories and beginning with *Okina* standardized an emergent structure by accepting and promoting claims of its "original and correct" character.

48. See, for example, Harrison's *Themis: A Study of the Social Origins of Greek Religion* (Cambridge: Cambridge University Press, 1912). Harrison was a member of the "Cambridge ritualist" school, which seems to have developed a number of its readings under the influence of Nietzsche's 1886 *Birth of Tragedy*, and which is arguably continued throughout the modern performance studies and ritual studies approaches of Ronald Grimes, Richard Schechner, and their many disciples.

49. Zeami Motokiyo, *Kakyō*, 14; "The Mirror Held to the Flower," trans. Thomas Rimer, in *On the Art of the Nō Drama*, 97–98. The opening quotation is attributed to Gertan Sōkō (1316?–89), a priest of the Rinzai sect of Zen Buddhism. Note that Zeami normally refers to his art as *sarugaku* or *sarugaku-nō*.

50. Categorization of performance arts—or anything else, for that matter—as religious or secular is inherently problematic, as the last few decades of theoretical scholarship on religion has shown. In the present discussion, I intend merely to recapitulate historiography on Nō and other early Japanese dramatic arts, in which to my knowledge such classification has not been adequately theorized. Such work as has been available to me has generally taken "religion" to be a relatively straightforward classifier. Gardner's dissertation ("The Art in Nō") goes some way toward challenging this, but his focus is primarily on undermining the invidious distinction between "religion" and "art."

51. Ortolani provides an excellent overview of these and other arguments (*Japanese Theatre*, 85–93); for discussion of the many Kamakura (1192–1333) arts that may have influenced Nō, see Ortolani, *Japanese Theatre*, 54–84. Ortolani is rightly cautious about wholeheartedly supporting any of these theories and appears to suggest that all have their points but none is sufficient, that is, that the origins of Nō are too complex to define simply. Ortolani's references here are Akima Toshio, "The Songs of the Dead: Poetry, Drama, and Ancient Death Rituals of Japan," *Journal of Asian Studies* 41 (May 1982): 485–509; Matsumoto Shinhachirō, "Nō no hassei" (Origins of Nō), *Bungaku* 25, no. 9 (1957): 13–30; Honda Yasuji, *Okina sono hoka* (Okina and other matters) (Tokyo: Meizendō, 1958); and Gotō Hajime, *Nōgaku no kigen* (The origins of *nōgaku*) (Tokyo: Mokujisha, 1975).

52. Ortolani, *Japanese Theatre*, 104.

53. Ibid., 105–6. Ortolani mentions the total corpus of three thousand or so plays on page 132, where he notes:

> The plays surviving in the canon were chosen in fact according to the taste of the Tokugawa period, which did not follow the criterion of popularity and success with wider audiences, but rather the sophisticated taste of the ruling class. Some of Zeami's best known masterpieces, such as *Matsukaze*, *Nonomiya* and *Kinuta*, evidently composed to please the elite at court, do not seem to have

been particularly welcome to the larger mixed audiences of the big festivals in Zeami's time. These, on the contrary, loved plays of no literary value, now vanished from the stage.

54. These binaries are not all present in precisely this form in every nativist, and issues of emphasis also greatly color particular uses. Furthermore, many important *kokugakusha* after Motoori often formulated new binaries to add to the list. But this may perhaps be taken as a representative sample.

55. For a detailed survey of Motoori's ideas, see Harootunian, *Things Seen and Unseen*, 76–117. More recently, Ann Wehmeyer has translated the first volume of *Ko-jiki-den*: Motoori Norinaga, *Kojiki–Den*, trans. Wehmeyer, *Cornell East Asia Series* 87 (Ithaca: Cornell University Press, 1997), including a preface by Naoki Sakai and a biographical introduction by Wehmeyer.

56. Quoted in Harootunian, *Things Seen and Unseen*, 122.

57. I emphasize that I do not know of any discussion of Nō by Motoori or Hirata, the nativists on whom I focus here. Within the huge body of kokugaku (and certainly the later *minzokugaku* of Yanagita Kunio and his ilk) there must surely be such studies, but as I am primarily limited to secondary sources and translations I have been unable to track this down. Given the recent interest in late kokugaku-oriented and *nihonjinron* nativisms among American scholars, it is entirely possible I have missed a recent, seminal work. Certainly the 2003 book by Susan Burns importantly develops the protonationalist implications of kokugaku and, from my reading, strengthens the notional connection of Nō to kokugaku: Susan Burns, *Before the Nation: Kokugaku and the Imagining of Community in Early Modern Japan* (Durham: Duke University Press, 2003).

58. Harootunian, *Things Seen and Unseen*, 144–45.

59. Ibid., 146; this is a quote from Hirata Astutane, *Shinshū Hirata Atsutane zen-shū* (Tokyo: Meicho Shuppan, 1978), 5:28–29.

60. This is clearest in Harootunian, *Things Seen and Unseen*, 168–75 ("The Chronotope of Collective Time"). The term "chronotope" comes from Mikhail M. Bakhtin, "Forms of Time and Chronotope in the Novel," *The Dialogic Imagination*, ed. Michael Holquist, trans. Caryl Emerson and Michael Holquist (Austin: University of Texas Press, 1981), 84–151.

61. LaFleur, *Karma of Words*, 124.

62. LaFleur, *Karma of Words*, 127; quoting Dōgen, "Bendowa," in Nishio Minoru et al., eds., *Shōbōgenzō, Shōbōgenzō-zuimon-ki*, Nihon koten bungaku taikei 81 (Tokyo: Iwanami Shoten, 1966), 83: "Buppō ni wa, shushō kore ittō nari."

63. For Zeami's stages of an actor's spiritual progress, see his *Kyūi* ("Notes on the Nine Levels") and *Shikadō* ("The True Path to the Flower"), in Rimer, trans., *On the Art of the Nō Drama*, 120–25, 64–73.

64. Yanagita is clearly a major source for Joseph Kitagawa, and through him I suspect Eliade. Taking Yanagita's nativist folklore-studies (*minzokugaku*) on the one

hand and D. T. Suzuki's overwhelmingly influential and nativist-leaning presentations of Zen on the other, it seems plausible that many of the more romantic, idealist conceptions of "archaic ontology" in the later Eliade and his disciples must have come under the influence of the *kokugakusha*. Given that various nativisms became strongly complicit in the rise of Japanese fascism through (among other things) its emphasis on the unique character of the Japanese and their "folk" spirit, ideas concordant with German *Volksgeistliche* formulations, this suggests a more effective and historically sophisticated means by which to reveal the ideological underpinnings of the Eliadean project than the accounts of Steven Wasserstrom and his imitators: Wasserstrom, *Religion after Religion*.

65. Harootunian, *Things Seen and Unseen*, 407.

66. Ibid., 408.

67. Ibid., 374–406.

68. In this language of "trace" and "survival," Yanagita is probably influenced by the Victorian mode of ethnography pioneered by Edward B. Tylor, Sir James Frazer, and William Robertson Smith.

69. Harootunian, *Things Seen and Unseen*, 420; quoting Yanagita Kunio.

70. Ibid., 416.

71. On the discourse of "uniqueness" with respect to religion, see Jonathan Z. Smith, "Fences and Neighbors," in his *Imagining Religion* (Chicago: University of Chicago Press, 1982), 1–18. It would be instructive to follow up the ideological implications of such claims in contexts such as the present one; this would likely reveal yet again subtle and complex reasons for the Eliadean project's fatal attraction for fascistic ideas.

72. Grimes, "Sitting and Eating" and "Modes of Zen Ritual," *Beginnings in Ritual Studies* (Lanham, Md.: University Press of America, 1982), 87–100, 101–13.

73. One can of course partially avoid such complicity by imposing one's own ideological project and simply steamrollering over anything in the data that seems potentially difficult, but I assume that my readers will not find this option palatable, and I am certain that Grimes would not.

74. "Modes of Zen Ritual," 107.

75. On the nationalist implications of Zen, see Bernard Faure, *The Rhetoric of Immediacy: A Cultural Critique of Chan/Zen Buddhism* (Princeton: Princeton University Press, 1991), and the significant literature that has arisen in Faure's wake.

76. "Modes of Zen Ritual," 106.

77. Ibid.

78. Ibid, 103. The quoted phrase "ritual as symbol system" is from Clifford Geertz, "Religion as a Cultural System," *Anthropological Approaches to the Study of Religion*, ed. Michael Banton, *ASA Monographs* 3 (London: Tavistock, 1966), 1–46; reprinted in *The Interpretation of Cultures* (New York: Basic Books, 1973), 87–125.

79. "Modes of Zen Ritual," 103–104.

80. "Sitting and Eating," 92.

81. See Faure, *Rhetoric of Immediacy*, introduction and final chapter.

82. "Modes of Zen Ritual," 106; quoting John W. Dixon Jr., *The Physiology of Faiths: A Theory of Theological Relativity* (San Francisco: Harper and Row, 1979).

83. See Herman Ooms, *Tokugawa Ideology* (Princeton: Princeton University Press, 1985).

84. John Dee, "Compendious Rehearsal" (1593), in *Autobiographical Tracts of Dr. John Dee . . .* , ed. James Crossley, *Chetham Miscellanies* 1.5, Remains Historical and Literary Connected with the Palatine Counties of Lancaster and Chester published by the Chetham Society 24 (1851). Discussed in Woolley, *Queen's Conjuror*, 12–15.

85. Dee, *Monas Hieroglyphica*, 134–37. See also Håkansson, *Seeing the Word*, 298–99, 318–31; and Clulee, *Dee's Natural Philosophy*, 116–42, for discussion of this passage.

86. Håkansson, *Seeing the Word*, 321; as he rightly notes, the best discussion of this project, which dominates the *Libri Mysteriorum* angel conversations, is Harkness, *Dee's Conversations*, 195–214.

87. Dee, MS Sloane 3188, 6v; quoted in Szőnyi, 187–88, who gives the further references: *Mysteriorum Libri*, 22 December 1581–23 May 1583, in Christopher Whitby, *John Dee's Actions with Spirits* (New York: Garland, 1988), 2:8; *The Enochian Magick of Dr. John Dee*, ed. and trans. Geoffrey James (1983; St. Paul, Minn.: Llewellyn, 1994), 1:4.

88. "The Theater of Cruelty, First Manifesto," *The Theater and Its Double*, trans. Mary Caroline Richards (New York: Grove, 1958), 89–100.

4. THE MAGIC MUSEUM

1. Carlo Ginzburg, *Clues, Myths, and the Historical Method*, trans. John and Anne Tedeschi (Baltimore: Johns Hopkins University Press, 1989), x, xii. The "current work" to which Ginzburg refers was published as *Storia Notturna* (Turin: Einaudi, 1989); English: *Ecstasies: Deciphering the Witches' Sabbath*, trans. Raymond Rosenthal (New York: Random House, 1991). Interestingly, critics did attack the work on these grounds, if not usually in these terms.

2. Jonathan Z. Smith, "Acknowledgments: Morphology and History, part 1," *Relating Religion* (Chicago: University of Chicago Press, 2004), 72; Ginzburg quote, 64.

3. Smith, "Trading Places," *Relating Religion*, 219.

4. Ibid., 218.

5. Sir James Frazer, *The Golden Bough*, 1 vol. abridged ed. (London: Macmillan, 1955 [1922]), 49.

6. Giordano Bruno, *On the Composition of Images, Signs, and Ideas*, trans. and ed. Charles Doria and Dick Higgins (New York: Willis, Locker, and Owens, 1991), xxxvi–xxxvii. The volume is now so rare that the only copy I have seen for sale was offered at over $500! Given the interest in Bruno, it is peculiar that no one has undertaken a reprint.

7. "L'image ne peut pas être idée, mais elle peut jouer le rôle de signe, ou, plus exactement, cohabiter avec l'idée dans un signe; et, si l'idée n'est pas encore là, respecter

sa place future et en faire apparaître négativement les contours," *La pensée sauvage*, 34; "Images cannot be ideas but they can play the part of signs or, to be more precise, co-exist with idea in signs and, if ideas are not yet present, they can keep their future place open for them and make its contours apparent negatively," *Savage Mind*, 20.

8. See esp. Marie-Luce Demonet, *Les voix du signe: Nature et origine du langage à la Renaissance, 1480–1580* (Paris-Geneva: Champion-Slatkine, 1992).

9. Bruno, *On the Composition*, 235–41. Notes in square brackets are the editors'; those in curly braces are mine. I have at times silently corrected punctuation to a more standard English.

10. Gatti, *Giordano Bruno and Renaissance Science*, 178–79.

11. Ibid., 179; citing Rita Sturlese, "Il *De imaginum, signorum et idearum composi-tione* di Giordano Bruno ed il significato filosofico dell'arte della memoria," *Giornale critico della filosofia italiana* (May–August 1990), and "Per un'interpretazione del *De umbris idearum* di Giordano Bruno," *Annali della Scuola Normale Superiore di Pisa*, 3rd ser., 22, no. 3 (1992).

12. Gatti, *Giordano Bruno*, 200–201.

13. See Yates, *Giordano Bruno*, 131; cf. Lehrich, *Language of Demons and Angels*, 41.

14. On the seriousness of Bruno's playfulness, see Nuccio Ordine, *La cabala del-l'asino: Asinità e conoscenza in Giordano Bruno*, 2nd ed. (Naples: Liguori, 1996); trans-lated as *Giordano Bruno and the Philosophy of the Ass*, by Henryk Baraánski in collabo-ration with Arielle Saiber (New Haven: Yale University Press, 1996).

15. Bruno, *On the Composition*, 48.

16. To my knowledge, the precise layout of these rooms is not entirely under-stood, despite Sturlese's important work. There are clearly a number of problems with the diagrams and charts in the 1591 text, and unless the logical key can be found—probably cryptographically—it will be impossible to correct them. It does seem clear that there are both perspectival and combinatoric logics at work, such that the letter of the atrium produces a transformation on the letters of the relevant images, and further the various subsections are viewed from the center of the atrium in question (Bruno places the eye there) such that perspective is indirect like a knight move in chess or per-haps even mirrored around corners. My suspicion is that there is a very simple prin-ciple, rigidly and consistently applied—and a great many errors in the text.

17. In keeping with some recent scholarship on these issues, I use the spelling "phantasy" to distinguish the phantasmic or image-making faculty of the mind, as understood by early modern thinkers, from the modern "fantasy," which has entirely other and inappropriate connotations.

18. See al-Kindī, *De radiis*, trans. in Sylvain Matton, *La magie Arabe traditionelle* (Paris: Bibliotheca Hermetica, 1977). For a discussion, see Lehrich, *Language of Demons and Angels*, 116–19.

19. Bruno, *On the Composition*, bk. 1, pt. 1, chap. 5, 16.

20. Ibid., chap. 1, 8.

21. "Les espèces animales et végétales ne sont pas connues pour autant qu'elles

sont utiles: elles sont décrétées utiles ou intéressantes parce qu'elles sont d'abord connues" (*La pensée sauvage*, 21); cf. the slightly different translation in *The Savage Mind*,
9.

22. For recent work in English, see Paula Findlen, ed., *Athanasius Kircher: The
Last Man Who Knew Everything* (New York: Routledge, 2004); Daniel Stolzenberg,
ed., *The Great Art of Knowing: The Baroque Encyclopedia of Athanasius Kircher*
(Fiesole: Stanford University Libraries and Edizione Cadmo, 2001); Ingrid D. Rowland, *The Ecstatic Journey: Athanasius Kircher in Baroque Rome* (Chicago: University
of Chicago Press, 2000). Joscelyn Godwin's volume of images, *Athanasius Kircher: A
Renaissance Man and the Quest for Lost Knowledge* (London: Thames and Hudson,
1979), is still useful. For translations and new editions, Findlen's contributors find
only *China Illustrata*, trans. Charles Van Tuyl (Bloomington: Indiana University
Press, 1986).

23. In this conception of collection, I am relying on Walter Benjamin's flâneur,
for which see his *Charles Baudelaire: A Lyric Poet in the Era of High Capitalism*, trans.
Harry Zohn (London: Verso, 1997) and *The Arcades Project*, ed. and trans. Howard
Eiland and Kevin McLaughlin (Cambridge: Harvard University Press, Belknap
Press, 1999). See also Susan Stewart, *On Longing: Narratives of the Miniature, the Gi-
gantic, the Souvenir, the Collection* (Durham: Duke University Press, 1993).

24. As a young man Kircher had wanted to do missionary work in China, but he
was rejected in 1628.

25. Florence Hsia, "Athanasius Kircher's *China Illustrata* (1667): An Apologia
Pro Vita Sua," in Findlen, ed., *Last Man*, 383; quoting Oldenburg to Robert Boyle
(25 August 1664), in *The Correspondence of Henry Oldenburg*, ed. A. Rupert and
Marie B. Hall, vol. 2 (1663–65) (Madison: University of Wisconsin Press, 1966),
532.

26. For example, Johann Burkhard Mencke described with great amusement a
number of academic pranks played on Kircher, such as the time he was given "silk
paper inscribed with Chinese-like characters. Unable to interpret it, he finally expressed his bewilderment . . . to the bearers of this gift. With great glee, they held it
up to a mirror, and the following words appeared: *Noli vana sectari et tempus perdere
nugis nihil proficientibus* ('Do not seek vain things, or waste time on unprofitable tri-
fles')": Findlen, "The Last Man Who Knew Everything . . . or Did He?," in Findlen,
Last Man, 7; citing Mencke, *The Charlatanry of the Learned (De charaltaneria eruditorum, 1715)*, trans. Francis E. Litz, ed. H. L. Mencken (New York: Knopf, 1937), 85–86.
Other examples appear throughout this volume of essays. Amusingly, Findlen tran-
scribes "Mencken" as "Mencke," raising the suspicion that one witty exposer of intellectual follies might be descended from another.

27. Hsia, "Athanasius Kircher's *China Illustrata*," 385.

28. Stolzenberg, "Egyptian Oedipus: Antiquarianism, Oriental Studies, and Occult Philosophy in the Work of Athanasius Kircher," PhD diss., Stanford University,
2003, 23–24; quoting a letter of Peiresc to Dupuy, Aix, 11 October 1632, Philippe

Tamizey de Larroque, ed., *Lettres de Peiresc*, Collections de documents inédits sur l'histoire de France (Paris: Imprimerie Nationale, 1888–98), 2:359.

29. Stolzenberg, "Egyptian Oedipus," 26–27; quoting Peiresc to Gassendi, Aix, 2 March 1633, *Lettres de Peiresc*, 4:295.

30. Stolzenberg, "Egyptian Oedipus," 45; quoting Peiresc to Kircher, Aix, 30 March 1635, Archivio della Pontifica Università Gregoriana 568, 364r–65v.

31. Stolzenberg, "Egyptian Oedipus," 23–69, tells the story of the Abnephius (Barachias Nephi, etc.) manuscript in full, and explicates effectively the ways in which these events were in a sense paradigmatic for others in Kircher's career.

32. "All Things Considered," May 22, 2002. The symposium at the New York Institute for the Humanities proposed the question, "Was Athanasius Kircher just about the coolest guy ever, or what?"

33. It is worth considering the extent to which this project, of comparing (implicitly, at least) universes of discourse, falls into the same difficulties as did the Pan-Babylonians and those later historians of Judaism whom Jonathan Z. Smith criticizes in "In Comparison a Magic Dwells"; I note in particular Smith's discussion of E. P. Sanders, *Paul and Palestinian Judaism: A Comparison of Patterns of Religion* (Philadelphia: Fortress, 1977), who wanted to compare religions "parts and all": Smith, *Imagining Religion*, 26–35, esp. 33–34.

34. Romano, "Epilogue: Understanding Kircher in Context," trans. Paula Findlen and Derrick Allums, in Findlen, ed., *Last Man*, 405.

35. Michel Foucault, *Les mots et les choses* (Paris: Gallimard, 1966), xxx; also trans. in *The Order of Things: An Archaeology of the Human Sciences* (New York: Random House, 1970), xv. The passage is from "El idioma analítico de John Wilkins" in *Otras inquisiciones*; a translation by Ruth L. C. Simms may be found in Jorge Luis Borges, *Other Inquisitions 1937–1952* (Austin: University of Texas Press, 1993), 101–5.

36. Paolo Rossi, *Clavis Universalis: Arti della memoria e logica combinatoria da Lullo a Leibniz*, 2nd ed. (Bologna: Società editrice il Mulino, 1983), xxx; I have relied primarily on Stephen Clucas's translation, *Logic and the Art of Memory: The Quest for a Universal Language* (Chicago: University of Chicago Press, 2000), in which this preface appears on pages xxi–xxviii.

37. "In Comparison a Magic Dwells," *Imagining Religion*, 25.

38. Antonella Romano, "Epilogue: Understanding Kircher in Context," in Findlen, ed., *Last Man*, 405.

39. Stolzenberg, *Great Art of Knowing*; Rossi, *Logic and the Art of Memory*, 141–42.

40. Horapollo, *The Hieroglyphics of Horapollo*, trans. George Boas (Princeton: Princeton University Press, 1950), 43.

41. See, for example, Erwin Panofsky, *Studies in Iconology: Humanistic Themes in Art* (Oxford: Oxford University Press, 1939).

42. Findlen, *Possessing Nature: Museums, Collecting, and Scientific Culture in Early Modern Italy* (Berkeley: University of California Press, 1994).

43. Athanasius Kircher, *China Monumentis . . . Illustrata* (1667), trans. Charles D. Van Tuyl (Bloomington: Indiana University Press, 1987), 214 (6.1). I have slightly amended Van Tuyl's translations throughout and have also retransliterated the Chinese into the now-standard pinyin system.

44. Kircher, *China*, 216 (6.2).

45. Ibid., 218–20, fig. 9 (6.3, fig. 9).

46. Ibid., 222 (6.4).

47. For Intorcetta's manuscript, see Knud Lundbaek, ed. and trans., *The Traditional History of the Chinese Script: From a Seventeenth Century Jesuit Manuscript* (Aarhus, Denmark: Aarhus University Press, 1988), 192. For Chinese sources, see Lundbaek, "Imaginary Ancient Chinese Characters," in *China Mission Studies (1550–1800), Bulletin V* (1983); it refers to *Wen Lin Sha Jin Wan Bao Quan Shu*, which probably served as Kircher's source as it was given to him around 1650. Saussy, "*China Illustrata*: The Universe in a Cup of Tea," in Stolzenberg, ed., *Great Art of Knowing*, 111, suggests a late Ming collection of fanciful calligraphic styles on the *Diamond Sutra*: Kumarajiva, attr., *Sanshi'er zhuanti Jingang jing* (The Diamond Sutra in thirty-two seal character styles) (Ming Wan-li period edition; repr. Tianjin: Guji shudian, 1985 [not seen]).

48. Brian Vickers, "On the Function of Analogy in the Occult," in *Hermeticism and the Renaissance*, ed. Ingrid Merkel and Allen G. Debus (Washington, D.C.: Folger Shakespeare Library; London: Associated University Presses, 1988), 265–92. The original conference was held in March 1982.

49. Vickers, "Function of Analogy," 289.

50. Ibid., 272.

51. Ibid.; the reference is to D. P. Walker, *Spiritual and Demonic Magic*.

52. Stanley J. Tambiah, "The Magical Power of Words," *Man*, n.s., 3 (1968): 175–208; "Form and Meaning of Magical Acts," in *Modes of Thought: Essays on Thinking in Western and Non-Western Societies*, ed. Robin Horton and Ruth Finnegan (London: Faber and Faber, 1972); "A Performative Approach to Ritual," *Proceedings of the British Academy* 65 (1979): 113–69; *Magic, Science, Religion, and the Scope of Rationality* (Cambridge: Cambridge University Press, 1990).

53. Vickers, "Function of Analogy," 266.

54. "La vraie question n'est pas de savoir si le contact d'un bec de pic guérit les maux de dents, mais s'il est possible, d'un certain point de vue, de faire 'aller ensemble' le bec de pic et la dent de l'homme . . . et, par le moyen de ces groupements de choses et d'êtres, d'introduire un début d'ordre dans l'univers; le classement, quel qu'il soit, possédant une vertu propre par rapport à l'absence de classement," *La pensée sauvage*, 21–22; *The Savage Mind*, 9.

55. Stephen Jay Gould, "Father Athanasius on the Isthmus of a Middle State: Understanding Kircher's Paleontology," in Findlen, *Last Man*, 208.

56. Ibid., 219.

57. Ibid., 222, emphasis added; quoting Kircher, *Mundus Subterraneus*, 2 vols. (Amsterdam, 1665), 2:48.

58. "Nous répondrons d'abord que cette association supposée procède d'une pétition de principe. Si l'on a convenu de définir le totémisme par la présence simultanée de dénominations animales ou végétales, de prohibitions portant sur les espèces correspondantes, et d'interdiction du mariage entre gens partageant le même nom et la même prohibition, alors il est clair que la liaison entre ces observances pose un problème. Mais, comme on l'a remarqué depuis longtemps, chacune peut se rencontrer sans les autres, ou deux quelconques d'entre elles sans la troisième," *La pensée sauvage*, 120; the translation in *The Savage Mind*, 97, is not legitimate, much less intelligible, English grammar.

59. Stewart, *On Longing*, 151–52, emphasis in original.

60. "Nous croyons que les anciens ethnologues se sont laissé duper par une illusion.": *La pensée sauvage*, 7; *Savage Mind*, xi. Le *Totémisme aujourd'hui* (Paris: PUF, 1962); *Totemism*, trans. Rodney Needham (Boston: Beacon, 1963).

61. S. K. Heninger Jr., *Touches of Sweet Harmony: Pythagorean Cosmology and Renaissance Poetics* (San Marino, Calif.: Huntington Library, 1974), and *The Cosmographical Glass: Renaissance Diagrams of the Universe* (San Marino, Calif.: Huntington Library, 1977).

62. Heninger and Vickers render this as *The Universal Work of the Muses*. The title is certainly somewhat ambiguous; I follow the translation used in Stolzenberg, *Great Art of Knowing*.

63. Heninger, *Sweet Harmony*, 331, quoted in Vickers, "Function of Analogy," 274.

64. Vickers, "Function of Analogy," 274.

65. Ibid., 275–76; the quote is from Heninger, *Sweet Harmony*, 338.

66. Vickers, "Function of Analogy," 276.

67. Ibid., 277.

68. In the weak analogy (aka false analogy, faulty analogy, questionable analogy), the argument runs: *a* is like *b*; *b* has property *P*; therefore *a* has property *P*: a crow is like a lump of coal; crows can fly; therefore coal can fly. Another reading of the slippage here is as a question-begging analogy, in which there is an implied "given that *a* is like *b*," which begs the question. In any event, the implied claim here is that Heninger's analysis is not only accurate to Kircher but equivalent, and thus can be analyzed in Kircher's stead.

69. Vickers, "Function of Analogy," 266.

70. See Penelope Gouk, "Making Music, Making Knowledge: The Harmonious Universe of Athanasius Kircher," in Stolzenberg, *Great Art of Knowing*, 71–83; Gouk, *Music, Science, and Natural Magic in Seventeenth-Century England* (New Haven: Yale University Press, 1999). George J. Buelow, "Kircher, Athanasius," *Grove Music Online*, ed. L. Macy (accessed September 2005–May 2006), http://www.grovemusic .com, provides a useful overview and bibliography. Kircher's most important work of

music theory has been reprinted in facsimile, with a foreword and indexes by Ulf Scharlau: Athanasius Kircher, *Musurgia Universalis* (Hildesheim: G. Olms Verlag, 1970).

71. Goethe, letter to Herder, May 17, 1787; trans. in Heller, *Disinherited Mind*, 10; quoted in Smith, "Acknowledgments," *Relating Religion*, 71.

72. Vickers, "Function of Analogy," 288.

73. Ibid., 288.

74. Ibid., 289.

75. Sahlins's *How "Natives" Think: About Captain Cook, for Example* (Chicago: University of Chicago Press, 1995) makes this point elegantly in response to Gananath Obeyesekere's dubious criticisms in *The Apotheosis of Captain Cook* (Princeton: Princeton University Press, 1992).

76. Pierre Bourdieu, *The Logic of Practice*, trans. Richard Nice (Cambridge: Polity Press, 1990), 285n7.

77. Again, this is not to lend credence to Obeyesekere's points, which are genuinely reductive in collapsing all "natives" into one category—that to which Obeyesekere belongs and in which common sense and reason are applied—and all "whites" into another—to which Sahlins and Cook belong, in which common sense and reason are not applied, in which all "natives" are collapsed into singularity. As Sahlins points out, this view of the native/white division reduces all natives to middle-class bourgeoisie, disregards their particularity and interest, and is at base a racist conception.

78. Derrida, "Structure, Sign, and Play in the Discourse of the Human Sciences," *Writing and Difference*, trans. Alan Bass (Chicago: University of Chicago Press, 1978), 278–94.

79. Émile Durkheim in 1912 noted that science's claims to certainty are at least as dependent on social categories as on logic, a point repeated by Foucault, Kristeva, et al. What is frustrating about the "science wars" replying to Kristeva's critique (especially) is that few involved—perhaps especially scientists—seemed to know that *The Elementary Forms* had long since made the crucial argument, and that much of what remained for post-1968 scholars was historical detail.

80. "Dès lors, on comprend qu'une observation attentive et méticuleuse, tout entière tournée vers le concret, trouve, dans le symbolisme, à la fois son principe et son aboutissement. La pensée sauvage ne distingue pas le moment de l'observation et celui de l'interprétation, par plus qu'on n'enregistre d'abord, en les observant, les signes émis par un interlocuteur pour chercher ensuite à les comprendre: il parle, et l'émission sensible apporte avec elle sa signification. C'est que le langage articulé se décompose en éléments dont chacun n'est pas un signe, mais le moyen d'un signe: unité distinctive qui ne saurait être remplacée par une autre sans que change la signification, et qui peut être elle-même dépourvue des attributs de cette signification, qu'elle exprime en se joignant ou en s'opposant à d'autres unités," *La pensée sauvage* 266–67; cf. the disastrous translation in *The Savage Mind*, 222–23.

81. See Derrida, *Of Grammatology*, 27–93.

82. On this problem in Tambiah, see Lehrich, *Language of Demons and Angels*, 164–71.

83. See Derrida, "Structure, Sign, and Play."

84. "La fourrure, les plumes, le bec, les dents, peuvent être *de moi* parce qu'ils sont ce par quoi l'animal éponyme et moi différons l'un de l'autre: cette différence est assumée par l'homme à titre d'emblème, et pour affirmer son rapport symbolique avec l'animal; tandis que les parties consommables, donc assimilables, sont l'indice d'une consubstantialité réelle, mais qu'à l'inverse de ce qu'on imagine la prohibition alimentaire a pour véritable but de nier," *La pensée sauvage*, 132; *Savage Mind*, 107.

85. See Lévi-Strauss, *La pensée sauvage*, 186–93; *Savage Mind*, 154–60.

86. Derrida, "Structure, Sign, and Play"; *Of Grammatology*.

87. Note that the translation of *The Savage Mind* omits the epilogue on *viola tricolor*.

88. Lévi-Strauss, *Tristes Tropiques*, chap. 28; cf. Derrida, *Of Grammatology*, 107–40.

89. Claude Lévi–Strauss, *Myth and Meaning* (New York: Schocken, 1995 [1978/79]), 15: "people we call, usually and wrongly, 'primitive'—let's describe them rather as 'without writing,' because I think this is really the discriminatory factor between them and us."

90. One is reminded of Lévi-Strauss's citation of E. E. Evans-Pritchard on Azande interpretations of a granary falling down and killing a man, which for Lévi-Strauss proves that "magic postulates a complete and all-embracing determinism" (postule un déterminisme global et intégral): *La pensée sauvage*, 24; *Savage Mind*, 11.

91. Rey Chow, "How (the) Inscrutable Chinese Led to Globalized Theory," *PMLA* 116, no. 1 (January 2001): 69–74.

92. Stolzenberg, "Egyptian Oedipus," 3–4, 173–78, 282–85.

93. Ibid., 156–67.

94. Ibid., 120.

95. See Haun Saussy, "The Prestige of Writing: [wen], Letter, Picture, Image, Ideography," *Sino-Platonic Papers* 75 (February 1997): 1–40.

96. For an overview of the system, see Erik Iversen, *The Myth of Egypt and Its Hieroglyphs* (Princeton: Princeton University Press, Bollingen, 1993 [1961]), 11–37.

97. See Iversen, *Myth of Egypt*, 38–56; also Erik Hornung, *The Secret Lore of Egypt: Its Impact on the West*, trans. David Lorton (Ithaca: Cornell University Press, 2001), 19–25.

98. The first chapters of both Iversen, *Myth of Egypt*, and Hornung, *Secret Lore*, suggest this reading indirectly, and although I am confident that Iversen would reject it Hornung appears somewhat more open. The first chapter of Iversen is also a remarkable demonstration of Derrida's points about logocentrism in the historiography of writing.

99. For an introduction to the very complex problem of Chinese grammatology, see Saussy, "Prestige of Writing"; Saussy's *Great Walls of Discourse and Other Adven-*

tures in Cultural China (Cambridge: Harvard University Asia Center, 2002) is worth perusing as well. Jonathan Spence's *The Memory Palace of Matteo Ricci* (London: Penguin, 1985) includes exceptionally accessible discussions.

100. Hornung, *Secret Lore*, 11–13; Iversen, *Myth of Egypt*, 11–38.

101. Eric A. Havelock, "Chinese Characters and the Greek Alphabet," *Sino–Platonic Papers* 5 (December 1987), 1–4.

102. Denis Diderot and Jean le Rond d'Alembert, *Encyclopédie, ou Dictionnaire raisonné des sciences, des arts et des metiers, par une societé de gens de lettres*, 17 vols. (Paris, 1751–65), "Botanique," 2:340–45 (342); quoted in Rossi, *Logic and the Art of Memory*, 172.

103. Herodotus, *The Histories*, bk. 2, trans. Aubrey de Sélincourt, rev. A. R. Burn (London: Penguin Classics, 1972), 188–89.

104. Findlen, "The Last Man," in Findlen, *Last Man*, 1–48; for example, "It was not Kircher's ignorance but the complex and compelling nature of his intellectual convictions that led him down a particular path, which, it turns out, was not the road to modernity but a rather different project" (8).

105. *Encyclopedia Britannica; or, A Dictionary of Arts and Sciences Compiled Upon a New Plan. . . . By a Society of Gentlemen in Scotland*, 3 vols. (Edinburgh, 1771), "Anatomy," 1:145–310, and "Anatoria," 310: "ANATORIA, a small city of Greece, upon the river Asopa, five miles from the straits of Negropont."

106. See Jonathan Z. Smith, "Fences and Neighbors," *Imagining Religion*, 1–18, esp. 1–5.

107. F. Scott Fitzgerald, *The Crack-Up*, ed. Edmund Wilson (New York: J. Laughlin, 1945).

108. Anthony Grafton, "Kircher's Chronology," in Findlen, ed., *Last Man*, 183–84.

109. Stolzenberg, "Egyptian Oedipus."

110. Eliade, *Cosmos and History*.

111. *La pensée sauvage*, chap. 9.

112. For example, *La pensée sauvage*, 70; *Savage Mind*, 52—where it is opposed to the axis "of simultaneities."

5. TAROCCO AND FUGUE

1. Antoine Court de Gébelin's account of this party appears in volume 8 of *Le Monde Primitif* (Paris, 1781), 367. The hostess is probably Madame Helvetius, wife of the Encyclopedist: see Antoine Court de Gébelin, *Le tarot*, ed. Jean-Marie Lhôte (Paris: Berg International, 1983), 86.

2. On collections, see Susan Stewart, *On Longing*, 151–66, and chapter 4 above.

3. "The Structural Study of Myth," in *Structural Anthropology*, trans. Claire Jacobson and Brooke Grundfest Schoepf (New York: Basic Books, 1963), 212–13.

4. "The Structural Study of Myth," originally in "Myth, a Symposium," *Journal of*

American Folklore 78, no. 270 (October–December 1955): 428–44; reprinted "with slight modifications" in *Structural Anthropology*, 206–31. "Structure et Dialectique," in *For Roman Jakobson, Essays on the Occasion of His Sixtieth Birthday* (The Hague, 1956), 289–94; reprinted in translation in *Structural Anthropology*, 232–41. *La pensée sauvage* (Paris, 1962); translated as *The Savage Mind* (Chicago: University of Chicago Press, 1966). The four volumes of *Mythologiques* were published in Paris by Librairie Plon, and in English, translated by John and Doreen Weightman, were originally published by Harper and Row, but reprinted by the University of Chicago Press. The volumes are: *Le cru et le cuit* (1964); *The Raw and the Cooked* (ed. cit. Harper, 1969; Chicago, 1983). *Du miel aux cendres* (1966); *From Honey to Ashes* (Harper, 1973; ed. cit. Chicago, 1983). *L'Origine des manières de table* (1968); *The Origin of Table Manners* (Harper, 1978; ed. cit. Chicago, 1990). *L'Homme nu* (1971); *The Naked Man* (Harper, 1981; ed. cit. Chicago, 1990). Also of major importance here is *Regarder, Écouter, Lire* (Paris: Librairie Plon, 1993); *Look, Listen, Read*, trans. Brian C. J. Singer (New York: Basic Books, 1997).

5. Apart from the brief discussion in Marcel Hénaff, *Claude Lévi-Strauss and the Making of Structural Anthropology*, trans. Mary Baker (Minneapolis: University of Minnesota Press, 1998), 175–78 and 209–11, I initially found no significant examination of Lévi-Strauss, *Mythologiques*, and music. In my attempt at an exhaustive search, I was aided by David Wood, Chris Nelson, and Andrew Von Hendy; if something of a nontechnical musicological nature was passed over, it must be said that it is not easy to find.

Later, however, I stumbled on a rich trove of material in the little-known field of musical semiotics or semiology, of which Jean-Jacques Nattiez is now perhaps the leading figure. The specialist journal *Musique en jeu*, now defunct, ran an issue (no. 5, Nov. 1971) partly devoted to the question, unfortunately well before the completion of *Mythologiques*. My reading of this journal and several of Nattiez's fascinating works reveals much of considerable interest, and I plan to return to music and the occult at length in a future work. Unfortunately, however, very little of this material is of direct value here: the primary focus for music semiologists, unsurprisingly, is music itself, and as such their discussions are minimally concerned with the broad questions of myth and history addressed here. See Nattiez, *Music and Discourse: Toward a Semiology of Music*, trans. Carolyn Abbate (Princeton: Princeton University Press, 1990); *De la sémiologie à la musique* (Montreal: University of Quebec at Montreal, 1988), 189–234; and "Reflections on the Development of Semiology in Music," trans. Katherine Ellis, *Music Analysis* 8, no. 1–2 (1989): 21–74, a translation of chapter 10 of *De la sémiologie à la musique* together with a lengthy and valuable bibliography.

On Lévi-Strauss's mathematics, see Mauro W. Barbosa de Almeida, "Symmetry and Entropy: Mathematical Metaphors in the Work of Lévi-Strauss," *Current Anthropology* 31.4 (Aug.-Oct. 1990), 367–85. Lévi-Strauss himself, however, remarks that these formulae "should not be taken too seriously. There is only a superficial resemblance between my formulas and the equations of the mathematician. . . . Their purpose is quite different. Certain analyses of myths are so long and detailed that it would be impossible to carry them through to the end, if one did not have at one's disposal some abbreviated form of writing—a kind of shorthand" (*The Raw and the Cooked*, 30). We need not be bound by an author's intentions, stated or implicit, but it is problematic to analyze in detail the analogy Lévi-Strauss dismisses while ignoring that on which he tells us to focus. At any rate, the issue should not be relegated to musicology alone.

6. The historical connection between the formation of the tarot pack and that of our "modern" playing cards is unclear and much debated, particularly in the specialist journal *The Playing Card*; see also Michael Dummett, *The Game of Tarot* (London: Duckworth, 1980); and Ronald Decker, Thierry Depaulis, and Michael Dummett, *A Wicked Pack of Cards: The Origins of the Occult Tarot* (New York: St. Martin's, 1996).

7. The etymology of *tarocco* (tarot) is unclear. For a discussion, see Dummett, *Game of Tarot*.

8. Detailed information on the early origins of the tarot may be found in Stuart Kaplan, *The Encyclopedia of Tarot*, vol. 1 (New York: U.S. Games Systems, 1978); *Game of Tarot*, particularly pages 3–92; and Dummett's catalogue of the earliest surviving deck, *The Visconti-Sforza Tarot Cards* (New York: George Braziller, 1986). It is also worth noting that the "modern" suits are dominant only in North America, Britain, France, and Holland. Italian decks still use the suits listed above, with Spanish decks essentially equivalent (*espadas, bastos, copas, oros*). German and Swiss decks use a rather different set: *Laube, Grüne,* or *Schilten; Eicheln; Herzen* or *Rosen; Schellen*.

9. On the archetypal tarot, see *Wicked Pack*, 25–26. On *Sermones de Ludo cum Aliis*, see *Encyclopedia of Tarot*, vol. 1. For the late occult decks, see Arthur Edward Waite, *Pictorial Key to the Tarot* (London: Rider, 1911), and Aleister Crowley, *The Book of Thoth* (York Beach, Maine: Samuel Weiser, 1986). Note that these three sample decks cannot readily be compared with the early nineteenth-century Etteilla tarots, the first decks printed expressly for the purpose of cartomancy, which had a quite different structure; on Etteilla and his contributions to the history of Tarot cartomancy, see *Wicked Pack*, 74–100.

10. See *Wicked Pack*, 45. Dummett, *Visconti-Sforza Tarot*, 122, gives several citations for the early meaning of Time. Waite, generally more reliable as a critic than an interpreter, except as a primary occult source, insists that a star shines within the lantern and that "therefore the Hermit is not, as Court de Gébelin explained, a wise man in search of truth. . . . His beacon intimates that 'where I am, you also may be.' . . . [Furthermore] the idea of occult isolation. . . . is one of the frivolous renderings which we owe to Eliphas Lévi" (*Pictorial Key*, 104).

11. Decker et al. argue that cartomancy "does not appear to have been practised in Western Europe with cards of any kind until much before the XVIII century," although they note a 1690 deck designed for a similar purpose. At the same time, their definition of cartomancy is problematic, as it does not include "a light-hearted practice of telling fortunes, probably practised for amusement at home rather than by

professionals charging fees." Indeed, the 1690 deck "was not cartomancy as we understand it, based on symbolic meanings attached to the individual cards" (47–51). For these authors, then, cartomancy is either "serious" or "professional": to be a cartomancer, one must either believe in the cards' higher truths or charge fees for one's services, or both. One wonders how a distinguished logician such as Dummett could have fallen into the old fallacy of assuming that he can divine what people really believe; see also note 23 below. As a further point, note that this whole approach assumes that cartomancy is only "serious" if it locks meaning to specific cards on an individual basis. Oddly, this seems to require that only occultists and philosophers are mad enough to accept the arbitrariness of the sign. Although I suspect there is some truth to this, the reality is that Decker et al. probably intend little by their remark, presuming that occult thought is insufficiently important to deserve logical rigor.

12. Near the end of his life, Court de Gébelin became enamored of Mesmerism and, in fact, died of electrocution in 1784, while undergoing magnetic therapy. An unknown wag penned the following epitaph (*Wicked Pack*, 64, and 271n52):

> Ci-gît ce pauvre Gébelin,
> Qui parloit Grec, Hébreu, Latin;
> Admirez tous son héroisme:
> Il fut martyr du magnétisme.

13. Antoine Court de Gébelin, *Le Monde Primitif, analysé et comparé avec le monde moderne,* . . . 9 vols., vol. 8 (Paris: 1781), 365.

14. Court de Gébelin consistently uses the term *allegorie* in a broad sense of symbolic representation, perhaps thinking of the Greek ἀλληγορέω, which carries a more general sense of the symbolic or figurative.

15. *Le Monde Primitif*, vol. 1 (Paris: 1774), 4: "il ne faut que bien connoître celui d'aujourd'hui pour connoître ceux de tous les siecles: le séries physique & le séries morales sont nécessaires en elles-mêmes; elles sont sous nos yeux, sous notre main."

16. *Le Monde Primitif*, vol. 2 (Paris, 1775), 38, 40, and 275; these translations are taken from Gérard Genette, *Mimologics*, trans. Thaïs E. Morgan, (Lincoln: University of Nebraska, 1995), 92; Genette's chapter "Generalized Hieroglyphics" (91–115) is the best short discussion of *Le Monde Primitif* available. Some lengthy quotations from volumes 3, 6, and 7 may be found in Jean Roudaut, *Poètes et grammariens au XVIIIe siècle: Anthologie* (Paris: Gallimard, 1971), 288–323; see also Roudaut's discussion of Court de Gébelin and Charles de Brosses in ibid., 223–61.

17. The identity of "M. le C. de M." was apparently first discovered by Jean-Marie Lhôte, who explains how this identification was made in his annotated facsimile edition of *Le Monde Primitif* tarot essays: Antoine Court de Gébelin, *Le Tarot*, ed. Jean-Marie Lhôte (Paris: Berg International, 1983), 144, s.v. "M. le C. de M."; see also Dummett, *Game of Tarot*, 105n13.

18. *Le Monde Primitif*, 8:368.

19. Referring to trump II, the Popess (*la papessa*), now usually called "the high priestess" in occult terminology.

20. *Le Monde Primitif*, 8:372. Note that the original symbolism probably refers to a traitor, given the old Italian practice of hanging such criminals by their heels, as was done to Mussolini (*Wicked Pack*, 45–46). Decker et al., 269n13, credit Gertrude Moakley, *The Tarot Cards Painted by Bonifacio Bembo for the Visconti-Sforza Family: An Iconographic and Historical Study* (New York: New York Public Library, 1966), 95, with this identification.

21. This theory of the four suits has been repeated ever since, as for example in Joseph Campbell's introduction essay "Symbolism of the Marseilles Deck," in Joseph Campbell and Richard Robert, *Tarot Revelations* (San Anselmo, Calif.: Vernal Equinox Press, 1979), which is also the sole source for an article by Richard W. Thurn in the *Encyclopedia of Religions*, ed. Mircea Eliade, s.v. "Cards." In this article the proposition is stated baldly enough: "The pictorial symbolism of the deck is known to have much in common with the symbolism of spiritual initiation rites and instruction in Hellenistic mystery cults, ancient astrology, and medieval alchemy, wherein the processes of manifesting divine energies are represented in the progression of visual and numerical symbols." I cannot agree with Mr. Thurn's claims, nor with his assessment of *Tarot Revelations*, which he describes as "a detailed work summarizing the phenomenological evidence linking the tarot to Hellenistic religion and alchemy as well as the tarot's place in nineteenth-century esoteric societies."

22. *Le Monde Primitif*, 8:380, 385–86, 388–89, 393–94.

23. *Le Monde Primitif*, 8:395. The definitions used by de Mellet for this etymology are not original to him but come from earlier volumes of *Le Monde Primitif*. Decker et al. seem convinced that de Mellet and Court de Gébelin do not agree about much, that the latter more or less cribbed or stole the idea of the occult tarot from the former, and so forth (*Wicked Pack of Cards*, 64–68); the evidence for this depends on various hypothetical sins of omission in Court de Gébelin. At the same time, Decker et al. do not seem to have examined much of the rest of *Le Monde Primitif*, and do not notice the many times that de Mellet borrows from Court de Gébelin, equally without citation or reference. A more likely explanation of this mutual borrowing is that de Mellet, a subscriber since at least volume 2, wrote his essay as a kind of extension of Court de Gébelin's work, and the latter, recognizing the sincere flattery of such an extension, published it. It is also possible that Court de Gébelin removed citations, since after all they would be cross-references; there is no reason to assume that Court de Gébelin simply published de Mellet's essay without any editing.

24. *Le Monde Primitif*, 8:396. In the trick-taking game of tarot, the Fool is unnumbered because it is not properly part of the sequence of trumps, but rather may be played at any time in order to avoid following suit within a trick.

25. *Le Monde Primitif*, 8:400.

26. Ibid., 404.

27. Ibid., 405. The names Jannes and Mambres refer to 2 Timothy, 3:8, in the Vulgate; the Revised Standard Version has Jannes and Jambres.

28. *Le Monde Primitif*, 8:407.

29. Ibid., 408. Although it is certainly possible that the entire discussion of fortune-tellers in de Mellet is simply the product of his somewhat fevered imagination, this strikes me as unlikely, given the content of the text (408–10). If this text has any accuracy at all, it clearly refers to professional cartomancers, perhaps those based in the Maine and Perche, where de Mellet was governor. At any rate, the text should be taken as serious evidence of cartomancy that was something other than a "light-hearted game," as Decker et al. would have it.

I have not been able to find all of these letter-meanings in the previous seven volumes of *Le Monde Primitif*, but it seems probable that a careful search would turn them up. For example, de Mellet tells us that the Hebrew letter ס *sameh* means "adhesion," and in Court de Gébelin's "Dictionnaire Etymologique de la Langue Latine" (vols. 6 and 7), we are told that this Hebrew letter derives from a picture of a belt or cincture. Similarly, de Mellet says that "zayin [ז] announces inconstancy, error, violated faith, crime," which is why he assigns it to card XV, Typhon (the Devil); the same article in Court de Gébelin tells us that "la signification propre de Z, est celle de se mouvoir, s'agiter." See Roudaut, *Poètes et grammariens*, 322–23, s.v. "Z."

30. "Were we to *tell* the myth, we would disregard the columns and read the rows from left to right and from top to bottom. But if we want to *understand* the myth, then we will have to disregard one half of the diachronic dimension (top to bottom) and read from left to right, column after column, each one being considered as a unit": *Structural Anthropology*, 214.

31. *The Raw and the Cooked*, "Overture," 1–32, esp. 14–30.

32. *Le Monde Primitif*, 8:369.

33. Ibid., 369–73.

34. See Eliphas Lévi (Alphonse Louis Constant), *Transcendental Magic*, trans. A. E. Waite (London, 1896; repr. York Beach, Maine: Samuel Weiser, 1972), 393.

35. For the following discussion, I have referred to *The New Harvard Dictionary of Music*, ed. Don Michael Randel (Cambridge: Harvard University Press, Belknap Press, 1986), and the online www.grovemusic.com, which comprises *The New Grove Dictionary of Music and Musicians*, 2nd ed., ed. Stanley Sadie and John Tyrrell (London, 2001), *The New Grove Dictionary of Opera*, ed. Stanley Sadie (London, 1992), and *The New Grove Dictionary of Jazz*, 2nd ed., ed. Barry Kernfeld (London, 2002).

36. Technically speaking, it is not entirely clear whether the well-tempered scale was a particular system or a rough class of tempering systems, but this refinement clearly has no impact on Lévi-Strauss's arguments.

37. *The Raw and the Cooked*, 21. The reference here is to Arnold Schoenberg's twelve-tone system, which Schoenberg first labeled "Method of Composing with Twelve Tones Which Are Related Only with One Another." Schoenberg's considerable theoretical oeuvre is most readily approached through the many essays in *Style*

and Idea: Collected Writings, ed. Leonard Stein, trans. Leo Black, rev. ed. (Berkeley: University of California Press, 1984), particularly pt. 5, "Twelve-Tone Composition," 207–50. On a more technical level, his 1911 (rev. 1922) *Harmonielehre* is excellent reading: *Theory of Harmony*, trans. Roy E. Carter (Berkeley: University of California Press, 1978); the older translation by Robert D. W. Adams (New York: Philosophical Library, 1948) omits all the theoretical discussions to make the work a practical manual, which may be in keeping with Schoenberg's general intent but makes it much less useful for understanding Schoenberg. See also the unfinished *The Musical Idea and the Logic, Technique, and Art of Its Presentation*, ed. and trans. Patricia Carpenter and Severine Neff (New York: Columbia University Press, 1995).

38. *The Raw and the Cooked*, 23–24; the quotation is from Boulez, "Serie," in *Encyclopédie de la musique*, edited by F. Michel, F. Lesure, and V. Fédorov, 3 vols. (Paris, 1958–61) 2:696–67, which provides a dense and nuanced overview of serialism not well represented by this isolated remark. It is worth noting that properly speaking Schoenberg was not a serialist, but again the distinction is not entirely relevant here: Lévi-Strauss is discussing relatively broad conceptual issues, and since the serialists did indeed look to Schoenberg as their master inspiration, one should not overemphasize this elision.

39. *The Raw and the Cooked*, 24.

40. *The Naked Man*, 652; Lévi-Strauss mentions prior occurrences of the fugue metaphor in *The Naked Man*, 115, 182, 337, and *The Raw and the Cooked*, 147–63, 240–55.

41. *The Naked Man*, 660. Note that the lines "chasing each other and overlapping" may be intended as a literal rendering of the French term *fugue* in its original, nonmusical meaning. As Alfred Mann notes, however, there is considerable difficulty determining the origin of the term *fugue*: Alfred Mann, *The Study of Fugue* (New York: W. W. Norton, 1965), 9–30.

42. The simplest form of canon in this sense is the strict canon, essentially equivalent to a round, like "Row, Row, Row Your Boat." Canon requires "imitation of a complete subject [melodic theme] by one or more voices at fixed intervals of pitch and time" (*New Harvard Dictionary of Music*, s.v. "Canon"). In complex canons, this imitation may involve transposition up or down the scale, inversion (reversing intervals up and down), retrogression (reversing chronologically), and many other devices. From the most complex forms of canon comes the fugue, in which all such devices are used more or less simultaneously, and the subject itself may be complex. If we add to this classification of polyphonic forms the serialist "polyphony of polyphonies," we might rather loosely express the relations thus: round : canon :: canon : fugue :: fugue : serialism.

43. This may not be clear to those who have never studied music: when one plays a wind or string instrument, significant adjustment of any given note may be obtained by alteration of embouchure or finger position. This does not require retuning, or changing hand/finger position as for playing a new note; merely opening or

tightening the throat or lips, angling the pressure of the finger pads, and so forth, produces a shift in pitch. The point here is that a performer required to hit a perfect A-440, an acoustic purity important in the tight harmonies of Brahms, for example, cannot usually also improvise a perfectly harmonic line and keep track of what all the other players of a symphony orchestra are doing with their own individual lines. It was largely this increasing complexity that led to the modern institution of the orchestral conductor. Incidentally, it is worth considering that Lévi-Strauss's understanding of myth could usefully be paralleled to improvisational jazz, for any and all of the reasons stated above, and with potentially valuable results in the affective dimension. Lévi-Strauss's avoidance of the jazz metaphor is perhaps due to a dislike of the form, or perhaps merely to ignorance.

44. An enigma or riddle canon is one that contains "neither signs nor figures nor letters marking the four voices, and often there is not even a clef indication. In order to solve the riddle . . . various intervals, such as the upper or lower third, must be tried until the proper answer is found. Often one must experiment with the techniques of inversion, retrograde motion, inverted retrograde motion, or with the use of the three clefs and their transpositions": Johann Georg Albrechtsberger, "The Canon," *Gründliche Anweisung zur Komposition*, translated in Mann, *Study of Fugue*, 255–62. Mann gives several of Albrechtsberger's examples of enigma canons and their solutions.

45. *The Raw and the Cooked*, 17.

46. These three definitions are from *The Raw and the Cooked*, 199.

47. Boulez, "Série," 697: "La pensée du compositeur, utilisant une méthodologie déterminée, crée les objets dont elle a besoin et la forme nécessaire pour les organiser, chaque fois qu'elle doit s'exprimer." Quoted in *The Raw and the Cooked*, 23.

48. "Son univers instrumental est clos, et la règle de son jeu est de toujours s'arranger avec les 'moyens du bord,' c'est-à-dire un ensemble à chaque instant fini d'outils et de matériaux, hétéroclites au surplus, parce que la composition de l'ensemble n'est pas en rapport avec le projet du moment, ni d'ailleurs avec aucun projet particulier, mais est le résultat contingent de toutes les occasions qui se sont présentées de renouveler ou d'enrichir le stock, ou de l'entretenir avec les résidus de constructions et de destructions antérieures. L'ensemble des moyens du bricoleur n'est donc pas définissable par un projet." *La pensée sauvage*, 31; *Savage Mind*, 17.

49. Umberto Eco, "Unlimited Semiosis and Drift: Pragmaticism vs. 'Pragmaticism,'" in *The Limits of Interpretation* (Bloomington: Indiana University Press, 1990), 24. Note that Eco does not tar Derrida himself with this brush; on the contrary, he notes: "In *Grammatology* [Derrida] reminds his readers that without all the instruments of traditional criticism 'critical production will risk developing in almost any direction at all and authorize itself to say almost anything. But this indispensable guard-rail has always only *protected*, it has never *opened* a reading'" (Eco, "Unlimited Semiosis," 37). Eco uses this as support for his contention that "frequently Derrida—in order to stress nonobvious truths—disregards very obvious truths that nobody can

reasonably pass over in silence. . . . I think . . . that Derrida takes many of these obvious truths for granted—while frequently some of his followers do not" (ibid., 36). Eco's citation is from Derrida, *Of Grammatology*, 158.

50. Max Paddison, *Adorno's Aesthetics of Music* (Cambridge: Cambridge University Press, 1993), 151, quoting Adorno, *Aesthetic Theory*, trans. Christian Lenhardt (London: Routledge and Kegan Paul, 1984), 213 (*Gesammelte Schriften* 7:222). See also Adorno, *Philosophy of Modern Music*, trans. Anne G. Mitchell and Wesley V. Blomster (New York: Seabury Press, 1973), and *Essays on Music*, ed. Richard Leppert (Berkeley: University of California Press, 1992), esp. part 1, 113–209.

51. Paddison, *Adorno's Aesthetics*, 152.

52. Schoenberg, "Composition with Twelve Tones (1)," 1941, in *Style and Idea*, 216.

53. *The Naked Man*, 649.

6. De(mon)construction

1. In the course of an interesting experiential defense of "magic" as a useful category, Ariel Glucklich provides extensive examples of such dismissals, especially in his discussion of "Theories of Magic": *The End of Magic* (New York: Oxford University Press, 1997), 17–79.

2. For a general discussion, see Lehrich, *Language of Demons and Angels*, 5–8.

3. Aleister Crowley, *Magick in Theory and Practice* (1929; facsimile repr. Secaucus, N.J.: Castle Books, 1991), xi.

4. A. R. Radcliffe-Brown, *Taboo* (Cambridge: Cambridge University Press, 1939); repr., *Reader in Comparative Religion*, ed. William A. Lessa and Evon Z. Vogt, 4th ed. (New York: Harper and Row, 1979), 46–56.

5. Mauss, *Esquisse d'une théorie générale de la magie*, in *Sociologie et anthropologie* (Paris: PUF, 1960), 1–141. See also the translation by Robert Brain, *A General Theory of Magic* (London: Routledge and Kegan Paul, 1972).

6. For an examination of the mana problem, see Jonathan Z. Smith, "Manna, Mana Everywhere and /ˇ/ˇ/, *Relating Religion* (Chicago: University of Chicago Press, 2004), 117–44, esp. 125–34; the endnotes contain a considerable library of references.

7. Radcliffe-Brown, *Taboo*, 51.

8. *Introduction to the Work of Marcel Mauss*, trans. Felicity Barker (London: Routledge and Kegan Paul, 1987), 53; "Introduction à l'oeuvre de Marcel Mauss," in Marcel Mauss, *Sociologie et anthropologie* (Paris: PUF, 1960), xliii.

9. Lévi-Strauss, *Introduction*, 53; "Introduction," xliii.

10. Ibid., 55–56; xliv.

11. Ibid., 60; xlvii.

12. Ibid., 61; xlviii.

13. Smith, "Manna," 133.

14. For specific criticism of the signifier-totality, see Maurice Godelier, *The*

Enigma of the Gift, trans. Nora Scott (Chicago: University of Chicago Press, 1999), 17–31 esp. 23–25; for mana-specific criticisms, see the notes to Smith, "Manna," which also drew my attention to Godelier's work.

15. Lévi-Strauss, *Introduction*, 57; "Introduction," xlv: "Là vraiment, le *mana* est *mana*."

16. Smith, "Manna," 134.

17. *La pensée sauvage*, 24; *Savage Mind*, 11.

18. "Dès lors, on comprend qu'une observation attentive et méticuleuse, tout entière tournée vers le concret, trouve, dans le symbolisme, à la fois son principe et son aboutissement. La pensée sauvage ne distingue pas le moment de l'observation et celui de l'interprétation, par plus qu'on n'enregistre d'abord, en les observant, les signes émis par un interlocuteur pour chercher ensuite à les comprendre: il parle, et l'émission sensible apporte avec elle sa signification. C'est que le langage articulé se décompose en éléments dont chacun n'est pas un signe, mais le moyen d'un signe: unité distinctive qui ne saurait être remplacée par une autre sans que change la signification, et qui peut être elle-même dépourvue des attributs de cette signification, qu'elle exprime en se joignant ou en s'opposant à d'autres unités" (*La pensée sauvage* 266–67); cf. the dreadful translation on pages 222–23 of *Savage Mind*.

19. Smith, "Trading Places," *Relating Religion*, 215.

20. Lévi-Strauss, *La pensée sauvage*, 23; *Savage Mind*, 10–11. The citation is from Mauss, *Esquisse*, 56; *General Theory*, 78.

21. Lehrich, *Language of Demons and Angels*, esp. chap. 3.

22. Wouter J. Hanegraaff, *New Age Religion and Western Culture* (Albany: State University of New York Press, 1998), 6–7. Hanegraaff's quotes are from J. G. Platvoet, *Comparing Religions: A Limitative Approach* (The Hague: Mouton, 1983), 4–5.

23. The use of the Marvin Harris-style division emic/etic is extremely problematic here, not least because, as so many cultural anthropologists have noted, all data concerned with thought and meaning is necessarily emic. The defensive positivism of Hanegraaff's usage is also marked here by the phrase "scientific legitimacy," and in many respects undercuts whatever theoretical or methodological contribution the book might have made. Nevertheless, Hanegraaff's important book provides a clear and readable survey of a wide range of New Age texts, and constructs a kind of preliminary phenomenological classification of ideas and types. It thus lays a solid foundation for analysis.

24. Smith, "Trading Places," *Relating Religion*, 215–19.

25. Ibid., 219. As an example of the concluding point, Smith cites the "Moses phylactery" from Acre and, as a reference, R. D. Kotansky, "Texts and Studies in the Greco-Egyptian Magic Lamellae" (PhD diss., University of Chicago, 1988), text 36 (esp. 220–22) and the treatment of "counter-magic" in the introduction (8–10).

26. Smith, "Trading Places," 219–22.

27. Ibid., 218.

28. Ibid., 221.

29. Ibid., 227.

30. Ibid., 226.

31. In rendering the French *différance* as "differance," I must note that this is contrary to the usage of Alan Bass, Derrida's best translator. Bass argues with justification that the term is literally untranslatable; his italics and orthography thus demarcate an alterity of (or within) ordinary language. But too often the same orthographic devices have been taken to indicate an alterity *above* language, such that the Derridean neographism transforms itself into a hypostatization, from which differance could not more greatly differ. For this reason I prefer (like Gayatri Spivak) "differance."

32. The term "autonomous negation" comes from Dieter Henrich, "Hegels Grundoperation: Eine Einleitung in die 'Wissenschaft der Logik,'" *Der Idealismus und seine Gegenwart: Festschrift für Werner Marx*, ed. Ute Guzzoni et al. (Hamburg: Meiner, 1976), 215; cited and discussed in Manfred Frank, *What Is Neostructuralism?* trans. Sabine Wilke and Richard Grey (Minneapolis: University of Minnesota Press, 1987), lecture 17, 262–78.

33. This analysis presumes, with Derrida, a particular (semi-Hegelian) reflection model of subjectivity. But as Manfred Frank has noted, in a singularly lucid and eloquent treatment of Derrida's philosophical work, precisely these problems with a reflection model were already noted and criticized by Schelling, and it is unfortunate indeed that Derrida seems not to have escaped Hegel to the extent that his criticisms, devastating and elegant though they are, do not take into consideration alternative models. Frank argues that Schelling's model, and in a different context aspects of Peirce's and Schleiermacher's systems of signification and text, would be able to demonstrate that Derrida has particularly gracefully identified the slippery subject in its *Dasein* precisely within—but not reducible to—differance. Frank, *What Is Neostructuralism?*, esp. lecture 18, 279–87. On the vexed problem of Kabbalah and Derrida, see Elliot R. Wolfson's precise corrective reading: "Assaulting the Border: Kabbalistic Traces in the Margins of Derrida," *Journal of the American Academy of Religion* 70, no. 3 (September 2002): 475–514.

34. *Of Grammatology*, 24.

35. Ibid., 37.

36. Ibid., 41. Curly braces are my interpolations.

37. Ibid., 44.

38. Ibid., 107–40; Lévi-Strauss, *Tristes Tropiques*, chap. 28.

39. "Comme on vient de le voir, les logiques pratico-théoriques qui régissent la vie et la pensée des sociétés appelées primitives sont mues par l'exigence d'écarts différentiels": *La pensée sauvage*, 95; *Savage Mind*, 75.

40. "Différance," in *Margins of Philosophy*, trans. Alan Bass (Chicago: University of Chicago Press, 1982), 6. I have taken the liberty of transposing differance for Bass's *différance*. The ellipsis at the end marks a passage included in the printed version but not in the original lecture, a passage referring to a debate with Jacques Lacan that need not concern us here.

41. Frank, *What Is Neostructuralism?*, 215–17.

42. This is not to invalidate every redeployment of the analogy, by any means; literary critics, for example, who use bricolage for their own purposes and without further analytical remark on Lévi-Strauss can hardly be faulted for borrowing a useful conception. But to criticize Lévi-Strauss for thinking that tribal peoples' myths *are* bricolage is to misunderstand the initial argument.

43. Derrida, "Structure, Sign, and Play."

44. Richard Rorty's criticism of "differance" as a self-defeating neologism is worth taking seriously here: Rorty, "Deconstruction and Circumvention," *Critical Inquiry* 11 (1984): 1–23; also cited in Christopher Norris, *Derrida* (Cambridge: Harvard University Press, 1987), 16.

45. Frank, *What Is Neostructuralism?* Lectures 5 (48–64) and 14–18 (215–87) examine Derrida in light of Saussure and then phenomenology (Husserl) and idealism (Hegel). The concluding two lectures (410–49) lay a groundwork for a hermeneutical rethinking of both subjectivity and signification on a combined base of Schleiermacher, Peirce, and Saussure, significantly informed by Derrida.

46. Schelling encountered this material through the intellectual lineage of Jakob Boehme, via Friedrich Christoph Oetinger and other Romantics, some of them friends. For an introduction to this problem, see the essays in Eveline Goodman–Thau, Gerd [*sic*, Gert] Mattenklott, and Christoph Schulte, eds., *Kabbala und Romantik* (Tübingen: Niemeyer, 1994) and Eveline Goodman–Thau, Gert Mattenklott, and Christoph Schulte, eds., *Kabbala und die Literatur der Romantik: Zwischen Magie und Trope* (Tübingen: Niemeyer, 1999). Elliot R. Wolfson, in *Language, Eros, Being* (New York: Fordham University Press, 2005), and *Alef, Mem, Tau: Kabbalistic Musings on Time, Truth, and Death* (Berkeley: University of California Press, 2006), considers Schelling's encounter with Jewish mysticism largely outside of the narrow typologies of Gershom Scholem and Moshe Idel.

47. Frank is deeply, even brutally, critical of Foucault and Deleuze (and Guattari) but evinces considerable respect for Lyotard, Lacan, and most especially Derrida, the latter having in his estimation provided a most stimulating conversation partner for a hermeneutics in need of redirection. He also appears to agree with Fredric Jameson that Sartre, particularly his *Critique of Dialectical Reason*, has not yet received appropriate engagement within the philosophical world. See Jameson's foreword to the new edition of Sartre's *Critique*, vol. 1, trans. Alan Sheridan-Smith (London: Verso, 2004), xiii–xxxiii.

Adorno, Theodor. *Aesthetic Theory*. Translated by Christian Lenhardt. London: Routledge and Kegan Paul, 1984.

——. *Essays on Music*. Edited by Richard Leppert. Berkeley and Los Angeles: University of California Press, 1992

——. *Philosophy of Modern Music*. Translated by Anne G. Mitchell and Wesley V. Blomster. New York: Seabury Press, 1973.

Akima Toshio. "The Songs of the Dead: Poetry, Drama, and Ancient Death Rituals of Japan." *Journal of Asian Studies* 41 (May 1982): 485–509.

Al-Kindi. *De radiis*. Translated in *La magie Arabe traditionelle*, edited by Sylvain Matton. Paris: Bibliotheca Hermetica, 1977.

Albrechtsberger, Johann Georg. "The Canon." *Gründliche Anweisung zur Komposition*. Translated in Mann, *Study of Fugue*, 255–62.

Artaud, Antonin. "The Theater of Cruelty, First Manifesto." In *The Theater and Its Double*, translated by Mary Caroline Richards, 89–100. New York: Grove, 1958.

Ashworth, William. "Natural History and the Emblematic World View." In Lindberg and Westman, eds., *Reappraisals of the Scientific Revolution*, 303–32.

Bakhtin, Mikhail M. "Forms of Time and Chronotope in the Novel." In *The Dialogic Imagination*, edited by Michael Holquist, translated by Caryl Emerson and Michael Holquist, 84–151. Austin: University of Texas Press, 1981.

Barbosa de Almeida, Mauro W. "Symmetry and Entropy: Mathematical Metaphors in the Work of Lévi-Strauss." *Current Anthropology* 31, no. 4 (August–October 1990): 367–85.

Bell, Catherine M. *Ritual Theory, Ritual Practice*. Oxford: Oxford University Press, 1992.

Benjamin, Walter. *The Arcades Project*. Edited and translated by Howard Eiland and Kevin McLaughlin. Cambridge: Harvard University Press, Belknap Press, 1999.

——. *Charles Baudelaire: A Lyric Poet in the Era of High Capitalism*. Translated by Harry Zohn. London: Verso, 1997.

——. "Unpacking My Library." In *Illuminations*, translated by Harry Zohn, edited by Hannah Arendt, 59–67. New York: Schocken, 1969.

Betz, Hans Dieter. "Magic and Mystery in the Greek Magical Papyri." In *Magika Hiera: Ancient Greek Magic and Religion*, edited by Christopher A. Faraone and D. Obbink, 244–59. Oxford: Oxford University Press, 1991.

Blacker, Carmen. *The Catalpa Bow: A Study of Shamanistic Practices in Japan*. London: Allen and Unwin, 1975.

Blavatsky, H[elena] P[etrovna]. *Isis Unveiled*. 2 vols. New ed. Wheaton, Ill.: Theosophical Publishing House, 1972; 1st ed., 1877.

——. *The Secret Doctrine*. 2 vols. London: Theosophical Publishing Company, 1888.

Bono, James. *The Word of God and the Languages of Man: Interpreting Nature in Early Modern Science and Medicine; Ficino to Descartes*. Madison: University of Wisconsin Press, 1995.

Borges, Jorge Luis. "The Analytical Language of John Wilkins." In *Other Inquisitions 1937–1952*, translated by Ruth L. C. Simms, 101–5. Austin: University of Texas Press, 1993. Original: "El idioma analítico de John Wilkins," *Otras inquisiciones* (Buenos Aires: Emece Editores, 1964).

Boulez, Pierre. "Serie." In *Encyclopédie de la musique*, edited by F. Michel, F. Lesure, and V. Fédorov. 3 vols., 2:696–67. Paris: Fasquelle, 1958–61.

Bourdieu, Pierre. *The Logic of Practice*. Translated by Richard Nice. Cambridge: Polity Press, 1990.

Brann, Noel L. *Trithemius and Magical Theology: A Chapter in the Controversy over Occult Studies in Early Modern Europe*. Albany: State University of New York Press, 1998.

Broadbent, Simon. "Simulating the Ley Hunter." *Journal of the Royal Statistical Society*, ser. A (General) 143, no. 2 (1980): 109–40.

Bruno, Giordano. *The Ash-Wednesday Supper*. Translated by Edward A. Gosselin and Lawrence S. Lerner. Hamden, Conn.: Archon/Shoestring, 1977.

——. *Cause, Principle and Unity, and Essays on Magic*. Edited and translated by Robert de Lucca and Richard J. Blackwell. Cambridge: Cambridge University Press, 1998.

——. *On the Composition of Images, Signs, and Ideas*. Translated and edited by Charles Doria and Dick Higgins. New York: Willis, Locker, and Owens, 1991.

Buelow, George J. "Kircher, Athanasius." *Grove Music Online*, edited by L. Macy. Accessed September 2005–May 2006, http://www.grovemusic.com.

Buisset, Christiane. *Eliphas Lévi: Sa vie, son oeuvre, ses pensées*. Paris: G. Trâedaniel, Editions de La Maisnie, 1984.

Burns, Susan. *Before the Nation: Kokugaku and the Imagining of Community in Early Modern Japan*. Durham: Duke University Press, 2003.

Calcagno, Antonio. *Giordano Bruno and the Logic of Coincidence: Unity and Multiplicity in the Philosophical Thought of Giordano Bruno*. New York: P. Lang, 1998.

Calder, I. R. F. "John Dee Studied as an English Neoplatonist." 2 vols. PhD diss., Warburg Institute, 1952.

Campbell, Joseph. "Symbolism of the Marseilles Deck." Introduction to Joseph Campbell and Richard Robert, *Tarot Revelations*. San Anselmo, Calif.: Vernal Equinox Press, 1979.

Cassirer, Ernst. *The Problem of Knowledge: Philosophy, Science, and History since Hegel*.

Translated by William H. Woglom and Charles Hendel. New Haven: Yale University Press, 1950.

Chacornac, Paul. *Eliphas Lévi, renovateur de l'occultisme en France, 1810–1875*. Paris: Chacornac frères, 1926.

Chow, Rey. "How (the) Inscrutable Chinese Led to Globalized Theory." *PMLA* 116, no. 1 (January 2001): 69–74.

Churchward, James. *The Lost Continent of Mu: The Motherland of Man*. New York: William Edwin Rudge, 1926.

Claudel, Paul. *Mes idées sur le théatre*. Edited by Jacques Petit and Jean-Pierre Kempf. Paris: Gallimard, 1968 [1926].

Clulee, Nicholas H. *John Dee's Natural Philosophy: Between Science and Religion*. London: Routledge, 1989.

Cohen, H. Floris. *The Scientific Revolution: A Historiographical Inquiry*. Chicago: University of Chicago Press, 1994.

Copenhaver, Brian P. *Hermetica: The Greek "Corpus Hermeticum" and the Latin "Asclepius" in a New English Translation with Notes and Introduction*. Cambridge: Cambridge University Press, 1992.

——. "Natural Magic, Hermeticism, and Occultism." In Lindberg and Westman, eds., *Reappraisals of the Scientific Revolution*, 261–302.

Court de Gébelin, Antoine. *Le Monde Primitif, analysé et comparé avec le monde moderne. . . .* 9 vols. Paris, 1777–96.

——. *Le tarot*. Edited by Jean-Marie Lhôte. Paris: Berg International, 1983. (Facsimile reprint of the Tarot essays in vol. 8 of *Le Monde Primitif*.)

Crowley, Aleister. *The Book of Thoth*. York Beach, Maine: Samuel Weiser, 1986.

——. *Magick in Theory and Practice*. London, 1929; facsimile repr., Secaucus, N.J.: Castle Books, 1991.

Däniken, Erich von. *Chariots of the Gods? Unsolved Mysteries of the Past*. Translated by Michael Heron. New York: Putnam Berkeley, 1999 [1968].

Debus, Allen G. *Man and Nature in the Renaissance*. Cambridge: Cambridge University Press, 1978.

Decker, Ronald, Thierry Depaulis, and Michael Dummett. *A Wicked Pack of Cards: The Origins of the Occult Tarot*. New York: St. Martin's Press, 1996.

Dee, John. "Compendious Rehearsal." 1593. In *Remains Historical and Literary Connected with the Palatine Counties of Lancaster and Chester published by the Chetham Society*, edited by James Crossley, vol. 224 (1851), chap. 1.

——. *The Enochian Magick of Dr. John Dee*. Edited and translated by Geoffrey James. St. Paul, Minn.: Llewellyn, 1994 [1983].

——. *The Hieroglyphic Monad*. Translated by J. W. Hamilton-Jones. London: John M. Watkins, 1947.

——. *Jean Dee de Londres, Le Monade Hiéroglyphique*. Translated by Émile-Jules Grillot de Givry. Paris: Bibliothèque Chacornac, 1925.

——. *Monas Hieroglyphica*. Antwerp: William Silvius, 1564.

——. *A True & Faithful Relation of What Passed for Many Yeers Between Dr. John Dee . . . and Some Spirits. . . .* Edited by Meric Casaubon. London: D. Maxwell, for T. Garthwait, 1659; facsimile, New York: Magickal Childe, 1992.

Demonet, Marie-Luce. *Les voix du signe: Nature et origine du langage à la Renaissance, 1480–1580*. Paris: Champion-Slatkine, 1992.

Derrida, Jacques. "Différance." *Margins of Philosophy*, translated by Alan Bass, 1–27. Chicago: University of Chicago Press, 1982.

——. *Of Grammatology*. Translated by Gayatri Chakravorty Spivak. Baltimore: Johns Hopkins University Press, 1976.

——. "La parole soufflée." In *Writing and Difference*, translated by Alan Bass, 169–95. Chicago: University of Chicago Press, 1978.

——. "Plato's Pharmacy." In *Dissemination*, translated by Barbara Johnson, 61–171. Chicago: University of Chicago Press, 1981.

——. "Structure, Sign, and Play in the Discourse of the Human Sciences." In *Writing and Difference*, translated by Alan Bass, 278–94. Chicago: University of Chicago Press, 1978.

Devereux, Paul. "Leys/'Ley-lines'." Abridgment of paper presented at "Wege Des Geistes—Wege Der Kraft" conference, October 1996, in Germany (city not given); available at http://www.pauldevereux.co.uk/.

Diderot, Denis, and Jean le Rond d'Alembert, eds. *Encyclopédie, ou Dictionnaire raisonné des sciences, des arts et des metiers, par une societé de gens de lettres*. 17 vols. Paris, 1751–65.

Dixon, John W., Jr. *The Physiology of Faiths: A Theory of Theological Relativity*. San Francisco: Harper and Row, 1979.

Donnelly, Ignatius. *Atlantis, the Antediluvian World*. New York: Harper, 1882.

Dummett, Michael. *The Game of Tarot*. London: Duckworth, 1980.

——, ed. *The Visconti-Sforza Tarot Cards*. New York: George Braziller, 1986.

Durkheim, Émile. *The Elementary Forms of Religious Life*. Translated by Carol Cosman. New York: Oxford University Press, 2001.

——. *The Elementary Forms of Religious Life*. Translated by Karen E. Fields. New York: Free Press, 1995.

Eco, Umberto. "Unlimited Semiosis and Drift: Pragmaticism vs. 'Pragmatism.'" In *The Limits of Interpretation*. Bloomington: Indiana University Press, 1990.

Eliade, Mircea. *Cosmos and History*. Translated by Willard R. Trask. New York: Harper Torchbooks, 1959. Original: *Le Mythe de l'éternel retour: archétypes et répétition* (Paris: Gallimard, 1949).

——. *The Forge and the Crucible*. Translated by Stephen Corrin. 1956. Chicago: University of Chicago Press, 1962.

——. "The Occult and the Modern World." In *Occultism, Witchcraft, and Cultural Fashions: Essays in Comparative Religions*, 47–68. Chicago: University of Chicago Press, 1986.

Bibliography

——. *Patterns in Comparative Religion: A Study of the Element of the Sacred in the History of Religious Phenomena*. Translated by Rosemary Sheed. 1949. New York: Sheed and Ward, 1958; ed. cit. Cleveland: Meridian, 1963. Compare to *Traité d'histoire des religions*, new ed., preface by Georges Dumézil, *Bibliothèque Scientifique* (Paris: Payot, 1970).

——. "Religion, Magic, and Hermetic Traditions before and after the Reformation." Chapter 38 of *A History of Religious Ideas*, vol. 3, translated by Alf Hiltebeitel and Diane Apostolos-Cappadona. Chicago: University of Chicago Press, 1985.

——. *Shamanism: Archaic Techniques of Ecstasy*. Translated by Willard R. Trask. 1951. Princeton: Bollingen, 1964.

——. "Some Observations on European Witchcraft." In *Occultism, Witchcraft, and Cultural Fashions: Essays in Comparative Religions*, 69–92. Chicago: University of Chicago Press, 1986.

Elkins, James. *The Poetics of Perspective*. Ithaca: Cornell University Press, 1994.

Encyclopedia Britannica; or, A Dictionary of Arts and Sciences Compiled Upon a New Plan. . . . By a Society of Gentlemen in Scotland. 3 vols. Edinburgh, 1771.

Evans-Pritchard, E[dward] E[van]. *Theories of Primitive Religion*. Oxford: Clarendon, 1965.

Faure, Bernard. *The Rhetoric of Immediacy: A Cultural Critique of Chan/Zen Buddhism*. Princeton: Princeton University Press, 1991.

Festugière, A.-J. *La révelation d'Hermès Trismégiste*. 4 vols. Paris: J. Gabalda, 1950–54.

Findlen, Paula. "The Last Man Who Knew Everything . . . or Did He?" In Findlen, ed., *Last Man*, 1–48.

——. *Possessing Nature: Museums, Collecting, and Scientific Culture in Early Modern Italy*. Berkeley: University of California Press, 1994.

——, ed. *Athanasius Kircher: The Last Man Who Knew Everything*. New York: Routledge, 2004.

Fitzgerald, F. Scott. *The Crack-Up*. Edited by Edmund Wilson. New York: J. Laughlin, 1945.

Foucault, Michel. *The Order of Things: An Archaeology of the Human Sciences*. London: Tavistock, 1970. Original: *Les mots et les choses* (Paris: Gallimard, 1966).

Fowden, Garth. *The Egyptian Hermes: A Historical Approach to the Late Pagan Mind*, new ed. Princeton: Princeton University Press, 1993.

Frank, Manfred. *What Is Neostructuralism?* Translated by Sabine Wilke and Richard Grey. Minneapolis: University of Minnesota Press, 1987.

Frazer, Sir James G. *The Golden Bough*. 1 vol. abridged ed. 1922. London: Macmillan, 1955.

Gardner, Martin. *Fads and Fallacies in the Name of Science*. Rev. and expanded ed. New York: Dover, 1957.

——. *The New Age: Notes of a Fringe Watcher*. Buffalo, N.Y.: Prometheus Books, 1988.

Gardner, Richard A. "The Art in Nō: A Reconsideration of the Relation of Religion and Art." PhD diss., University of Chicago, 1988.

Gatti, Hilary. *Giordano Bruno and Renaissance Science*. Ithaca: Cornell University Press, 1999.

Geertz, Clifford. "The Cerebral Savage: On the Work of Claude Lévi-Strauss." In *The Interpretation of Cultures*, 345–59. New York: Basic Books, 1973.

——. "Religion as a Cultural System." In *Anthropological Approaches to the Study of Religion*, edited by Michael Banton, ASA Monographs 3, 1–46. London: Tavistock, 1966; repr., *The Interpretation of Cultures*, 87–125. New York: Basic Books, 1973.

Genette, Gérard. *Mimologics*. Translated by Thaïs E. Morgan. Lincoln: University of Nebraska Press, 1995.

Ginzburg, Carlo. *Clues, Myths, and the Historical Method*. Translated by John and Anne Tedeschi. Baltimore: Johns Hopkins University Press, 1989.

——. *Ecstasies: Deciphering the Witches' Sabbath*. Translated by Raymond Rosenthal. New York: Random House, 1991. Original: *Storia Notturna* (Turin: Einaudi, 1989).

Glucklich, Ariel. *The End of Magic*. New York: Oxford University Press, 1997.

Godelier, Maurice. *The Enigma of the Gift*. Translated by Nora Scott. Chicago: University of Chicago Press, 1999.

Godwin, Joscelyn. *Athanasius Kircher: A Renaissance Man and the Quest for Lost Knowledge*. London: Thames and Hudson, 1979.

Goethe, Johann Wolfgang von. *Goethes Naturwissenschaftliche Schriften*. 5 vols. Edited by Rudolf Steiner. Dornach: Rudolf-Steiner-Verlag, 1973.

——. *Scientific Studies*. Edited and translated by Douglas Miller. Vol. 12 of *Goethe: The Collected Works*. Princeton: Princeton University Press, 1988.

Goodman–Thau, Eveline, Gerd [Gert] Mattenklott, and Christoph Schulte, eds. *Kabbala und Romantik*. Tübingen: Niemeyer, 1994.

Goodman–Thau, Eveline, Gert Mattenklott, and Christoph Schulte, eds. *Kabbala und die Literatur der Romantik: Zwischen Magie und Trope*. Tübingen: Niemeyer, 1999.

Gosselin, Edward A. "Bruno's 'French Connection': A Historiographical Debate." In Merkel and Debus, eds., *Hermeticism and the Renaissance*, 166–81.

Gouk, Penelope. "Making Music, Making Knowledge: The Harmonious Universe of Athanasius Kircher." In Stolzenberg, ed., *Great Art of Knowing*, 71–83.

——. *Music, Science and Natural Magic in Seventeenth-Century England*. New Haven: Yale University Press, 1999.

Gould, Stephen Jay. "Father Athanasius on the Isthmus of a Middle State: Understanding Kircher's Paleontology." In Findlen, ed., *Last Man*, 207–37.

Grafton, Anthony. "Kircher's Chronology." In Findlen, ed., *Last Man*, 171–87.

Grimes, Ronald. *Beginnings in Ritual Studies*. Lanham, Md.: University Press of America, 1982.

——. *Deeply into the Bone: Re-inventing Rites of Passage*. Berkeley: University of California Press, 2000.

——. *Reading, Writing, and Ritualizing: Ritual in Fictive, Liturgical, and Public Places.* Washington, D.C.: Pastoral Press, 1993.

——. *Research in Ritual Studies: A Programmatic Essay and Bibliography.* [Chicago]: American Theological Library Association; Metuchen, N.J.: Scarecrow Press, 1985.

——. *Ritual Criticism: Case Studies in Its Practice, Essays on Its Theory.* Columbia: University of South Carolina Press, 1990.

Håkansson, Håkan. *Seeing the Word: John Dee and Renaissance Occultism.* Ugglan Minervaserien 2. Lund: Lunds Universitat, 2001.

Hanegraaff, Wouter J. "Beyond the Yates Paradigm: The Study of Western Esotericism between Counterculture and New Complexity." *Aries* 1 (2001): 5–37.

——. "Empirical Method in the Study of Esotericism." *Method and Theory in the Study of Religion* 7 (1995): 99–129.

——. *New Age Religion and Western Culture.* Albany: State University of New York Press, 1998.

Harkness, Deborah E. *John Dee's Conversations with Angels: Cabala, Alchemy, and the End of Nature.* Cambridge: Cambridge University Press, 1999.

Harootunian, H[arry] D. *Things Seen and Unseen: Discourse and Ideology in Tokugawa Nativism.* Chicago: University of Chicago Press, 1988.

Harrison, Jane. *Themis: A Study of the Social Origins of Greek Religion.* Cambridge: Cambridge University Press, 1912.

Havelock, Eric A. "Chinese Characters and the Greek Alphabet." *Sino–Platonic Papers* 5 (December 1987).

Heller, Erich. *The Disinherited Mind: Essays in German Literature and Thought.* New York: Harcourt, Brace, Jovanovich, 1959.

Hénaff, Marcel. *Claude Lévi-Strauss and the Making of Structural Anthropology.* Translated by Mary Baker. Minneapolis: University of Minnesota Press, 1998.

Heninger, S. K., Jr. *The Cosmographical Glass: Renaissance Diagrams of the Universe.* San Marino, Calif.: Huntington Library, 1977.

——. *Touches of Sweet Harmony: Pythagorean Cosmology and Renaissance Poetics.* San Marino, Calif.: Huntington Library, 1974.

Henrich, Dieter. "Hegels Grundoperation: Eine Einleitung in die 'Wissenschaft der Logik.'" In *Der Idealismus und seine Gegenwart: Festschrift für Werner Marx*, edited by Ute Guzzoni et al. Hamburg: Meiner, 1976.

Herodotus. *The Histories.* Translated by Aubrey de Sélincourt, revised by A. R. Burn. London: Penguin Classics, 1972.

Heyerdahl, Thor. *Aku-Aku: The Secret of Easter Island.* Chicago: Rand McNally, 1958.

Horapollo. *The Hieroglyphics of Horapollo.* Translated by George Boas. Princeton: Princeton University Press, 1950.

Hornung, Erik. *The Secret Lore of Egypt: Its Impact on the West.* Translated by David Lorton. Ithaca: Cornell University Press, 2001.

Hsia, Florence. "Athanasius Kircher's *China Illustrata* (1667): An Apologia Pro Vita Sua." In Findlen, ed., *Last Man*, 383–404.

Hutton, Ronald. *The Triumph of the Moon*. Oxford: Oxford University Press, 1999.

Iversen, Erik. *The Myth of Egypt and Its Hieroglyphs*. 1961. Princeton: Princeton University Press, Bollingen, 1993.

Jacobs, Louis. *The Jewish Religion*. Oxford: Oxford University Press, 1995.

Jameson, Fredric. Foreword to Jean-Paul Sartre, *Critique Of Dialectical Reason*, vol. 1, translated by Alan Sheridan-Smith, xiii–xxxiii. London: Verso, 2004.

Josten, C. H. "A Translation of John Dee's *Monas Hieroglyphica* (Antwerp, 1564), With an Introduction and Annotations." *Ambix* 12 (1964): 112–221.

Kaplan, Stuart. *The Encyclopedia of Tarot*. 4 vols. New York: U.S. Games Systems, 1978–90.

Keller, William B. *A Catalogue of the Cary Collection of Playing Cards in the Yale University Library*. 4 vols. New Haven: Yale University Library, 1981.

Kernfeld, Barry, ed. *The New Grove Dictionary of Jazz*. 2nd ed. London, 2002. www .grovemusic.com.

Kircher, Athanasius. *China Monumentis . . . Illustrata*. Amsterdam: apud Joannem Janssonium à Waesberge and Elizeum Weyerstraet, 1667. Translated as *China Illustrata*, by Charles Van Tuyl. Bloomington: Indiana University Press, 1986.

——. *Magnes, sive, De Arte Magnetica Opus Tripartitum . . .* Rome: ex typographia Ludouici Grignani, sumptibus Hermanni Scheus, 1641.

——. *Mundus Subterraneus, in XII Libros Digestus . . .* 3rd ed. Amsterdam: apud Joannem Janssonium à Waesberge and filios, 1678.

——. *Musurgia Universalis, sive Ars Magna Consoni et Dissoni*. 10 vols. in 1. Rome: ex typographia haeredum Francisci Corbelletti, 1650; facsimile, Hildesheim: G. Olms, 1970.

——. *Obelisci Aegyptiaci: Nuper inter Isaei Romani Rudera Effossi Interpretatio Hieroglyphica*. Rome: ex typographia Varesij, 1666.

——. *Sphinx Mystagoga: sive Diatribe Hieroglyphica qua Mumiae . . .* Amsterdam: ex officina Janssonio–Waesbergiana, 1676.

——. *Turris Babel, sive Archontologia . . .* Amsterdam: ex officina Janssonio–Waesbergiana, 1679.

Komparu Kunio. *The Noh Theater: Principles and Perspectives*. Translated by Jane Corddry. New York: Weatherhill/Tankosha, 1983.

Kotansky, Roy David. "Texts and Studies in the Greco-Egyptian Magic Lamellae." PhD diss., University of Chicago, 1988.

LaFleur, William R. *The Karma of Words: Buddhism and the Literary Arts in Medieval Japan*. Berkeley: University of California Press, 1983.

Lehrich, Christopher I. *The Language of Demons and Angels: Cornelius Agrippa's Occult Philosophy*. Leiden: Brill, 2003.

Lévi, Eliphas [Alphonse Louis Constant]. *Transcendental Magic*. Translated by A. E. Waite. London, 1896; repr. York Beach, Maine: Samuel Weiser, 1972.

Bibliography

Lévi-Strauss, Claude. *From Honey to Ashes*. Translated by John and Doreen Weightman. 1966. New York: Harper and Row, 1973; ed. cit. Chicago: University of Chicago Press, 1983.

——. "Introduction à l'oeuvre de Marcel Mauss." Introduction to Mauss, *Sociologie et anthropologie*. Translation: *Introduction to the Work of Marcel Mauss*, translated by Felicity Barker. London: Routledge and Kegan Paul, 1987.

——. *Look, Listen, Read*. 1993. Translated by Brian C. J. Singer. New York: Basic Books, 1997.

——. *Myth and Meaning*. 1978. New York: Schocken, 1995.

——. *The Naked Man*. Translated by John and Doreen Weightman. 1971. New York: Harper and Row, Harper, 1981; ed. cit. Chicago: University of Chicago Press, 1990.

——. *The Origin of Table Manners*. Translated by John and Doreen Weightman. 1968. Chicago: University of Chicago Press, 1990.

——. *La pensée sauvage*. Paris: Plon, 1962; ed. cit. Paris: Brodard et Taupin, 1990. Translation: *The Savage Mind* (Chicago: University of Chicago Press, 1966).

——. *The Raw and the Cooked*. Translated by John and Doreen Weightman. 1964. New York: Harper and Row, 1969.

——. *Structural Anthropology*. Translated by Claire Jacobson and Brooke Grundfest Schoepf. New York: Basic Books, 1963.

——. *Tristes Tropiques*. Translated by John and Doreen Weightman. 1955. London: Penguin, 1992.

——. *Totemism*. Translated by Rodney Needham. Boston: Beacon, 1963.

Lincoln, Bruce. "Dumézil's German War God." *Theorizing Myth*, 121–37. Chicago: University of Chicago Press, 2000.

Lindberg, David C., and Robert S. Westman, eds. *Reappraisals of the Scientific Revolution*. Cambridge: Cambridge University Press, 1990.

Lundbaek, Knud. "Imaginary Ancient Chinese Characters." *China Mission Studies (1550–1800)* 5 (1983).

——, ed. and trans. *The Traditional History of the Chinese Script: From a Seventeenth Century Jesuit Manuscript*. Aarhus, Denmark: Aarhus University Press, 1988.

MacKie, E. W. "Archaeological Tests on Supposed Prehistoric Astronomical Sites in Scotland." *Philosophical Transactions of the Royal Society of London*, ser. A (Mathematical and Physical Sciences) 276.1257, "The Place of Astronomy in the Ancient World" (May 2, 1974): 169–94.

Maggi, Armando. *Identità e impresa rinascimentale*. Ravenna: Longo, 1998.

Mancini, Sandro. *La sfera infinita: Identità e differenza nel pensiero di Giordano Bruno*. Milan: Mimesis, 2000.

Mann, Alfred. *The Study of Fugue*. New York: W. W. Norton, 1965.

Mauss, Marcel. *Sociologie et anthropologie*. Paris: PUF, 1950.

——, with Henri Hubert. *Esquisse d'une théorie générale de la magie*. In Mauss, *Sociologie et anthropologie*, 1–141. Translation: *A General Theory of Magic*. Translated by Robert Brain. London: Routledge and Kegan Paul, 1972.

McIntosh, Christopher. *Eliphas Lévi and the French Occult Revival*. London: Rider, 1972.

Mencke, Johann Burckhard. *The Charlatanry of the Learned (De charlataneria eruditorum, 1715)*. Translated by Francis E. Litz, edited by H. L. Mencken. New York: Knopf, 1937.

Merkel, Ingrid, and Allen G. Debus, eds. *Hermeticism and the Renaissance: Intellectual History and the Occult in Early Modern Europe*. Washington: Folger Shakespeare Library; London: Associated University Presses, 1988.

Michel, Aimé. *Mystérieux objets celestes*. Paris: Editions Arthaud, 1958.

Michell, John. *The New View over Atlantis*. London: Garnstone, 1972; London: Thames and Hudson, 1983.

——. *The View over Atlantis*. London: Sago Press, 1969.

Mitchell, W. J. T. *Iconology: Image, Text, Ideology*. Chicago: University of Chicago Press, 1987.

Moakley, Gertrude. *The Tarot Cards Painted by Bonifacio Bembo for the Visconti-Sforza Family: An Iconographic and Historical Study*. New York: New York Public Library, 1966.

Motoori Norinaga. *Kojiki–Den*. Vol. 1. Translated by Ann Wehmeyer. Ithaca: Cornell University Press, 1997.

Murray, Margaret A. *The God of the Witches*. London: Faber, 1934.

——. "Witchcraft." *Encyclopedia Britannica*, 23.687, 1965 ed.

——. *The Witch-Cult in Western Europe*. Oxford: Oxford University Press, 1921

Nattiez, Jean-Jacques. *De la sémiologie à la musique*. Montréal: Université du Québec à Montréal, 1988.

——. *Music and Discourse: Toward a Semiology of Music*. Translated by Carolyn Abbate. 1987. Princeton: Princeton University Press, 1990.

——. "Reflections on the Development of Semiology in Music." Translated by Katherine Ellis. *Music Analysis* 8, no. 1–2 (1989): 21–74.

Nelson, Buck. *My Trip to Mars, the Moon, and Venus*. Grand Rapids: UFOrum, Grand Rapids Flying Saucer Club, 1956.

Norris, Christopher. *Derrida*. Cambridge: Harvard University Press, 1987.

Obeyesekere, Gananath. *The Apotheosis of Captain Cook*. Princeton: Princeton University Press, 1992.

Oldenburg, Henry. *The Correspondence of Henry Oldenburg*. Edited by A. Rupert Hall and Marie Boas Hall. 9 vols. Madison: University of Wisconsin Press, 1965–86.

Ooms, Herman. *Tokugawa Ideology: Early Constructs*. Princeton: Princeton University Press, 1985.

Ordine, Nuccio. *La cabala dell'asino: asinità e conoscenza in Giordano Bruno*. 2nd ed. Naples: Liguori, 1996. Translation: *Giordano Bruno and the Philosophy of the Ass*. Translated by Henryk Baraánski in collaboration with Arielle Saiber. New Haven: Yale University Press, 1996.

Ortner, Sherry. "Theory in Anthropology since the Sixties." *Comparative Studies in Society and History* 126, no. 1 (1984): 126–66.

Ortolani, Benito. *The Japanese Theatre: From Shamanistic Ritual to Contemporary Pluralism*. Rev. ed. Princeton: Princeton University Press, 1995.

Otto, Rudolf. *The Idea of the Holy*. Translated by John W. Harvey. London: Oxford University Press, 1923.

Paddison, Max. *Adorno's Aesthetics of Music*. Cambridge: Cambridge University Press, 1993.

Panofsky, Erwin. *Studies in Iconology: Humanistic Themes in Art*. Oxford: Oxford University Press, 1939.

Picard, Michel. *Aimé Michel, ou la quête du surhumain*. Paris: JMG, Collection Science-Conscience, 2000.

Plato. *Phaedrus*. Translated by Robin Waterfield. Oxford: Oxford University Press, 2002.

Platvoet, J[ohannes] G[erhardus]. *Comparing Religions: A Limitative Approach*. The Hague: Mouton, 1983.

Popkin, Richard. *The History of Scepticism: From Savonarola to Bayle*. Oxford: Oxford University Press, 2003.

Radcliffe-Brown, A[lfred] R[eginald]. *Taboo*. Cambridge: Cambridge University Press, 1939; repr. in *Reader in Comparative Religions*, edited by William A. Lessa and Evon Z. Vogt, 4th ed., 46–56. New York: Harper Collins, 1979.

Randel, Don Michael, ed. *The New Harvard Dictionary of Music*. Cambridge: Harvard University Press, Belknap Press, 1986.

Randi, James. *Flim-Flam!* Buffalo, N.Y.: Prometheus, 1982.

Rennie, Bryan. *Reconstructing Eliade: Making Sense of Religion*. Albany: State University of New York Press, 1996.

Renondeau, Gaston. *Le bouddhisme dans le nō*. Tokyo: Maison franco-japonaise, 1950.

Romano, Antonella. "Epilogue: Understanding Kircher in Context." Translated by Paula Findlen and Derrick Allums. In Findlen, ed., *Last Man*, 405–19.

Rorty, Richard. "Deconstruction and Circumvention." *Critical Inquiry* 11 (1984): 1–23.

Rossi, Paolo. *Clavis Universalis: arti della memoria e logica combinatoria da Lullo a Leibniz*. 2nd ed. Bologna: Società editrice il Mulino, 1983. Translation: *Logic and the Art of Memory: The Question for a Universal Language*, translated by Stephen Clucas. Chicago: University of Chicago Press, 2000.

Roudaut, Jean. *Poètes et grammariens au XVIIIe siècle: Anthologie*. Paris: Gallimard, 1971.

Rowland, Ingrid D. *The Ecstatic Journey: Athanasius Kircher in Baroque Rome*. Chicago: University of Chicago Press, 2000.

Sadie, Stanley, ed. *The New Grove Dictionary of Opera*. London, 1992. www.grovemusic.com.

Sadie, Stanley, and John Tyrrell, eds. *The New Grove Dictionary of Music and Musicians*. 2nd ed. London, 2001. www.grovemusic.com.

Sahlins, Marshall. *Apologies to Thucydides: Understanding History as Culture and Vice Versa*. Chicago: University of Chicago Press, 2004.

———. *How "Natives" Think: About Captain Cook, for Example*. Chicago: University of Chicago Press, 1995.

Sandell, Roger. "Notes towards a Social History of Ley–Hunting." *Magonia* 29 (April 1988).

Sanders, E. P. *Paul and Palestinian Judaism: A Comparison of Patterns of Religion*. Philadelphia: Fortress, 1977.

Sansom, George. *Japan: A Short Cultural History*. Rev. ed. New York: Appleton-Century-Crofts, 1962.

Saussy, Haun. *Great Walls of Discourse and Other Adventures in Cultural China*. Cambridge: Harvard University Asia Center, 2002.

———. "Magnetic Language: Athanasius Kircher and Communication." In Findlen, *Last Man*, 263–82.

———. "The Prestige of Writing: [wen], Letter, Picture, Image, Ideography." *Sino-Platonic Papers* 75 (February 1997): 1–40.

Schoenberg, Arnold. *Harmonielehre*. 1911, rev. 1922. Translated as *Theory of Harmony* by Roy E. Carter (Berkeley: University of California Press, 1978); *Theory of Harmony*, translated by Robert D. W. Adams (New York: Philosophical Library, 1948).

———. *The Musical Idea and the Logic, Technique, and Art of Its Presentation*. Edited and translated by Patricia Carpenter and Severine Neff. New York: Columbia University Press, 1995.

———. *Style and Idea: Collected Writings*. Edited by Leonard Stein, translated by Leo Black, rev. ed. Berkeley: University of California Press, 1984.

Scott, Walter, ed. and trans. *Hermetica: The Ancient Greek and Latin Writings Which Contain Religious or Philosophical Teachings Ascribed to Hermes Trismegistus*. 4 vols.; vol. 4 completed by A. S. Ferguson. 1924–36. London: Dawsons, 1968.

Segal, Robert A. "In Defense of the Comparative Method." *Numen* 48, no. 3 (2001): 339–73.

Sherman, William H. *John Dee: The Politics of Reading and Writing in the English Renaissance*. Amherst: University of Massachusetts Press, 1997.

Smith, Jonathan Z. "Acknowledgments: Morphology and History in Mircea Eliade's *Patterns in Comparative Religion* (1949–1999)." 2 parts. *History of Religions* 39, no. 4 (May 2000): 315—51; repr. in Smith, *Relating Religion*, 61–100.

———. *Imagining Religion*. Chicago: University of Chicago Press, 1982.

———. *Map Is Not Territory*. Leiden: E. J. Brill, 1978; repr. University of Chicago Press, 1993.

———. *Relating Religion*. Chicago: University of Chicago Press, 2004.

———. *To Take Place: Toward Theory in Ritual*. Chicago: University of Chicago Press, 1987.

Smyth, Piazzi. *Our Inheritance in the Great Pyramid*. London: A. Straham, 1864.

Spence, Jonathan. *The Memory Palace of Matteo Ricci*. London: Penguin, 1985.

Steiner, Rudolf. *Goethes Weltanschauung*. Weimar: E. Felber, 1897. *Goethe's Conception of the World*. London: Anthroposophical Publishing, 1928; *Goethe's World View*. [n.p.]: Mercury Press, 1985.

——. *Nature's Open Secret: Introductions to Goethe's Scientific Writings*. Translated by John Barnes and Mado Spiegler. New York: Anthroposophic Press, 2000.

——. *The Origins of Natural Science*. Spring Valley, N.Y.: Anthroposophic Press, 1985.

——. *The Spiritual–Scientific Basis of Goethe's Work*. London: Rudolf Steiner Press, 1982.

——. *A Theory of Knowledge Based on Goethe's World Conception*. Translated by Olin D. Wannamaker. New York: Anthroposophic Press, 1968.

Stewart, Susan. *On Longing: Narratives of the Miniature, the Gigantic, the Souvenir, the Collection*. Durham: Duke University Press, 1993.

Stolzenberg, Daniel. "Egyptian Oedipus: Antiquarianism, Oriental Studies, and Occult Philosophy in the Work of Athanasius Kircher." PhD diss., Stanford University, 2003.

——, ed. *The Great Art of Knowing: The Baroque Encyclopedia of Athanasius Kircher*. Fiesole: Stanford University Libraries and Edizione Cadmo, 2001.

Stuckrad, Kocku von. "Western Esotericism: Towards an Integrative Model of Interpretation." *Religion* 35 (2005): 78–97.

Sturlese, Rita. "Il *De imaginum, signorum et idearum compositione* di Giordano Bruno ed il significato filosofico dell'arte della memoria." *Giornale critico della filosofia italiana* 10 (May–August 1990): 182–203.

——. "Per un'interpretazione del *De umbris idearum* di Giordano Bruno," *Annali della Scuola Normale Superiore di Pisa*, 3rd ser., 22, no. 3 (1992).

Sullivan, Danny. "Ley Lines: Dead and Buried: A Reappraisal of the Straight Line Enigma." *3rd Stone* 27 (Autumn 1997): 44–49.

Suzuki, D[aisetz] T[eitaro]. *Zen and Japanese Culture*. Princeton: Bollingen, 1959.

Szőnyi, György Endre. *John Dee's Occultism: Magical Exaltation through Powerful Signs*. Albany: State University of New York Press, 2005.

Tambiah, Stanley J. "Form and Meaning of Magical Acts." In *Modes of Thought: Essays on Thinking in Western and Non-Western Societies*, edited by Robin Horton and Ruth Finnegan. London: Faber and Faber, 1972.

——. "The Magical Power of Words." *Man*, n.s., 3 (1968): 175–208.

——. *Magic, Science, Religion, and the Scope of Rationality*. Cambridge: Cambridge University Press, 1990.

——. "A Performative Approach to Ritual." *Proceedings of the British Academy* 65 (1979): 113–69.

Thurn, Richard W. "Cards." In Mircea Eliade, ed., *The Encyclopedia of Religion*. New York: Macmillan, 1986; repr. in *Hidden Truths: Magic, Alchemy, and the Occult*, edited by Lawrence E. Sullivan, 163–64. New York: Macmillan, 1989.

Trachtenberg, Joshua. *Jewish Magic and Superstition*. New York: Behrman's Jewish Book House, 1939; repr., Philadelphia: University of Pennsylvania Press, 2004.

Velikovsky, Immanuel. *Worlds in Collision*. London: Gollancz, 1950.

Vickers, Brian. "Frances Yates and the Writing of History." *Journal of Modern History* 51, no. 2 (June 1979): 287–316.

——. "On the Function of Analogy in the Occult." In Merkel and Debus, eds, *Hermeticism and the Renaissance*, 265–92.

——, ed. *Occult and Scientific Mentalities in the Renaissance*. Cambridge: Cambridge University Press, 1984.

Waite, Arthur Edward. *Pictorial Key to the Tarot*. London: Rider, 1911.

Waley, Arthur. *The Nō Plays of Japan*. London: Allen and Unwin, 1921.

Walker, D[aniel] P[ickering]. "The *Prisca Theologia* in France." *Journal of the Warburg and Courtauld Institutes* 17 (1954): 204–59.

——. *Spiritual and Demonic Magic from Ficino to Campanella*. London: Warburg Institute, 1958; repr. Notre Dame: University of Notre Dame Press, 1975, and University Park: Pennsylvania State University Press, 2000.

Wasserstrom, Steven M. *Religion after Religion: Gershom Scholem, Mircea Eliade, and Henry Corbin*. Princeton: Princeton University Press, 1999.

Watkins, Alfred. *Archaic Tracks around Cambridge*. London: Simpkin Marshall, 1932.

——. *The Old Straight Track: Its Mounds, Beacons, Moats, Sites and Mark Stones*. London: Methuen, 1923; repr. London: Abacus (Little, Brown) 1974.

Watkins, Allen. *Alfred Watkins of Hereford*. London: Garnstone, 1972.

Wedd, J[ohn] A[nthony] D[unkin]. *Skyways and Landmarks*. 1961; repr. Hull: P. Heselton, 1972.

Westman, Robert S. "Magical Reform and Astronomical Reform: The Yates Thesis Reconsidered." In *Hermeticism and the Scientific Revolution*, edited by Robert S. Westman and J. E. McGuire, 5–91. Los Angeles: William Andrews Clark Memorial Library, 1977.

Whitby, Christopher. *John Dee's Actions with Spirits*. 2 vols. New York: Garland, 1988.

Wilding, Nick. "Publishing the Polygraphy." In Findlen, ed., *Last Man*, 283–96.

Williams, Thomas A. *Eliphas Lévi: Master of Occultism*. Tuscaloosa: University of Alabama Press, 1975.

Wolfson, Elliot R. *Alef, Mem, Tau: Kabbalistic Musings on Time, Truth, and Death*. Berkeley: University of California Press, 2006.

——. "Assaulting the Border: Kabbalistic Traces in the Margins of Derrida." *Journal of the American Academy of Religion* 70, no. 3 (Sept. 2002): 475–514.

——. "Divine Suffering and the Hermeneutics of Reading: Philosophical Reflections on Lurianic Mythology." In Robert Gibbs and Elliot R. Wolfson, eds., *Suffering Religion*, 101–62. New York: Routledge, 2002.

——. *Language, Eros, Being: Kabbalistic Hermeneutics and Poetic Imagination*. Bronx, N.Y.: Fordham University Press, 2005.

Woolley, Benjamin. *The Queen's Conjurer*. New York: Henry Holt, 2001.

Yates, Frances A. *The Art of Memory*. London: Routledge and Kegan Paul, 1966.

——. *Giordano Bruno and the Hermetic Tradition*. London: Routledge and Kegan Paul, 1964; repr. Chicago: University of Chicago Press, 1979.

——. "The Hermetic Tradition in Renaissance Science." In *Art, Science, and History in the Renaissance*, edited by C. S. Singleton. Baltimore: Johns Hopkins University Press, 1967. Repr. in Yates, *Ideas and Ideals in the North European Renaissance*, 227–46.

——. *Ideas and Ideals in the North European Renaissance: Collected Essays*, vol. 3. London: Routledge and Kegan Paul, 1984.

——. *The Occult Philosophy in the Elizabethan Age*. London: Routledge and Kegan Paul, 1979.

——. *The Rosicrucian Enlightenment*. London: Routledge and Kegan Paul, 1972.

Yelle, Robert A. *Explaining Mantras: Magic, Rhetoric, and the Dream of a Natural Language*. London: Routledge, 2003.

Zeami Motkiyo. *On the Art of the Nō Drama: The Major Treatises of Zeami*. Translated by Thomas J. Rimer and Masakazu Yamazaki. Princeton: Princeton University Press, 1984.

⁞⁞⁞ INDEX

Hermeticism, 13–14, 16, 28–32, 51, 60; and Bruno, 29, 34, 39, 43; and Dee, 57; and Kircher, 120; and science, 29, 35. *See also* Yates, Frances A.; Yates thesis

Herodotus, 121, 124–25

hieroglyphics: Ægyptian, 7–9, 80, 140–42, 171; and alphabets, 121–22; and Chinese writing, 100–102; Copernican cosmos and, 39–40, 43–44; in Dee, 48–49; Egyptian, 123, 126, 132; in Kircher, 92, 96–97, 120–23; and perfect language, 42–43, 97. *See also* Hermes Trismegistus; writing

Higgins, Dick 84–85

Hirata Atsutane, 63, 69–71, 72

history: antagonism to, 14, 59; in comparison, 15–16, 56, 57–61, 80; epistemology of, 20, 46–47; as hierophany, 128; methodologies of, 20, 32–34, 105, 180; and morphology, 10–12, 82–84, 91, 108, 130–31, 153, 177–80; and music, 152–55; natural (*see* science); of science (*see* science, history of); and structure, 33, 58–61, 100, 126–31; and tarot, 133. *See also* classification; Eliade, Mircea; Kircher, Athanasius; Lévi-Strauss, Claude; Smith, Jonathan Z.; Yates, Frances A.

homology. *See* analogy

Honda Yasuji, 66

Horapollo, 96, 121

Horn, Georg, 92

Hubert, Henri, 160, 166. *See also* Mauss, Marcel

iconology, 97

illud tempus. See Eliade, Mircea

infinite, problem of, 38, 41–44, 85, 87, 128, 166. *See also* Bruno, Giordano; epistemology; mathematics

ingénieur. See bricolage

interdisciplinarity of magic, 159

Intorcetta, Prosper, 102, 121

Jannes and Mambres, 141, 156

Japaneseness, 63, 73, 76–78

Japanese soul, essentialized, 68, 71, 74

Johnny-jump-up, 119

Joseph, Genesis story of, 141, 155–57

Josten, C. H., 55

Kabbalah, 40, 51, 181; and tarot, 133, 145–46. *See also* Dee, John

Kabuki (dramatic form), 67, 68

kagura (possession ritual), 65

Kamo no Mabuchi, 68

Kan'ami Kiyotsugu, 62, 66

Kendall, David, 20

Kepler, Johannes, 37

al-Kindī, 90

Kircher, Athanasius, 91–116, 119–31, 180; classification in, 95–96, 106, 108–12, 115–31, 172–73; coherence of, 92–95, 106, 126–31; collecting in, 92, 95; and epistemic divide, 116; "great art of knowing" (*ars magna sciendi*), 94, 95, 96–97, 130; and Hermeticism, 120; and history, 127–31, 172–73; and language, 104, 124, 127; methodology of, 94, 96, 103; and music, 108–9, 111–13; and paleontology, 105–6, 113; and writing, 92–93, 96–102, 119–23. *See also* analogy; Vickers, Brian

Kojiki, 68–69, 78

kokugaku. See nativism

Komparu Kunio, 63, 64

Komparu Ujinobu Zenchiku. *See* Zenchiku

kyōgen (dramatic form), 64, 67

labyrinth, Egyptian, 124–25

LaFleur, William, 70

language: before fall, 7, 78; fall of, 42,

88, 91, 97; perfect, 42–43, 48–53, 92, 94–95. *See also* Ægypt; Bruno, Giordano; Dee, John; Hermes Trismegistus; Kircher, Athanasius; Saussure, Ferdinand de; sign; writing
Lawton, Arthur, 19
Leonardo da Vinci, 31
Lévi, Eliphas, 3, 133, 146
Lévi-Strauss, Claude: binarism in, 115–16, 154–55; and cartomancy, 133–34; and classification, 105, 106–8, 115–19, 175–76; and comparison, 95; and concrete thought, 33, 165, 176 (*see also* bricolage); and epistemology, 91, 129; *La pensée sauvage*, 104–5, 162; on mana, 161–64, 170; and mathematics, 134, 157; and music, 134, 142–43, 146–55; and myth, 133–34, 142–43, 151, 157, 181; and science, 36, 105, 111, 116–17; and signification, 85, 116–17; on time, 82, 130–31; "The Writing Lesson," 119, 174–75. *See also* Derrida, Jacques; structuralism; structure and event; synchrony and diachrony
Ley Hunter's Club, 19
leys, 3; and archaeology, 18–19, 20–22; as lines of force, 19–20, 23; and nostalgia, 24–25; statistical analysis of, 20; in Watkins, 18; in Yates, 27–28, 32–33
Linnaeus, 10, 115, 123–24, 126. *See also* classification: scientific
logocentrism, 116–17, 171, 173–75. *See also* Derrida, Jacques
Long, Mary, 19
Lundbaek, Knud, 102
Luria, Isaac, 181

magic: as analytical term, 83–84, 158–73, 175–82; definitions of, 83–84, 159–60, 165–66, 168–71, 172, 176; and differance, 171–82; and differentiation, 53,

159–60, 164–82; opposed to science and religion, 32, 164–71, 177–78; and philosophy, 181–82; as theory, 115, 163–64, 182. *See also* analogy
magus, 30–31, 40, 56, 59, 87. *See also* Dee, John; Sherman, William; Yates, Frances A.
mana, 160–64, 170
masks, in Nō, 62, 65
mathematics, 54, 166; in Bruno, 36–39, 85, 128; in Dee, 52; in Lévi-Strauss, 134, 157; and music, 113. *See also* Copernicus, Nicolaus; infinite, problem of; models: mathematical
Matsumoto Shinhachirō, 66
Mauss, Marcel, 159, 160–63, 166
Maximilian II (emperor), 52, 55
Mellet, Comte de (Louis Raphaël-Lucrèce de Fayolle), 138, 140–42, 143–45, 155–56. *See also* tarot
memory. *See* Ægypt; art of memory; nostalgia
Michel, Aimé, 19
Michell, John, 19–20, 22–23, 25, 188 n8
models: mathematical, 34, 36–39, 54, 158; occult (*see* analogy); scientific, 43–44, 110, 113. *See also* classification
Monas Hieroglyphica. *See* Dee, John
monomane (mimetic imitation), 62, 66, 68
mono no aware, 68–69, 78
morphology: and history, 10–12, 82–84, 91, 108, 130–31, 153, 177–80; as method, 12, 15–16. *See also* Eliade, Mircea; Ginzburg, Carlo; Goethe, Johann Wolfgang von; Smith, Jonathan Z.
Motoori Norinaga, 63, 68–69, 70, 78
Murray, Margaret, 3
museums, 92, 100, 108, 123–24. *See also* collecting; Findlen, Paula; Kircher, Athanasius

emblematic, 42; epistemology of, 31–32, 34–35, 43, 110–11, 113–14, 164; history of, 28–32, 36, 57, 58, 103, 119; and occultism, 32, 35, 115. *See also* Bruno, Giordano; Dee, John; Heninger, S. K., Jr.; Lévi-Strauss, Claude; Vickers, Brian; Yates, Frances A.; Yates thesis

science of the concrete, 44, 100, 104, 117–18, 119, 164. *See also* bricolage; Lévi-Strauss, Claude; *pensée sauvage*

semiotics: and analogy, 104; in Bruno, 84, 91; in Dee, 51, 54, 97; in Kircher, 97; in music, 211 n5; in ritual, 75–76. *See also* sign

serialism (musical form), 146–48, 150–53, 155

Sherman, William, 50, 55–57, 58–61

shite (in Nō), 63, 79

sign, arbitrariness and motivation of, 16, 91, 116–18, 150–51

skepticism, 51, 53, 132–33

Smith, Jonathan Z., 91, 162–63, 180; on comparison, 15–16, 56–57; on definitions of magic, 83–84, 165–66, 168–71; on morphology and history, 28, 82–84, 130–31, 179–80; on structuralism, 95

Smith, Thomas, 60

Star Fellowship, 19

Stewart, Susan, 108

Stolzenberg, Daniel, 92–94, 120–23

Stonehenge, 21, 22–23

Straight Track Club, 18–19

structuralism, 15–16, 115, 166; and Bruno, 44, 91; critiques of, 82, 94–95, 104, 115–16, 154–55. *See also* Lévi-Strauss, Claude

structure and event, 33, 80, 116, 118. *See also* epistemes; history; Lévi-Strauss, Claude; *pensée sauvage*; synchrony and diachrony

Sturlese, Rita, 87–88

subjectivity (philosophical problem), 172, 181–82

Suzuki, D. T., 76

Suzuki Shunryō, 76

synchrony and diachrony: in classification, 102; in comparison, 46–47, 80, 178–80; as epistemic problem, 33, 46–47, 118, 129–31, 178–80; in morphology and history, 82, 91, 129–31, 178–80; and music, 142–43, 148–54. *See also* Derrida, Jacques; Lévi-Strauss, Claude; Smith, Jonathan Z.

Szőnzyi, Győrgi, 50, 56, 79

Tambiah, Stanley Jeyaraja, 104, 117, 163

tarot, 132–45, 153–54, 155–57, 166, 180; composition of, 134–37; divination with, 140–42, 154, 155–57, 212–13 n11; and myth, 143–46, 151, 153–54; origins of, 133, 135, 137; and writing, 3, 140–42, 145–46

Thorndike, Lynn, 29

translation, 123

Trithemius, Johannes, 51–52

Turner, Victor W., 74, 161

Tycho Brahe, 34

UFOs, 19–20, 22–23

Velikovsky, Immanuel, 22, 128

Vickers, Brian, 29, 103–15, 115–17, 119, 123, 180; criticism of Frances Yates, 27–28, 32–33. *See also* analogy

Virgil, *Aeneid*, 85–88

Visconti, Filippo Maria, 135

Waite, Arthur Edward, 135

Walker, D. P., 3, 104

Watkins, Alfred, 3, 18, 20–21, 27, 45

wazaogi (comic pantomime), 66, 68

Wedd, Tony, 19, 22
Westman, Robert S., 28, 34–35, 39
witchcraft, 161
writing, 51, 66, 80, 119, 123, 170–71; alphabetic, 87, 120–123; Chinese, 68, 69, 92, 97, 100–102, 119–20, 120–22, 126, 129; in Dee, 48–49, 51; Egyptian (*see* hieroglyphics); epistemology of, 47, 53–56, 78, 117, 173–75; Hebrew, 3, 145–46; in Kircher, 96–102, 119–23; in Lévi-Strauss, 119, 174–75; and speech, 7, 68, 69, 174–76. *See also* Derrida, Jacques

Yanagita Kunio, 71–73
Yates, Frances A., 2, 25–26, 30, 51, 167, 180; and Bruno, 26–27, 34–35, 39–46, 85, 87–88; and Dee, 50, 56, 57, 58–59; and Hermeticism, 4, 12–14, 45; and historical scholarship, 16, 27–28, 32–34, 45, 111, 114; and nostalgia, 3, 12–14; as occultist, 26–28, 32; reactualizing methods of, 27, 30–32, 33–34, 45–46; and science, 26, 31. *See also* Vickers, Brian
Yates thesis, 26, 28–29, 36, 52. *See also* science: history of

Zeami Motokiyo, 62, 63, 70–71, 76; figure of marionette in, 65–66, 69, 71, 79; as theorist, 64, 67, 72
Zenchiku (Komparu Ujinobu Zenchiku), 62, 67
Zen ritual, 74–78